The Trade in Wildlife

The Trade in Wildlife

Regulation for Conservation

Edited by
Sara Oldfield

ResourceAfrica TRAFFIC

London • Sterling, VA

First published in the UK and USA in 2003
by Earthscan Publications Ltd

Reprinted 2005

ISBN: 1 85383 954 X paperback
1 85383 959 0 hardback

Typesetting by MapSet Ltd, Gateshead, UK
Printed and bound in the UK by Creative Print and Design (Wales), Ebbw Vale
Cover design by Danny Gillespie

For a full list of publications please contact:

Earthscan
8–12 Camden High Street, London, NW1 0JH, UK
Tel: +44 (0)20 7387 8558
Fax: +44 (0)20 7387 8998
Email: earthinfo@earthscan.co.uk
Web: **www.earthscan.co.uk**

22883 Quicksilver Drive, Sterling, VA 20166-2012, USA

A catalogue record for this book is available from the British Library

Library of Congress Cataloging-in-Publication Data

The trade in wildlife : regulation for conservation / edited by Sara Oldfield.
p. cm.
Includes bibliographical references (p.)
ISBN 1-85383-954-X (pbk.) – ISBN 1-85383-959-0 (hardback)
1. Wild animal trade. 2. Wild animal trade–Law and legislation. I. Oldfield, Sara.
SK591.T73 2002
333.95 417–dc21

2002152953

Earthscan is an imprint of James & James (Science Publishers) Ltd and publishes in association with the International Institute for Environment and Development

This book is printed on elemental chlorine-free paper

Contents

PART 3 CASE STUDIES

PART 4 LESSONS FROM ILLEGAL TRADE IN OTHER GOODS

List of Acronyms and Abbreviations

CAP	Common Agricultural Policy
CBD	Convention on Biological Diversity
CBI	Central Bureau of Investigation (India)
CCAMLR	Convention on the Conservation of Antarctic Marine Living Resources
CFC	chlorofluorocarbon
CIB	Congolaise Industrielle des Bois
CITES	Convention on International Trade in Endangered Species of Wild Fauna and Flora
CONAF	Corporación Nacional Forestal (Chile)
CoP	Conference of the Parties
CPIA	Convention on Cultural Property Implementation Act
DENR	Department of Environment and Natural Resources (Philippines)
DGFT	Director General of Foreign Trade (India)
EC	European Community
EEZ	exclusive economic zone
EPA	Environmental Protection Agency (US)
EU	European Union
FAO	Food and Agriculture Organization (United Nations)
FDA	Forestry Development Authority (Liberia)
FFI	Fauna & Flora International
FoB	free on board
FSC	Forest Stewardship Council
GATT	General Agreement on Tariffs and Trade
GEF	Global Environment Facility
GOI	Government of India
GTZ	Deutsche Gesellschaft für Technische Zusammenarbeit GMBH
G7	group of seven industrialized nations
G8	group of eight industrialized nations
HFC	hydrofluorocarbon
HIV	Human Immunodeficiency Virus
HS	Harmonized Commodity Description and Coding System
ICCAT	International Commission for the Conservation of Atlantic Tunas

IFAW	International Fund for Animal Welfare
IMPEL	European Network for the Implementation and Enforcement of Environmental Law
INECE	International Network for Environmental Compliance and Enforcement
IRS	Internal Revenue Service (US)
ITTA	International Tropical Timber Agreement
ITTO	International Tropical Timber Organization
IUCN	The World Conservation Union (formerly the International Union for the Conservation of Nature and Natural Resources)
IUU	illegal, unreported and unregulated
IWC	International Whaling Commission
LIRDP	Integrated Resource Development Project (now known as SLAMU) (Zambia)
Marpol	International Convention for the Prevention of Pollution from Ships at Sea
MACONAR	Maluku Conservation and Natural Resources Project (Indonesia)
MEA	multilateral environmental agreement
MOEF	Ministry of Environment and Forests (India)
MRDP	Maluku Regional Development Project (Indonesia)
MSC	Marine Stewardship Council
NGO	non-governmental organization
NWFP	non-wood forest product
ODS	ozone-depleting substance
OECD	Organisation for Economic Co-operation and Development
PHPA	Directorate General of Forest Protection and Nature Conservation (Indonesia)
POPs	Persistent Organic Pollutants
RIIA	Royal Institute of International Affairs
SGS	Société Générale de Surveillance
SLAMU	South Luangwa Area Management Unit (Zambia)
SRT	Save the Rhino Trust
SSC	Species Survival Commission
TRAFFIC	The wildlife trade monitoring programme of WWF and IUCN
UNCLOS	United Nations Convention on the Law of the Sea
UNCTAD	United Nations Conference on Trade and Development
UNEP	United Nations Environment Programme
UNEP–WCMC	United Nations Environment Programme–World Conservation Monitoring Centre
UNESCO	United Nations Organization for Education, Science and Culture

UNFF	United Nations Forum on Forests
USAID	United States Agency for International Development
WCMC	World Conservation Monitoring Centre (now UNEP-WCMC)
WCO	World Customs Organization
WCS	Wildlife Conservation Society
WHO	World Health Organization
WPA	Wildlife (Protection) Act, 1972 (India)
WPSI	Wildlife Protection Society of India
WTMU	Wildlife Trade Monitoring Unit (formerly part of WCMC)
WTO	World Trade Organization

List of Figures, Tables and Boxes

Figures

Tables

BOXES

About the Contributors

Evan Bowen-Jones is Manager of Fauna & Flora International (FFI) Americas Programme. He has worked as a wildlife biologist in West Africa, Central and South America and the Asia Pacific Region on a wide range of taxa and issues.

Duncan Brack is Head of the Sustainable Development Programme at the Royal Institute of International Affairs (Chatham House) in London, UK. The programme is one of the world's leading interdisciplinary research centres for a wide range of international energy, environmental and business issues. His work has focused in particular on trade and environment and international environmental crime.

Steven Broad has worked since 1996 as Executive Director of TRAFFIC International, the Cambridge-based head office of TRAFFIC – the wildlife-trade monitoring network, which has eight regional programmes, with around 90 staff based in 23 countries worldwide. He has worked on a wide range of wildlife-trade research projects and investigations in many parts of the world since the early 1980s.

Neil Brodie is Coordinator of the Illegal Antiquities Research Centre, McDonald Institute for Archaeological Research, University of Cambridge.

Rosie Cooney is CITES Treaties Officer with the WWF International Species Programme. She has a research background in international environmental law and zoology.

Barney Dickson is Senior Policy and Research Officer at FFI. His interests include CITES, the precautionary principle, sustainable use and the relationship between conservation and development.

Jon Hutton is Executive Director of Resource Africa, which works on policy issues with conservation and rural development partners in Africa, and Regional Director of the Africa programme at FFI. He has over 20 years' experience in wildlife management in Southern Africa and has been actively involved in CITES implementation at national and international levels for much of this time.

Hugo Jachmann is an expert in elephant ecology and management with over 20 years' experience in Africa. He is a member of the IUCN/SSC African Elephant Specialist Group and the CITES Monitoring of Illegal Killing of Elephants technical advisory group.

Paul Jepson is a former Chairman of the Oriental Bird Club and was Head of the BirdLife International – Indonesia Programme from 1991 to 1997. He is Co-director of Conservation Direct and an associate of the School of Geography and Environment in Oxford.

Nigel Leader-Williams is Professor of Biodiversity Management and Director of the Durrell Institute of Conservation and Ecology. He has been interested in the conservation of rhinos since studying the loss of black rhinos in Luangwa Valley during the 1980s.

Cyril Lombard is a member and Director of the Centre for Research, Information and Action for Development in Africa (Southern Africa – Development and Consulting) where he works on technical and market issues relating to the commercialization of botanical products. He is currently responsible for the research and development strategy of the Southern Africa Natural Products Trade Association (SANProTA).

Dave Lowe is Head of the specialist crime unit of the UK's National Criminal Intelligence Service.

Manoj Misra is an independent expert on wildlife trade. He is former Director of TRAFFIC India and former Conservator of Forests for the Government of India.

David Morgan is European Coordinator of the UK Nature and Landscape Office in Brussels, Belgium. Previously he worked for the Environment Directorate of the European Commission, where he was responsible for wildlife-trade issues.

Brendan Moyle is Senior Lecturer in the Department of Commerce at Massey University (Albany), Auckland, New Zealand.

Teresa Mulliken is Research and Policy Coordinator at TRAFFIC International.

Marshall Murphree is Emeritus Professor of applied social science at the University of Zimbabwe. He was Director of the Centre for Applied Social Sciences at the University of Zimbabwe from 1970 to 1996. He recently co-edited (with David Hulme) *African Wildlife and Livelihoods: The Promise and Performance of Community Conservation* (James Currey, 2001).

Sara Oldfield is Global Programmes Director at FFI. She has over 20 years' experience of international biodiversity conservation, with a particular interest in the conservation and sustainable use of plant species, and has worked on CITES issues throughout this time.

Pierre du Plessis is a member and Director of the Centre for Research, Information and Action for Development in Africa (Southern Africa – Development and Consulting) and coordinates the project promoting indigenous fruit in Namibia. He is also currently the Chairman of the management board of the Southern African Natural Products Trade Association (SANProTA).

Dilys Roe is Senior Research Associate in the biodiversity and livelihoods group at the International Institute for Environment and Development.

Nick Sinclair-Brown is Fellow of the Lauterpacht Research Centre for International Law and Fellow of Hughes Hall, Cambridge University.

Juan Carlos Vasquez is Legal and Trade Policy Officer at the CITES secretariat.

Grahame Webb is an expert in crocodile conservation. As Director of Wildlife Management International Pty Ltd., he has been involved in extending the sustainable use principles involved with crocodile conservation to other species.

Acknowledgements

This book is based on a seminar entitled *Regulation, Enforcement and the International Trade in Wildlife: New Directions for Changing Times*, which was held on 17–18 September 2001 at Hughes Hall, Cambridge University, UK. Special thanks are due to Hughes Hall for providing such a congenial setting for the seminar, to Nick Sinclair-Brown for chairing the meeting so ably and to Barbara Algar for ensuring that it ran smoothly. The seminar was facilitated by Africa Resources Trust (now Resource Africa) and TRAFFIC International in partnership with:

- Council of Agriculture Taiwan
- Department for Environment, Food and Rural Affairs
- European Commission
- Fauna & Flora International
- Hughes Hall, Cambridge University
- The World Conservation Union
- Lauterpacht Research Centre for International Law
- Royal Institute of International Affairs

The above organizations are thanked for their roles in bringing together the speakers and other participants in the seminar, which stimulated lively debate on crucial topics in biodiversity conservation. All who took part in the seminar are thanked for their contributions.

The editor is grateful for the support provided by an editorial committee which advised on the structure and content of the book and helped to ensure its timely production. Thanks are due to Crawford Allan (TRAFFIC International); Barney Dickson (FFI); Jon Hutton (Resource Africa and FFI); Stephanie Pendry (TRAFFIC International) and Nick Sinclair-Brown (Lauterpacht Research Centre for International Law). Simon Mickleburgh and Sarah Parker (FFI) are also thanked for their help in preparing the manuscript.

Publication of this book has been made possible by generous financial support from the UK Government, Department for Environment, Food and Rural Affairs.

Preface

I, like many people in this country, am concerned that some species are being pushed ever closer to extinction, partly as a consequence of the illegal wildlife trade.

The Government works hard to combat wildlife crime, and to ensure that the legal trade in wildlife is sustainable. Our commitment to working with other countries to protect the world's wildlife against over-exploitation through international trade was formalized in 1976 when we became a party to CITES. Now, with more than 150 parties, CITES is the leading international agreement in this area. Through the sustainable management of the trade in wild species, CITES can make a vital contribution to the overall goal of sustainable development, and we take our obligations under the convention very seriously.

But the convention can only make an impact if it is effectively implemented and enforced. The Government is also working hard in these areas. The National Wildlife Crime Intelligence Unit, which I was delighted to launch early in 2002, will help in the fight against wildlife crime at the highest level by targeting and disrupting these crimes and the people who commit them. We are also striving to raise awareness of the controls and promoting and supporting the enforcement of the legislation through the Partnership for Action Against Wildlife Crime. But there can be no room for complacency.

The regulation and enforcement of the trade in wildlife is the subject of this book. Its chapters contain an interesting collection of ideas, issues and suggestions for improvement, written by a variety of experts and practitioners in the wildlife field and also by people with knowledge of the trade in other valuable commodities. I very much welcome this forward-looking book, which will make an important contribution to our thinking on species conservation issues.

There is much more work to do if we want to make sure that endangered species are not lost. I believe that if we work together, we can ensure that wildlife species are there for future generations to enjoy.

Rt Hon Michael Meacher MP
Minister for the Environment and Agri-environment

Michael Meacher

Department for Environment,
Food & Rural Affairs
Nobel House
17 Smith Square
London SW1P 3TR

Introduction

The global trade in wildlife and its products is worth billions of pounds a year. The trade brings benefits through employment and income for rural communities, the business sector and national economies but can also pose serious conservation threats. The need to regulate international trade in wildlife has been seen as an important component of biodiversity conservation policy and practice for over 25 years, with regulation operating at various levels. The best known regulatory body is the Convention on International Trade in Endangered Species of Wild Fauna and Flora (CITES) – a multilateral institution. Regional groupings such as the European Community also impose their own regulations, as do individual states. There have been conservation successes and failures in the implementation of all these regulatory mechanisms and their application has provoked impassioned debate. Where regulation appears to fail, leading to declines in species abundance, threats to resource productivity and ecosystem functioning, lack of enforcement is often blamed. The fault may, however, be with the fundamental design of the regulation.

The context in which the regulation of the international trade in wildlife takes place has changed radically since CITES and other trade regulations first came into force. Global trade in all goods has expanded enormously and trade liberalization has become the order of the day. The understanding of the causes of biodiversity loss, and the place of international trade in that process, has also improved and there is a greater appreciation of the importance of equity and governance issues in biodiversity conservation. It is not always clear that wildlife policy has caught up with these changes. While some wildlife trade measures are becoming more flexible and sophisticated, others need to be refined to effectively conserve species within the framework of biodiversity conservation and the sustainable and equitable use of its components.

The content of this book is primarily based on a seminar, held at Hughes Hall, Cambridge University in September 2001, designed to address issues of wildlife trade regulation and enforcement in a changing global context. Facilitated by Africa Resources Trust (now renamed Resource Africa) and TRAFFIC International, the seminar brought together regulators, enforcement agencies, trade specialists and conservationists to reassess existing models of regulation and enforcement and to make recommendations for future policy. This book is the main output of the seminar. The chapters based on seminar presentations have been supplemented by additional contributions from leading experts.

The complexity of dealing with international wildlife trade issues results from the extent and diversity of trade in wildlife and the differing circumstances prevailing in different parts of the world. Lack of information and understanding of the scope and patterns of commercial use add to the difficulty of finding mechanisms for controlling the trade, where and when this is necessary. Expert views on both the very aims and means of regulation and enforcement also vary considerably as reflected by the diversity of opinions presented within this book.

REGULATION

Most of those concerned with the regulation of the international wildlife trade would agree that the overall goal is to promote the conservation of wild species. But they may differ, in practice, about the degree to which regulation should be coordinated with other efforts to promote that goal. Disagreements may also arise about whether regulation should be focused simply on the global status of species or should also concern itself with particular populations that are endangered. The latter issue, in turn, raises the question of how to reconcile the differing needs of individual states. More radically, proposals for regulation may be motivated by other objectives altogether. In many developed countries, there are significant constituencies that are opposed, on ethical or quasi-ethical grounds, to any trade in some species, whatever its impact on their conservation status. Rather differently, others argue that it is imperative to take account of the impact of regulation on the poor rural people who derive benefit from the trade in wild species. This second argument may be a pragmatic, conservationist one, that unless regulations do take account of the needs of the rural poor who live closest to the wildlife then those regulations will be unlikely to lead to successful conservation. Or it may be based on the ethical claim that there is no moral justification for ignoring basic human needs when devising conservation policy.

Whatever the merits of these different aims it is clear that regulation of the international trade, which often depends on cooperation among many different countries, will be more likely to be successful when there is a broad consensus on the goals of regulation than when there is substantial disagreement. Or, if consensus is not possible, it will probably help if the different goals are transparently recognized and appropriate protocols developed.

Assuming that the primary goal of regulation is species conservation (perhaps with a qualification that this should be pursued in an equitable way), there is still plenty of room for disagreement about the role that any particular piece of regulation plays in realizing that goal. Differences may arise because of different assessments of the role of international trade in causing species decline. While some advocate trade restrictions on the grounds that trade is an important factor endangering species, others may contend that the underlying causes lie elsewhere and that restricting international trade will have a minimal effect on conservation. Indeed, in some instances it is argued that the promotion of (sustainable) trade can have a positive conservation impact by providing incentives to conserve the species.

A specific problem with many trade measures is that they fail to take into account the socio-economic incentives that affect the behaviour of people at various stages of the trade process. The issue of illegal trade also appears in the questionable argument that any attempt to liberalize trade restrictions will inevitably lead to an escalation of the illegal trade. Having said that, well-designed regulation can play an important role in ensuring that trade is sustainable, particularly when it is combined with improved management of species in their country of origin.

Enforcement

The aim of enforcement within the context of this book is to ensure that wildlife trade laws are complied with and perpetrators of illegal activity are apprehended. Enforcement provides the 'teeth' to the regulation, allowing for the monitoring and control of trade, with penalties for offences against the regulation. How sharp and strong these teeth are depends on their legal basis, the resources available, how highly motivated the enforcement agency is and what methods it uses.

The motives for enforcement activity are not always related to conservation objectives. In general, the pressure to enforce regulations is shaped by the desire to ensure that the taxable revenues from the trade reach the national treasury. But many law enforcers believe that wildlife trade commodities are relatively low value compared to other commodities in trade and it is more difficult to determine standard values of the goods. Therefore, the enforcement of wildlife trade controls tends to be a low priority, particularly compared to controls on trade in drugs and weapons. In some countries a percentage of the value of the seizure is paid to the enforcement officer responsible. Again, this creates an incentive to focus on high value goods.

Resources required for effective enforcement are costly, as considerable staffing, equipment and the development of complex implementation systems need to be in place 24 hours a day. Despite the economic importance of wildlife trade, regulations are rarely seen as possessing social, political or financial importance and, accordingly, few resources are allocated for their enforcement. Enforcers recognize this and generally do not take regulation of the wildlife trade as seriously – within the enforcement community, lack of resources is typically seen as the main problem thwarting effective enforcement. But there is a case for thinking that the enforcement of wildlife trade regulation should be more efficient in the use of resources allocated by decision-makers.

Often the distance between the policy-makers who establish regulations and the enforcement agencies that apply them is vast. The views and experience of enforcement experts tend to be overlooked when trade regulations are being developed or revised and at the policy level there is little knowledge of how regulations are enforced in practice. The opportunities to ensure that regulations are easy to enforce are therefore limited.

Even in the developed world, enforcement of trade regulations can be surprisingly poor due to a lack of awareness, expertise and the low priority accorded to wildlife trade regulations. Controlling cross-border trade is not infrequently a 'rubber stamp' process where paperwork is almost never cross-checked by inspection of the shipment. Inspection is the exception rather than the norm in the majority of countries.

When analysing the penalties available and the penalties applied, lesser significance is afforded to perpetrators of illegal trade in wildlife, compared to the majority of other similar offences. However, the profits from the illegal wildlife trade are surprisingly high and criminal offences such as fraud, forgery, conspiracy and organized crime elements are often involved. The penalty for illegal cross-border movement is usually simply forfeiture of the goods without prosecution or other penalty. The reason for this is that it is costly, time and staff intensive and sometimes impractical to take the matter to prosecution (for example when the shipment is in transit). Due to the high profits to be made from successful illegal shipments that go undetected, some regular trading companies realize that potential forfeiture of goods alone is an acceptable business risk that occurs from time to time. The lost revenue from a seized shipment is reimbursed by the undetected shipments that they receive or send. If a trading company is detected consistently, the potential for prosecution is increased. However, most illegal shipments do often have accompanying permits and certificates but they may not be the appropriate papers – they may be counterfeit, adulterated or may not tally with the species or volumes in the shipment. Enforcers find it is not always prudent to prosecute for such paperwork offences as in court they are claimed to be minor administrative offences rather than premeditated smuggling. The penalties for breaches of wildlife trade regulations are rarely a deterrent; they are weak because so little significance is placed upon them. The lack of understanding of the environmental damage, scale of illegal trade, high profits and real criminal elements involved are the major reasons for this. Other means to deter illegal trade need to be established. Risk of detection may be a much greater deterrent than increasing penalties – yet the emphasis is generally on penalties.

Global Disparities

Globally there are huge disparities between the approaches to and resources for the enforcement of wildlife trade regulation. Biodiversity resources are generally concentrated in the developing countries where the resources for effective conservation and regulation of trade are limited. New financial mechanisms for supporting biodiversity conservation stimulated for example by the Convention on Biological Diversity are not yet sufficient to meet the needs. International regulations set out standard procedures, methods and uniform systems for enforcement, on the assumption that all nations will be able to meet these minimum standards. This assumption is often mistaken. The procedures agreed by international regulations are set by policy-makers who may be distanced from the realities of enforcement practice.

In the developing world, the equipment, training and infrastructure necessary to meet the minimum standards for enforcement are often lacking. There may not even be a computer at the port of entry so an automated intelligence profiling and targeting system for shipments and passengers is entirely out of the question. In some countries the sheer scale of the trade makes regulations unenforceable. Officials often have no resources or skills to identify the specimens and they have no facilities for holding the specimens should they decide to seize them. The need to supplement low incomes may induce them to seek bribes. Nevertheless, there is evidence that even a limited degree of training and some basic resources can increase detection of illegal shipments and facilitate procedural effectiveness.

In the developed world, generally the infrastructure and enforcement systems are in place to enforce regulations effectively, but as pointed out in Chapters 12 and 16 this may not be the case with the timber trade. There may also still be a lack of awareness of the detail of wildlife trade regulations and the range of controlled species or specimens and there is often the need for greater resources to allow for regular shipment inspections. Most enforcers know that commodities such as ivory, parrots and certain reptile skins are controlled but rarely little else. Specialist teams of enforcement personnel are becoming more common, pooling all resources for wildlife trade regulation into small units rather than attempting to achieve a broad and general level of expertise and resources across the country. The use of high technology and computerized systems is more commonplace and intelligence-based targeting of potential illegal shipments and smugglers is the main way of focusing effort more efficiently.

Organization of the Book

Following on from these brief comments on regulation and enforcement of international wildlife trade, the book is arranged in four parts. Part 1 provides more detailed background with a comprehensive overview chapter on international wildlife trade. This chapter highlights the huge range of species in trade around the world, only a fraction of which are covered by CITES controls. Part 1 also includes chapters on the nature of regulation and enforcement.

Some authors in this book, use the term 'regulation' to refer specifically to trade regulation. Others use the term in a more general sense to refer to any sort of conservation regulation. The context should make clear which sense is being employed. The appropriate relationship between trade regulation and other forms of conservation regulation is one of the themes running throughout the book.

Part 2 considers existing systems of regulation and enforcement which relate to international wildlife trade at international, regional and national levels. The chapter on CITES looks at implementation, compliance and enforcement of the provisions of the convention. Chapter 7 considers the impact of stricter domestic measures as allowed for by the convention in the context of the European Community Wildlife Regulation. Chapter 8 provides an example of regulation at a national level looking at legislation and enforcement in India.

Part 3 provides a series of case studies relating aspects of regulation and enforcement to different species and species groups. The scope of the case studies varies considerably from the situation faced by a particular species at a particular time to reviews of whole sectors of the international wildlife trade.

Part 4 looks at the lessons that can be drawn from tackling illegal trade in other goods including antiquities, drugs, ozone-depleting substances, timber and fisheries. The authors consider both the role of regulation and mechanisms for enforcement.

A concluding chapter draws together the themes running throughout the book and highlights issues that need to be considered further. The key issues are those which emerged from the seminar held at Hughes Hall, Cambridge in September 2001 and which are discussed further in this book. They provide a crucial agenda for improving the policy and practice of regulation to sustain both international wildlife trade and rural livelihoods. It is hoped that the ideas presented in this book will help to take forward and widen the ongoing debate on regulation and the effective enforcement of wildlife trade controls.

Part 1

Background

Chapter 1

The Nature and Extent of Legal and Illegal Trade in Wildlife

Steven Broad, Teresa Mulliken and Dilys Roe

INTRODUCTION

The sale and exchange by people of wild animal and plant resources – more simply 'wildlife trade' – is an issue at the very heart of the relationship between biodiversity conservation and sustainable development. Directly and indirectly, increasing demand and consumption are depleting the Earth's living natural resources at an alarming rate, yet these same resources offer the biological foundation upon which human society depends.

Although only one of a range of forces capable of driving this depletion, wildlife trade is related to some of the most important underlying causes of biodiversity loss. Widespread poverty and insecurity drive people to adopt ways of life that degrade the environment upon which they depend such that sustainable livelihoods cannot be maintained. At the same time, wealth often fuels consumption patterns that undervalue and drive the over-exploitation and depletion of natural resources. Linking the worlds of poverty and wealth, is an increasingly liberalized global economic system based on development and resource-use models that many believe to be flawed.

The historical impacts of wildlife trade on the security of biological resources have largely been negative, but the utilitarian value of wild animals, plants, their products and derivatives continues to make an important contribution to the fulfilment of human needs. This value may in some circumstances provide direct positive incentives for protection of natural habitats and systems. In turn, these incentives can compete with the overwhelming economic forces driving land conversion from natural ecosystems to biodiversity-poor agricultural systems, which represents the greatest cause of depletion of biodiversity today.

The trade in wild plants and animals and their parts and derivatives is big business, estimated to be worth billions of dollars and to involve hundreds of millions of plants and animals every year. The trade is diverse, ranging from live animals and ornamental plants to a vast array of wildlife products and derivatives. Fish and other food products, exotic leather goods, musical instruments, timber, tourist curios and medicines and other wildlife commodities can be found in markets around the globe.

This trade is complex and constantly evolving and, in many cases, poses a major challenge to conservation of biological diversity, either directly, through over-exploitation or indirectly, through impacts such as by-catch of non-target species and introduction of invasive species. Most of the trade is legal, but a significant portion of it is not. Both legal and illegal traders adapt to changing circumstances. They target new species when others become depleted, shift to new markets, or in the case of illegal trade develop new smuggling methods and routes to avoid detection. The increasing globalization of trade, creation of common markets and advances in technology all add further complications to the already difficult task of ensuring that trade is legal, maintained within sustainable levels, and that it does not have indirect negative impacts on the conservation of biodiversity.

COSTS AND BENEFITS

Detrimental impacts of unsustainable wildlife trade have been widely documented, notable examples including the depletion of populations of great whales, marine turtles and rhinoceroses through over-exploitation. Historical evidence of species extinction being caused primarily by human over-exploitation is patchy (Groombridge, 1992), though in combination with other threats, especially habitat loss, wildlife trade has been shown to result in significant declines in wild populations of many species. Over-exploitation can also have a negative impact on ecosystem functions, though such effects are often extremely difficult to demonstrate reliably (forest loss caused by timber extraction being one of the more tangible examples). A more obvious risk in many cases is loss of resource productivity and value resulting from population depletion, and in extreme circumstances leading to commercial extinction.

Beyond direct negative biological impacts, wildlife trade can cause indirect impacts of conservation concern, the two most obvious examples being detrimental by-catch of non-target species and introduction of harmful invasive alien species. Examples of detrimental by-catch are particularly well documented in the fisheries sector as with incidental catch of marine turtles and seabirds in capture fisheries. Terrestrial examples include impacts on non-target species from timber harvesting and waterfowl hunting (Freese, 1998). Negative conservation impacts of alien species introductions caused by wildlife trade are less well documented; some of the more problematic examples have been linked to deliberate movements of ornamental plants and food and game fish species outside their natural ranges.

Juxtaposed with these risks are the enormous benefits derived by people from consumptive use of wild plant and animal resources. Wildlife resources play a major and very often critical role in the livelihoods of a high proportion of the world's population and it is often the poorest people and households that are most dependent on these resources (Prescott-Allen and Prescott-Allen, 1982; Pimental et al 1997; Scoones et al, 1992; Arnold, 1995; Neumann and Hirsch, 2000; Nasi and Cunningham, 2001).

Numerous studies have noted the importance of wild food products, which are of particular importance to women, children and the poor for whom securing access to such resources is important for sustaining their livelihoods (Scoones et al, 1992; Warner, 1995; FAO, 1995; Cavendish, 1997; Barnett, 2000). Clarke et al, (1996), however, point out that the same cannot be said for big game in Africa, the household consumption of which increases with increased wealth. Some species are used daily while others are considered 'famine foods' and used only occasionally. Wild foods often fill a seasonal gap and are used when little else is available (Scoones et al, 1992). Wild foods include fruits, mushrooms, nuts, leaves and starches as well as meat and fish. Owing primarily to species conservation concerns, particular attention has been focused recently on the use of wild animal species for meat. According to Bennett and Robinson (2000), wild animals (including fish) contribute 20 per cent or more of the animal protein in rural diets in at least 62 countries. The use of wild meat varies by region and dietary custom. In West Africa for example, there is a high level of consumption – wild animals account for 75 per cent of meat intake in Liberia (Bennett and Robinson, 2000). In Ghana, an estimated 305,000 tonnes of wild meat is sold annually with a net value of approximately US$275 million (Government of the Republic of Ghana, 1998). In Côte d'Ivoire, an estimated 100,000 tonnes of wild meat was harvested in 1996, nearly twice as much meat as produced from domestic livestock (Caspary et al, 2001). A recent TRAFFIC study notes that reliance on wild meat is growing in Eastern and Southern Africa in response to increased human populations and poverty – for example, 80 per cent of rural Kenyan households depend on wild meat for the majority of meat protein (Barnett, 2000).

Wildlife in the form of trees and plants also provides an important source of fuel for cooking and heating, especially in rural areas, with 90 per cent of fuel-wood production taking place in developing countries (Bourke and Leitch, 2000). According to the Food and Agriculture Organization (FAO) data, nearly 464 million cubic metres of wood fuel were produced in Africa in 1998, of which all but a tiny fraction (less than one per cent) was consumed there. Nearly double that level – 883 million cubic metres – was produced in Asia with consumption once again equalling over 99 per cent of total production (FAO, 2001a). Fodder is considered the most important non-wood forest product (NWFP) in the drier regions of continental and South Asia, and to be of great importance in the arid and semi-arid zones of Africa (FAO, 2001b).

Wild species, both animal and plant, are also important components of traditional medicines, upon which an estimated 80 per cent of the world's population has been said to rely for primary health care. This frequently cited figure is attributed to the World Health Organization (WHO) (WHO, IUCN and WWF, 1993). Prescott-Allen and Prescott-Allen (1982) estimated that 95 per cent of traditional medicines were plant-based. However, a variety of animal species are also used for medicinal purposes, ranging from tigers *Panthera tigris* to medicinal leeches *Hirudo medicinalis*. Medicines are considered among the most important NWFPs throughout the world according to a recent FAO assessment of forest resources (FAO, 2001c). Wild plants are also an important source of materials for construction of furniture, housing, clothing, household utensils and ornamentation.

In these and other sectors of wildlife use, for all but strict subsistence purposes, benefits also derive from a wide range of economic activities along the marketing chain. These values are examined in greater detail later in this chapter.

Quantifying Wildlife Trade – an Overview

Wildlife trade is an economic activity carried out across the globe at local, national and international levels. The dividing line between purely subsistence use of wildlife, which plays a critical role in the livelihoods of a high proportion of the world's population, and wildlife trade is often blurred (Freese, 1998). Wildlife products such as fruits, mushrooms, nuts, leaves, fuel wood, wild meat and fish are both consumed directly and sold into the cash economy, sometimes by the same people in the same locations. Estimates of the number of people dependent on NWFPs for at least part of their income range from 200 million worldwide to one billion in the Asia and Pacific region alone (van Rijsoort, 2000).

For a wide variety of reasons, it is not easy to quantify the world's wildlife trade. Local use of wild plants and animals may account for the majority of global wildlife trade in terms of trade volume and perhaps even value. However, the nature of such trade is that it is often carried out through informal trade networks and beyond the reach of government statisticians. Even the more structured aspects of domestic trade in wildlife commodities, between regions within a country and to supply urban markets, is seldom closely monitored and even where it is, statistical records of trade volumes and values are dispersed and difficult to compile.

Specific analyses of domestic wildlife trade show some interesting results. Campbell and Brigham (1993) studied the relative importance of local, national and international trade for NWFPs in Zimbabwe and concluded that international trade involved far fewer species than subsistence use or domestic trade and was therefore likely to be less significant for the majority of rural communities. Similarly, Nash (1994) concluded in a review of the South-East Asian songbird trade that domestic trade in live birds within Indonesia (roughly estimated as at least 1.3 million wild-caught birds per year) greatly exceeded the export trade, previously perceived as the main conservation trade-related conservation issue for the bird species involved. Likewise, a review of wild meat use in Eastern and Southern Africa in the late 1990s indicated that commercial trade to urban centres, rather than subsistence use, had become the dominant driving force for rural hunters in many of the areas studied (Barnett, 2000).

Quantifying Wildlife Trade – Focus on International Trade

Information sources

Any effort to describe the international wildlife trade must unfortunately begin with the recognition that this cannot be done with any accuracy. The trade is very poorly documented in terms of the species or products involved, trade volumes and trade values. The international trade in timber and fisheries products is relatively better documented than the trade in most other wildlife commodities, which is a reflection of the greater monetary value of this trade.

There are two main sources of data on the international wildlife trade: customs data and annual reports compiled by parties to the Convention on International Trade in Endangered Species of Wild Fauna and Flora (CITES). Customs data include information on trade volumes and declared values upon export and import. These are compiled by national governments and organized according to commodity types, most often using the Harmonized Commodity Description and Coding System (HS). Customs data provide information on levels of processing and overall trade volumes, but rarely on the species or number of specimens involved. Much of the trade data compiled by the FAO and the UN Conference on Trade and Development (UNCTAD) are based on customs data and therefore have the same limitations. The International Tropical Timber Organization (ITTO) compiles more detailed data for the trade in tropical timbers, but again, these are often not specific to the species or even the genus level.

By virtue of CITES annual reporting requirements, the trade in CITES-listed species is relatively well documented. Information on the different species and the number of specimens reported in trade by CITES parties is compiled by the United Nations Environment Programme – World Conservation Monitoring Centre (UNEP–WCMC) on behalf of the CITES Secretariat. However, the number of species covered by CITES is small relative to the overall number of wildlife species in trade. Furthermore, problems with the accuracy of CITES trade reporting mean that trade data are indicative rather than actual. CITES trade data are better for live animal specimens than for plants or for animal and plant products.

Cross-border trade in many regions is likely to circumvent CITES or other trade control measures, for example customs controls, and therefore not to be accounted for within either customs or CITES data. By its very nature, illegal trade is also undocumented, with the exception of information available for seized shipments that is sometimes reported in the media or CITES trade data.

Although referring specifically to the trade in NWFPs, Iqbal (1993) summarizes the situation with regard to the wildlife trade in general when he states that:

> *Basic information ... is seriously lacking... Trade statistics, as far as they do exist, are to be handled with much thought, as a very large volume of NWFP are being traded unregistered. Under-reporting or not reporting at all, double counting, grouping of NWFP among themselves and with other products, and the use of unrealistic prices are among the systematic shortcomings of these statistics. Such statistics, however, are a starting point to get information and at best can be considered as indicative only.*

Scale of international wildlife trade

As indicated earlier, timber and fisheries products dominate the international wildlife trade in terms of volume and value. Approximately one billion cubic metres of wood products (including pulp and paper, but excluding fuel wood) were exported in 1999 (FAO, 2001a), with the total value of forest product exports (excluding fuel wood) during that year estimated at US$132 billion (FAOSTAT, 2002). According to FAO data, nearly 116 million cubic metres of sawn wood were traded internationally in 1998 (FAO, 2001a).

According to the FAO, 117 million tonnes of fish were produced via capture fisheries and aquaculture in 1998. Approximately one-third of fish (live-weight equivalent) produced during this year entered international trade, with 20 per cent of exports coming from 'low-income food deficit' countries. The total value of fish and fishery product exports in 1998 was US$51,300 million, of which developing countries accounted for 50 per cent. FAO estimates that 36 million people, comprising about 15 million full-time, 13 million part-time and 8 million occasional workers, are employed in primary capture and aquaculture fisheries production (FAO, 2000).

A 1993 study commissioned by the FAO (Iqbal, 1993) identified approximately 150 NWFPs considered of major significance in international trade based on a preliminary review of available trade data and other references. A list of products identified is reproduced in Table 1.1.

Relatively few of the commodity types identified by Iqbal are commonly thought of as being components of 'the wildlife trade', and most do not include species covered by CITES. Exceptions include wild animals and animal products, ornamental and medicinal plants and incense woods.

The scale of the annual international trade in more 'typical', if actually less common, wildlife products during the 1980s is illustrated in Table 1.2.

Table 1.1 *Commercially Significant NWFPs in International Trade*

Category	*Product*
Food products	Nuts: Brazil nuts, pine nuts, pignolia nuts, malva nuts, walnuts and chestnuts Fruits: jujube, sapodilla, ginkgo Fungi: morels, truffles, pine mushrooms Vegetables: bamboo shoots, osmunds, reindeer moss, palm hearts Starches: sago Bird nests Oils: shea nuts, babassu oil, illipe oil Maple sugar
Herbs and spices	Nutmeg, mace, cinnamon, cassia, cardamom, galanga, allspice, caraway, bay leaves, oregano etc
Industrial plant oils and waxes	Tung oil, neem oil, jojoba oil, kemiri (candle, lumbang) oil, akar wangi, babassu, oticica and kapok oils Carnauba wax
Plant gums	For food uses: gum arabic, tragacanth, karaya, carob Technological grade gums: talha, combretum
Natural pigments	Annatto seeds, logwood, indigo
Oleoresins	Pine oleoresin, copal, damar, gamboge, benzoin gum, dragon's blood (Benjamin), copaiba oil, amber
Fibres and flosses	Fibres: bamboo, rattan, xateattap, aren, osier, raffia, toquilla straw products, cork, esparto, Erica and other broom grasses Flosses: kapok or silk cotton
Vegetable tanning materials	Quebracho, mimosa, chestnut and catha/cutch
Latex	Natural rubber, gutta percha, jelutong, sorva and chicle
Insect products	Honey, beeswax, lac and lac-dye, silk, cochineal, aleppo galls, kermes
Incense woods	Sandalwood, gharu or aloewood [agarwood]
Essential oils	Various
Plant insecticides	Pyrethrum, derris, medang and peuak bong
Medicinal plants	Various
Wild plants	Various
Animals and animal products	Ivory, trophies, skins, feathers, eggs, butterflies, live animals and birds
Miscellaneous	Bidi leaves, soap nut, Quillaia bark, betel and cola nuts, chewing sticks, lacquer, dom nuts or ivory nuts

Source: Iqbal, 1993, as cited in Iqbal, 1995

More recent estimates for the trade in some CITES-listed taxa were provided by UNEP-WCMC (see Figure 1.1).

Table 1.2 *Wildlife Products in Trade during the 1980s*

Species group or product	*Quantity in trade*
Live primates	40,000
African elephant ivory	Tusks from 90,000 elephants
Pelts from wild furbearers	15 million
Live birds	4 million
Reptile skins	10 million
Tropical fish	350 million
Orchids	1 million

Source: Fitzgerald, 1989

Fauna (annual mean, 1995–1999)

- Over 1.5 million live birds (250,000 App II; 1,250,000 App III)
- 640,000 live reptiles
- 300,000 crocodilian skins (world trade is over 1,200,000 but mostly farmed)
- 1,600,000 lizard skins
- 1,100,000 snake skins
- 150,000 furs
- Almost 300 tonnes of caviar
- Over 1,000,000 pieces of coral
- 21,000 hunting trophies

Flora (1999)

- 19 million bulbs exported from Turkey
- Over 53,000 live wild-collected orchids exported from Central America and Vietnam
- Over 200 tonnes of dried orchid roots from Vietnam to the Republic of Korea
- 360,000 cacti 'rainsticks' exported from Chile and Peru
- 70 tonnes of *Aloe ellenbeckii* resin exported from Kenya to China
- Over 300 tonnes of *Aloe ferox* extract exported from South Africa
- 120 tonnes of Agarwood *Aquilaria malaccensis* chips exported from Indonesia and Malaysia
- 30 tonnes of American Ginseng *Panax quinquefolius* roots exported from the United States

Source: Caldwell, in litt, 2001

Figure 1.1 *Reported International Trade in CITES-listed Flora and Fauna*

Commodities in international wildlife trade

Wild species are traded internationally in many forms in order to produce a wide variety of products. Major uses include:

- Medicines. Many medicines, both traditional and 'western' are based on wild plants or compounds extracted from them. Approximately 1000 plant species have been identified in international trade in East Asia alone (Lee, in prep), and 700 imported for use within Europe. The global international trade in medicinal and aromatic plants exceeded 440,000 tonnes in 1996, and was valued at US$1.3 billion (Lange, 1998).
- Food. Although most wildlife hunted or collected for use as food is consumed for subsistence purposes, there is a substantial international trade in a variety of NWFPs, well-known examples including Brazil nuts *Bertholletia excelsa*, palm hearts, pine nuts, various mushrooms and spices. The trade in fisheries products dominates the food trade in animal species.
- Ornaments and furnishings. A wide variety of wildlife products are used for decoration and ornamental purposes including, ivory, coral, turtle and mollusc shells, reptile and other skins, and feathers. Tourist items are often crafted from local wildlife, including jewellery and ornaments crafted from corals and shells, curios such as insects or other small animals encased in plastic and stuffed animals.
- Wearing apparel. Skins, furs, feathers and fibres from many mammal, reptile, bird and fish species are traded internationally to make clothing, boots and shoes, bags and other items. These include expensive and high fashion items, for example shahtoosh shawls made from the endangered and Appendix I-listed Tibetan antelope *Pantholops hodgsonii* as well as more widely available and legally traded products such as snake-skin accessories.
- Pets/Hobbies. The increased availability of air transport around the world has greatly expanded the variety and numbers of wild species traded for use as pets or for hobbies. The international trade is dominated by reptiles, birds and ornamental fish, but includes invertebrate species such as scorpions and spiders. Imports of wild birds into the US, once one of the main markets for CITES-listed species, have declined significantly as a result of increased import restrictions. Imports of live reptiles have increased, however.
- Ornamental plants. Many common garden and indoor plants are the product of an international trade that has been taking place for centuries. This includes many bulbous species, for example snowdrops *Galanthus* spp and crocuses *Crocus* spp, cyclamens *Cyclamen* spp, orchids, tree ferns, bromeliads, cycads, palms and cacti. Although much of the trade now involves artificially propagated plants, there are still millions of wild plants traded internationally each year, including a specialist trade in rare species.
- Manufacturing and construction. Forest products including timber, rattan and bamboo for furniture making, plant oils and gums, dyes, resins and latex are all traded internationally in large volumes.

Key countries involved in the international wildlife trade

Research on the NWFP trade undertaken by the FAO identifies China as the exporter of the largest quantities, with other major suppliers being India, Indonesia, Malaysia, Thailand and Brazil. Approximately 60 per cent of all NWFPs in trade are imported by the EU, US and Japan and the general direction of wildlife trade flows is from developing to developed countries (Iqbal, 1995). It should also be noted that among those countries for whom wildlife trade is commercially significant are included some of the poorest countries and some of the countries richest in biodiversity resources (Roe et al, 2002).

In a recent analysis of wood production and consumption, FAO (2001a) reported the increasing importance of the Chinese market. Growing consumption and lack of adequate forest resources had contributed to a recent rapid increase in its imports. China was reported to be the world's third largest importer of primary forest products, after the US and Japan. The same report noted that global trade patterns were changing, largely as a result of increased trade among developing countries, especially between countries in the Asian region. Trade patterns have also become more diverse, and there had been increased intra-regional trade in other regions such as North America.

As for fisheries, a review of production and trade by the FAO (2000), noted that in 1998, China, Japan, US, the Russian Federation, Peru, Indonesia, Chile and India (in that order) were the top producing countries, together accounting for more than half of global capture fisheries production by weight for that year. China alone accounted for 32 per cent of the world total. As for consumption, the same report indicated that Japan was the largest importer of fishery products in 1998, accounting for some 23 per cent of total world imports, but Japanese imports of fish and fishery products had declined recently as a result of the economic recession. The EU had further increased its dependence on imports for its fish supply. The US, despite being the world's fifth major exporting country, was also its second main importer. More than 77 per cent of the total world import value was concentrated in these three areas.

Valuation of Wildlife Trade

Overview

The lack of information on wildlife use in general makes it very difficult to estimate total and relative levels of wildlife use for domestic and commercial use (Burgess, 1992). As noted by Wollenberg and Belcher (2001):

> *only a small subset of forest products possesses potential for significant cash income and employment generation... The majority of these products have low cash values and are used for consumption, rather than for sale.*

For some, however, wild products can be a significant source of cash income, particularly in marginal agricultural areas. As previously mentioned, estimates of the number of people dependent on NWFPs for at least part of their income range from 200 million worldwide to one billion just in Asia and the Pacific (van Rijsoort, 2000). According to Wollenberg and Belcher (2001), species with the most potential to contribute significantly to cash incomes include some rattan and bamboo species, resins, birds' nests, various fruits and nuts and medicinal plants. Timber was considered one of the most valuable forest products, but one that was rarely available to local communities for income generation on any significant scale.

The importance of the trade in NWFPs has been noted by the FAO, which stated that: 'Traded products contribute to the fulfilment of daily needs and provide employment as well as income, particularly for rural people and especially for women' (FAO 2001c). In their review of the literature on the trade in wild meat in West Africa, Kasim and Long (2000) determined that cash income, from sales of products such as wild meat, would become increasingly important for paying school fees and taxes, for example, as rural communities entered the cash economy.

International trade value

The value of the international wildlife trade is even less well documented than the quantities of specimens in trade. An estimate of US$4–5 billion per year, not including timber and fisheries has been credited to the United Nations Environment Programme (UNEP, 1989, cited in Roth and Merz, 1997), while Fitzgerald (1989) uses a figure of 'at least' US$5 billion for the wholesale value of products in trade. Iqbal (1995) provides a more recent estimate for the trade in NWFPs of over US$11 billion. TRAFFIC estimated an import value in the early 1990s approaching US$15 billion for all wildlife products – forest-related or not, climbing to nearly US$160 billion if wild-sourced timber and fish products are included (Table 1.3).

Although wildlife has often been considered under the umbrella of 'minor forest products', some species and specimens can command high prices. In Taiwan, the highest grade of agarwood, a fragrant resinous wood produced by some Indomalesian tree species of the genus *Aquilaria*, can sell for US$11,500/kg, and is now virtually unavailable (Barden et al, 2000). The retail price of a single blue and gold macaw *Ara ararauna*, of which approximately 42,000 were traded internationally from 1981–1992, could be as high as US$1200 in the early 1990s. Hyacinth macaws *Anodorhynchus hyacinthinus*, the largest parrot species in the world, and bright blue in colour, were offered for sale for upwards of US$8000 during the 1980s (Mulliken and Thomsen, 1995) – the price reflecting the fact that international trade in these very rare birds was banned both by range states and CITES.

Table 1.3 *Estimate of the Annual Value of Global International Trade in Wildlife in the early 1990s*

Commodity	*Estimated value US$*
Live animals	
Primates	10 million
Cage birds	60 million
Reptiles and amphibians	6 million
Ornamental fish	750 million
Animal products for clothing/ornament etc	
Mammal furs and fur products	750 million
Reptile skins	200 million
Reptile skin products	750 million
Mollusc shells	200 million
Ornamental corals	20 million
Natural pearls and products	90 million
Animal products for medicine	
Wild ungulate products for medicine (deer velvet, musk etc)	30 million
Chelonian products	5 million
Seahorses	5 million
Animal products for food (excluding fish)	
Game meat	120 million
Frogs legs	60 million
Swiftlet nests	65 million
Edible snails	460 million
Live ornamental plants	
'Wild' plant trade	250 million
Non-wood forest products	
Global NWFP estimate (Iqbal, 1995)	11.7 million
Subtotal excluding fisheries food products & timber	*14.9 billion*
Fisheries food products	40 billion
Timber	104 billion
TOTAL	**158.9 billion**

Source: TRAFFIC analysis based on declared import values from various sources, largely derived from published FAO and customs data.

Persistent demand for rare species such as hyacinth macaw *Anodorhynchus hyacinthinus* (listed in CITES Appendix I since 1987) and common species that are nevertheless restricted in international trade in some way (for example through national-level harvest or export controls and imposition of duties) collectively drive a widespread illegal trade in wildlife. The true size of the illegal trade is anyone's guess – and several have tried. One estimate states that the illegal component of the trade is US$5–8 billion (UNEP, 1998). Roth and Merz (1997) have claimed that the illegal trade in wildlife products is the world's second largest illegitimate business after narcotics. However the very nature of the illegal trade is such that no reliable data are available to support this assertion.

Understanding Trade Structure and Driving Forces

Beyond quantification of wildlife trade volumes, patterns and values, it is critical that any regulatory or non-regulatory interventions aimed to avoid risks and maximize benefits take into account the structure of the trade and the driving forces motivating this sector of commerce.

Structure of wildlife trade chains

The journey of any given wildlife product from the collector at source to the final consumer can involve a wide range of intermediaries and other stakeholders. While wildlife trade is often perceived as a predominantly rural activity, the urban dimension should not be underestimated. Barnett (2000) found that in Eastern and Southern Africa, complex rural to urban supply networks have developed for the wild-meat trade, which is driven by urban demand and lucrative prices. Kasim and Long (2000) similarly comment on the importance of urban markets, stating that there is evidence that much of the commercial trade in wild meat is in the hands of urban-based entrepreneurs who subcontract rural hunters, adding that wild-meat sales have moved beyond local urban markets to the international arena.

Warner (1995) describes the concessionaire system frequently used in the past in Asia, where collection and marketing of high value wildlife products for export or processing was often under a government-granted concession system, with the concessionaire having the right to sell all of a specified product that was collected from a designated area. This is the system that currently exists for collection of edible birds' nests. The concessionaire would need a number of collectors to ensure an adequate supply of the product and these collectors would often trade the collected products to the concessionaire for food and manufactured goods. If the collectors were in debt to the concessionaire (a common occurrence) they could easily enforce product collection and hence maintain supply. Warner notes that this form of 'debt bondage' is now decreasing in the Asia–Pacific region as the concessionaire system is being restructured or eliminated and as collectors increasingly form cooperatives and associations.

Even in systems where there is no concessionaire, few products are sold directly from collectors to wholesalers or processors because of the small

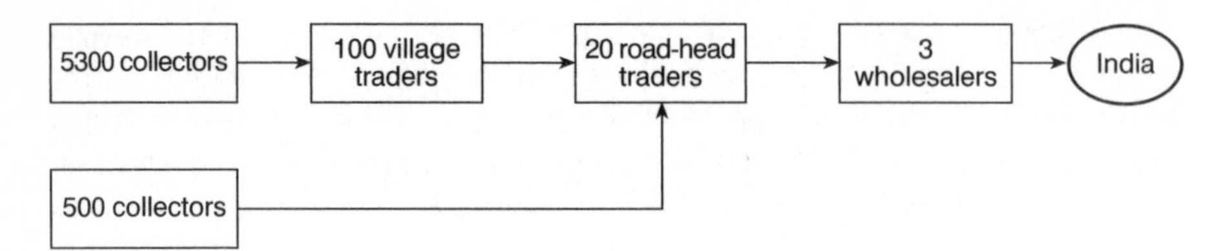

Source: Edwards, 1993, as depicted in Warner, 1995.

Figure 1.2 *Supply Chain for Trade in Medicinal Plants from East Nepal to India*

quantities involved. Middlemen – often local traders – are generally involved and handle storage and transport, for example. Edwards (1993) has described the trade chain for the export of medicinal plants from Eastern Nepal to India, noting the involvement of a series of middlemen between collectors and buyers in India, with the relatively small number of Terai-based wholesalers exerting the main influence over prices received by harvesters (Figure 1.2). Village traders were noted as providing an important marketing service to collectors, for example in transport and provision of credit.

The live bird trade in Tanzania usually has from two to three tiers – trappers, middlemen and exporters – with some trappers selling direct to exporters (Moyer, 1995). A three-tiered system is also described by Edwards (1992) with regard to the live bird trade in Guyana, where the majority of trappers were Amerindians. According to Parsaud (2001), Head of Guyana's Wildlife Division, Amerindians are not directly involved in the export of wildlife, which is dominated by seven or eight exporters, and are 'being fleeced all the time' with a lot of them 'being owed monies'. Potential reasons for their lack of participation in the export process included the remoteness of their communities or presumed lack of knowledge of the business.

As described by Neumann and Hirsch (2000):

> *the structure of relationships between collectors, middlemen, traders and wholesalers can be highly complex, involving various elements of exploitation, risk, cooperation, collusion and resistance … the character of these relationships can shift through time, from locale to locale and at different points along the marketing chain… Lack of access to information, transport, credit and storage facilities combine to keep collectors at a great disadvantage in the market place. And these conditions provide plenty of opportunities for intermediaries to position themselves as almost unavoidable links in the marketing chain.*

Shortening the supply chain is often seen as the answer to increasing income to collectors. However, as noted by Edwards (1993) with regard to the medicinal plant trade in Nepal, intermediaries also perform many vital functions including transport, packing and risk taking. Removing intermediaries would expose those with little resilience to a volatile industry. As Warner (1995) points out, middlemen are often perceived as being the villains, but the value of the services they provide should not be underestimated. If they are removed from the marketing chain then the services provided must be met from some other source. In the case of Nepal's medicinal plant trade, Edwards (1993) has recommended the formation of marketing collectives to increase the ability of collectors to access market information and sell direct to road-head traders, and Olsen and Helles (1997) recommended establishment of credit facilities and support to road-head traders to sell direct to India, as well as public dissemination of market information.

In other cases intermediaries add little or no value and simply capture a little (or a lot) of the income from the sale of wildlife. In the Tanzanian villages visited as part of a recent TRAFFIC study, village middlemen pay trappers only 50 per cent of what they themselves receive from city-based traders, yet have few costs. Since the majority of species are collected to order, they do not have significant risks such as paying collectors before they are paid.

Drivers

As for any other commercial activity, a primary motivating factor for many participants in wildlife trade is purely economic in nature. People derive direct revenues along the marketing chain of a wildlife product, through cash income or exchange of commercial services. As for other commodities, those involved in wildlife trade may be motivated by speculation about future values rather than immediate monetary benefits, particularly when dealing with non-perishable wildlife goods. Typically, revenue distribution along the trade chain for wildlife goods is uneven, with resource owners and harvesters receiving only a small fraction compared to intermediaries and retailers (Freese, 1996). Those involved in illegal activity may work at any point of the trade chain, gaining through direct trade revenues or indirect income, especially through corruption in regulatory systems.

However, the behaviour of participants in wildlife trade is not exclusively motivated by monetary benefits. Wildlife trade is driven by diverse socio-economic and cultural factors, including:

- food supply (from elements of staple diets to tonic and novelty foods);
- healthcare (from herbal remedies to ingredients of industrial pharmaceuticals);
- provision of industrial materials (including timber and a wide range of ingredients in manufacturing processes, such as gums and resins);
- religion (live animals, and a wide range of wild plant and animal parts);
- collecting (including live animals and plants and a range of wildlife specimens and curios);
- clothing and fashion (leather, furs, feathers etc);
- sport (including trophies and live birds).

These and other factors can often be equal or greater in importance than direct monetary benefits in driving wildlife trade patterns. Recent research into consumer perceptions about consumption of endangered species ingredients in traditional Asian medicines provides excellent illustration of the complexities of understanding wildlife demand and framing effective conservation interventions (Lee, 1998; Lee et al, 1998). For example Lee (1998) found that many traditional medicine consumers were motivated to avoid use of endangered species, but that awareness levels about the nature and origin of medicinal ingredients was often low. A small proportion of consumers, however, indicated that they would use medicines containing endangered species, despite understanding the conservation implications.

Framing a Response to Wildlife Trade Challenges

Responding to conservation problems associated with wildlife trade is not a straightforward challenge. In most situations, there is enormous uncertainty in almost every key variable related to decision-making, including:

- species status, population trends and other basic biological information;
- driving forces for harvests, monetary and non-monetary;
- causes of decline and the relative importance of wildlife trade impacts;
- definition of 'sustainable' wildlife exploitation;
- prediction of future changes in species and ecosystem status, economies and people's behaviour;

Unfortunately, remedial actions are often taken without due attention to such uncertainty and such actions are rarely linked to the establishment of means to judge their impact over time.

Over the past 25 years, the predominant response to concerns about over-exploitation of wildlife has been regulatory intervention by governments. Such regulation has been enacted through local and national laws and through multilateral instruments, particularly CITES, and a wide range of international agreements governing fisheries management.

Increasingly over this time, the 'precautionary principle' has been invoked in such regulatory decisions as a means to address the various aspects of uncertainty noted above. At risk of overgeneralizing this evolution in policy, it could be claimed that the burden of proof has shifted so that it is now more common for trade bans or strict limitations on trade volumes to be introduced and maintained until 'users' prove lack of conservation risk. This may be a pragmatic reaction to uncertainty and a counterbalance to earlier inaction by governments, traders and consumers in the face of overwhelming evidence of conservation damage for some wildlife species in trade. However, some argue that more flexible and adaptive approaches to wildlife management and regulation would be more effective.

Complicating this situation still further is the fact that wildlife trade regulations are often not motivated solely by specific conservation concerns, with many protective measures justified by concerns such as animal welfare, cultural values and wider commercial interests.

There is little doubt that regulatory measures have affected wildlife trade patterns, if nothing else in many cases by changing a lawful activity into an illegal one. However, application and enforcement of regulatory systems for wildlife trade often suffer from low prioritization by governments (as compared for example to controls on trade in narcotics and weapons), and resulting underinvestment, uneven application and failure to offer a deterrent to illegal activity. A common response to such concerns is a call for increased enforcement investment and effort and often this may be the best course of action to take. Nevertheless, there are also sound reasons in many cases to revisit the rationale for and design of wildlife trade regulations, focusing attention on what specific conservation and socio-economic impacts are intended and how best they can be achieved.

A range of non-regulatory approaches to wildlife trade concerns has gained increasing attention in recent years, especially initiatives such as certification and eco-labelling, aimed to encourage sustainable consumer behaviour. Again, such efforts struggle to address the uncertainties related to biological, management and economic factors.

Conclusion

This chapter provides just a glimpse of the complexities of the trade in wild animals and plants. Weighing the conservation impacts associated with the wildlife trade against the wide range of benefits that people derive from it is not an easy task. All too often in the past, the conservation risks of wildlife trade have not been adequately assessed or acknowledged before significant negative impacts have occurred. At the same time, interventions aimed to resolve such problems have typically been hampered by a partial understanding of trade dynamics and drivers and tended to be over-reliant on a limited range of remedial strategies. To minimize risk and maximize benefits in future it is essential that there is a greater emphasis on multidisciplinary analysis of wildlife trade issues and development of adaptive responses focused on clear conservation and socio-economic goals and the motivating factors that will ensure that such goals are achieved.

Acknowledgements

This chapter contains substantial extracts from Chapters 1 and 2 of *Making a Killing or Making a Living: Wildlife Trade, Trade Controls and Rural Livelihoods*, by Dilys Roe, Teresa Mulliken, Simon Milledge, Josephine Mremi, Simon Mosha and Maryanne Grieg-Gran, published by IIED in March 2002 (*Biodiversity and Livelihoods Issues*, no 6).

References

Arnold, J E M (1995) Socio-economic benefits and issues in non-wood forest products use, in FAO (ed), *Report of the International Expert Consultation on Non-Wood Forest Products, Yogyakarta, Indonesia,* 17–27 January 1995, Food and Agriculture Organization, Rome

Barden, A, Awang Anak, N, Mulliken, T and Song, M (2000) *Heart of the Matter: Agarwood use and trade and CITES implementation for* Aquilaria malaccensis, TRAFFIC International, Cambridge

Barnett, R (ed) (2000) *Food for Thought: The Utilization of Wild Meat in Eastern and Southern Africa,* TRAFFIC East/Southern Africa, Nairobi

Bennett, E L and Robinson, J G (2000) *Hunting of Wildlife in Tropical Forests. Implications for Biodiversity and Forest Peoples,* Biodiversity Series – Impact Studies, World Bank, Washington DC

Bourke, I J and Leitch, J (2000) *Trade Restrictions and Their Impact on International Trade in Forest Products,* Food and Agriculture Organization, Rome

Burgess, J C (1992) *The Impact of Wildlife Trade on Endangered Species,* LEEC Discussion Paper 9202, International Institute for Environment and Development, London

Caldwell, J (2001) CITES wildlife trade data. In litt to T Mulliken, TRAFFIC International, J Caldwell, UNEP-WCMC

Campbell, B and Brigham, T (1993) *Non-wood Forest Products Zimbabwe,* paper prepared for the FAO expert consultation on non-wood forest products (anglophone Africa), Food and Agriculture Organization, Rome

Caspary, H-U, Koné, I, Prouot, C and de Pauw, M (2001) *La Chasse et la Filière Viande de Brousse dans l'Espace Taï, Côte d'Ivoire,* Tropenbos, Abidjan

Cavendish, M (1997) *The Economics of Natural Resource Utilisation by Communal Area Farmers of Zimbabwe,* University of Oxford

Clarke, J, Cavendish, W and Coote, C (1996) Rural households and Miombo woodlands: use value and management, in B Campbell (ed), *The Miombo in Transition: Woodlands and welfare in Africa,* CIFOR, Bogor

Edwards, S R (1992) Wild bird trade: perceptions and management in the Cooperative Republic of Guyana, in Thomsen, J B, Edwards, S R and Mulliken, TA (eds), *Perceptions, Conservation and Management of Wild Birds in Trade,* TRAFFIC International, Cambridge

Edwards, D M (1993) *The Marketing of Non-timber Forest Products from the Himalayas: The Trade between East Nepal and India.* Rural Development Forestry Network, paper 156, ODI, Regent's College, London

FAO (1995) *Non Wood Forest Products for Rural Income and Sustainable Forestry,* Non Wood Forest Products Series no 7, Food and Agriculture Organization, Rome

FAO (2000) *The State of World Fisheries and Aquaculture 2000,* Food and Agriculture Organization, Rome

FAO (2001a) *State of the World's Forests 2001,* Food and Agriculture Organization, Rome

FAO (2001b) *Global Forest Resources Assessment 2000,* Food and Agriculture Organization, Rome

FAO (2001c) *What are NWFPs?,* Food and Agriculture Organization, Rome, http://www.fao.org/forestry/FOP/FOPW/NWFP/what-e.stm, 18 January 2002
FAOSTAT (2002). *FAOSTAT Forestry Data,* http://apps.fao.org/page/collections?subset=forestry
Fitzgerald, S (1989) *International Wildlife Trade: Whose business is it?*, World Wildlife Fund, Washington DC
Freese, C H (1996) *The Commercial, Consumptive Use of Wild Species: Managing it for the benefit of biodiversity*, WWF, Washington DC
Freese, C H (1998) *Wild Species as Commodities: Managing markets and ecosystems for sustainability,* Island Press, Washington DC
Government of the Republic of Ghana (1998) *Wildlife Development Plan 1998–2003,* Wildlife Department, Accra
Groombridge, B (1992) *Global Biodiversity: Status of the earth's living resources*, Chapman and Hall, London
Iqbal, M (1993) *International Trade in Non Wood Forest Products: An overview,* FAO: Misc/93/11 Working Paper, Food and Agriculture Organization, Rome
Iqbal, M (1995) *Trade Restrictions Affecting International Trade in Non-Wood Forest Products*, Non-Wood Forest Products Series, Food and Agriculture Organization, Rome
Kasim, I and Long, S A (2000) *The Bushmeat Trade in West Africa: A review of recent literature focusing specifically on the ecological and livelihood implications of the trade (DRAFT)*, Natural Resources Institute, Chatham
Lange, D (1998) *Europe's Medicinal and Aromatic Plants: Their use, trade and conservation,* TRAFFIC International, Cambridge
Lee, S (in prep) *Medicinal Plant Trade in East Asia,* TRAFFIC East Asia, Hong Kong
Lee, S (1998) *Attitudes of Hong Kong Chinese Towards Wildlife Conservation and the Use of Wildlife as Medicine and Food,* TRAFFIC East Asia, Hong Kong
Lee, S, Hoover, C, Gaski, A and Mills, J (1998) *A World Apart: Attitudes toward traditional Chinese medicine and endangered species in Hong Kong and the United States,* TRAFFIC East Asia, TRAFFIC North America and WWF–US, Washington DC
Moyer, D C (1995) *The Status of Fischer's Lovebird* Agapornis fischeri *in the United Republic of Tanzania,* IUCN Species Survival Commission, Gland and Cambridge
Mulliken, T A and Thomsen, J B (1995) International trade, in Abramson, J, Speer, B L and Thomsen, J B (eds), *The Large Macaws: Their care, breeding and conservation*, Raintree Publications, Hong Kong
Nash, S V (1994) *Sold for a Song: The trade in Southeast Asian non-CITES birds*, TRAFFIC International, Cambridge
Nasi, R and Cunningham, T (2001) *Sustainable Management of Non-Timber Forest Resources: A review with recommendations for the SBSTTA,* Secretariat to the Convention on Biological Diversity, Montreal
Neumann, R P and Hirsch, E (2000) *Commercialisation of Non-Timber Forest Products: Review and analysis of research,* CIFOR, Bogor
Olsen, C S and Helles, F (1997) Medicinal plants, markets and margins in the Nepal Himalaya: trouble in paradise, *Mountain Research and Development,* 17(4), 363–374.
Parsaud, B (2001) *Efficient Monitoring of Wildlife Trade Top Priority,* Conservation International, http://www.conservation.org/xp/CIWEB/programs/awards/2001/guyana/judges/entries/guy_02.xml, 18 January 2002

Pimental, D, McNair, M, Buck, L, Pimental, M and Kamil, J (1997) The value of forests to world food security, *Human Ecology,* 25, 91–120

Prescott-Allen, R and Prescott-Allen, C (1982) *What's Wildlife Worth? Economic Contribution of Wild Plants and Animals to Developing Countries*, IIED–Earthscan, London

Roe, D, Mayers, J, Grieg-Gran, M, Kothari, A, Fabricius, C and Hughes, R (2000) *Evaluating Eden: Exploring the myths and realities of community-based wildlife management,* Evaluating Eden Series 8, IIED, London

Roe, D, Mulliken, T, Milledge, S, Mremi, J, Mosha, S and Grieg-Gran, M (2002) *Making a Killing or Making a Living: Wildlife trade, trade controls and rural livelihoods,* IIED Biodiversity and Livelihoods Issues no 6

Roth, H and Merz, G (1997) *Wildlife Resources: A global account of economic use,* Springer Verlag, Berlin

Scoones, I, Melnyk, M and Pretty, J N (1992) *The Hidden Harvest. Wild Foods and Agricultural Systems. A Literature Review and Annotated Bibliography,* IIED, London

UNEP (1998) *Policy Effectiveness and Multilateral Environmental Agreements,* Environment and Trade Series, UNEP Economics, Trade and Environment Unit, Geneva

van Rijsoort, J (2000) *Non-Timber Forest Products (NTFPs): Their role in sustainable forest management in the tropics,* Theme Studies Series, National Reference Centre for Nature Management, Wageningen

Warner, K (1995) Marketing, Valuation and Pricing of NWFPs, in Durst, P B and Bishop, A (eds), *Beyond Timber: Social, economic and cultural dimensions of non-wood forest products in Asia and the Pacific*, Proceedings of a Regional Expert Consultation, 28 November–2 December 1994, FAO/RAP, Bangkok

WHO, IUCN and WWF (1993) *Guidelines on the Conservation of Medicinal Plants*, IUCN, Gland

Wollenberg, E and Belcher, B (2001) NTFPs – Income for rural populations or not?, *ETFRN News*, 32(1), 30–32.

Chapter 2

What is the Goal of Regulating Wildlife Trade? Is Regulation a Good Way to Achieve this Goal?

Barney Dickson

Introduction

The debate about the regulation of the international trade in wildlife has been characterized by differences over the goal of trade regulation and disputes about whether regulation is a good way to achieve the goal. By way of an introduction to the more detailed discussions that appear later in the book, this chapter offers a brief but critical examination of these two issues. It is argued that there is a case for the differences over goals to be made more explicit and, more particularly, for the conservation goals of regulation to be integrated more closely with sustainable development goals. It is also contended that the common assumption that trade measures are a universally appropriate tool for conserving species threatened by trade, is mistaken. The primary reference point for the discussion is CITES, the most important instrument for regulating the wildlife trade.

What is the Goal of Regulating Wildlife Trade?

It is a striking fact that, even among those who accept that the regulation of the international trade in wildlife has a valuable role to play, there are significant differences about what the goal of that regulation is.

The CITES treaty does not spell out what the goal of the treaty is, although the preamble does indicate that it is concerned with protecting wild species from over-exploitation through international trade. The recently adopted

'Strategic Vision Through 2005' is more explicit. It states that the purpose is: 'to ensure that no species of wild fauna or flora becomes or remains subject to unsustainable exploitation because of international trade' (CITES Secretariat, 2000). Thus the treaty has a conservationist goal and addresses one particular threat to the realization of that goal. The goal does appear to be accepted by many of the parties to CITES, although, not surprisingly, their acceptance may be tempered on occasion by what they perceive to be their more immediate economic or political interests. But within this broad conservationist perspective there may be specific differences. For example, while an objective, 'scientific' outlook might treat species which are equally threatened by trade with approximately equal seriousness (with perhaps some allowance for the varying ecological significance of different species), in practice the parties and others involved in CITES have certainly not treated all species equally. For a combination of cultural, political, economic and aesthetic reasons some species have been treated as more important than others. CITES has paid greater attention to animals than plants and, even more obviously, to what are sometimes called 'charismatic megafauna' than to other animal species. The large amount of time and resources that CITES has devoted to the African elephant is the most glaring example of this bias.

There have been other differences with the conservationist perspective. Some have taken the view that CITES should be concerned only with the global status of species, while others have taken the view that the status of particular populations (especially populations defined by national boundaries) may also be legitimate objects of concern. In practice, this difference has been of some importance in shaping debates within CITES. On occasion parties have argued that trade measures should be introduced on the grounds of the deteriorating situation in individual states, while others have argued that such measures are unnecessary because the global status of the species does not merit such action.

The differences about the goals of CITES regulation can be more radical than this and can encompass objectives that are not strictly conservationist. Where this is so, the differences are frequently not fully articulated, since all actors have an incentive to present their views as ones that fall within the explicit goals of the regulatory system. There is a significant constituency within the broad environmental movement in the developed world that is opposed to any trade in (certain) animal species, particularly where it is premised upon the killing of those animals. This view typically has its origins in an ethical perspective on animals and the appropriate way for humans to relate to them. It is a view that entails that the goal of regulation should be to halt the trade in the preferred species. This constituency, through its direct and indirect influence on parties, has affected the regulation CITES has introduced, often strengthening the support for restrictions on trade in wildlife. Some developing countries that take a more pro-use stance have objected to this influence, on the grounds that while there are provisions within CITES relating to the welfare of animals in trade, there is nothing to suggest that trade, as such, is wrong. They have attempted to portray the anti-use perspective as an illegitimate imposition of specific moral values on the wider conservation community. They have sometimes gone on to criticize the anti-use camp for ignoring other morally relevant aspects of the trade in wildlife, notably the role that the use of wildlife can play in supporting rural livelihoods in the developing world. This last point raises the question of the appropriate relationship between the conservationist goals of CITES and the broader aim of sustainable development.

The view that the policies of CITES should be situated within the overall objective of promoting sustainable development did not find expression in the original treaty, but it has become increasingly significant in recent years. The 'Strategic Vision' links the trade in wildlife to sustainable development in the following way:

> *The Strategic Plan confirms the recognition by the parties that sustainable trade in wild fauna and flora can make a major contribution to securing the broader and not incompatible objectives of sustainable development and biodiversity conservation* (CITES Secretariat, 2000).

This somewhat opaque endorsement of the relevance of sustainable development – a concept which is itself notoriously difficult to define – leaves it unclear what the implications might be for specific CITES policies. But it does open the way for countries from the South to press the point that developmental concerns should be taken account of in the formulation of wildlife trade regulations. There are some grounds (independently of what appears in the Strategic Vision) for thinking that this is a legitimate point. Many of the species with which CITES is most concerned are located in developing countries and CITES measures can impose significant costs on those states. Moreover, it is often the rural poor in developing countries who live in closest proximity to wild species and who typically constitute the primary harvesters. If CITES measures affect their livelihoods, then there is an obligation on the parties to CITES to take this into account. Finally, there is the pragmatic point that even from a purely conservationist perspective, there may be a need to take cognizance of the needs of the rural poor and of developing countries in general, since the success of CITES measures can depend on their support. Nevertheless, even if the case for a closer integration of conservation goals and developmental concerns is accepted, the practical implications of this have yet to be determined. What constraints, if any, does this place on the policies CITES adopts? Who decides if those constraints have been met? Determining the appropriate relationship between sustainable development and CITES remains a major task for the parties, and is not something that has already been achieved. If, as is suggested in the following section, CITES is increasingly addressing the issue of species management within range states, the political necessity of clarifying this relationship, as well as the opportunities for doing so, may increase.

But before moving on to that issue, it can be noted that the differences that exist about the goal of regulation – whether they are differences within a broadly conservationist perspective or whether they extend beyond that – are one factor that sometimes make it difficult for parties to CITES to reach agreement. Disputes that are ostensibly about how to realize an agreed goal, are sometimes caused by disguised differences about the goal itself. Greater clarity would be achieved if differences about the goals were debated more openly. Having said that, even when there is agreement that the goal of CITES trade regulation is species conservation, perhaps with the proviso that the regulations must be consistent with the goals of sustainable development, there may still be fierce differences about the role that trade regulations play in realizing that end.

Is Regulation a Good Way to Achieve this Goal?

One of the assumptions underlying the original CITES treaty is that, for wild species for which trade is a threat, trade regulations – of the sort provided for in the treaty – are an effective way of achieving its conservationist goals. This is apparent from the way in which the basic mechanism of the treaty functions. At the heart of the operation of CITES are two of its three appendices: Appendix I and II. The question of whether a species should be listed on either of these appendices is to be determined by its biological and trade status. Appendix I is for the species that are most seriously threatened by trade and Appendix II is for those species that are less seriously threatened. But once a species is listed on either one of the appendices, certain trade regulations are automatically imposed. The idea that trade may be a threat to a species but that trade regulation may not be the most appropriate policy response to that threat is not one that finds expression in the treaty. Nor is there any room within the mechanisms established by the treaty for consideration of alternative policy responses.

Despite the underlying assumption that trade measures are an appropriate policy response for species that are threatened by trade, during the course of CITES history doubts have arisen about their efficacy. This has been fuelled, in part, by the recognition that species that were subject to CITES measures were continuing to decline. Some diagnosed these apparent failures as due to inadequate enforcement and called for more resources to be devoted to enforcement. Others suggested that the trade measures themselves might not always be an effective way of promoting the conservation of species threatened by trade. By 1994 there was sufficient recognition that the question of efficacy was an important one, for the parties to decide to commission an independent study of the convention's effectiveness. This study (Environmental Resources Management, 1996) did not produce a ringing endorsement of trade measures as a conservation tool. One commentator noted that the study examined the status of 12 species that were subject to CITES measures and could conclude only that 2 species appeared to have improved as a result of the listing on CITES (Martin, 2000). Others expressed disappointment at the methodology of the study itself, since it failed to carry out a new assessment of whether trade measures were contributing to the conservation status of the species. It was seen as a gathering of views rather than an assessment of effectiveness.

More recently, the World Conservation Union (IUCN) has carried out a study of the effectiveness of CITES trade measures on behalf of the United Nations Environment Programme (UNEP). This study explicitly recognized the difficulty and complexity of assessing CITES trade measures. While the authors offered what they described as a 'cursory evaluation' of the effectiveness of listing some species on the appendices of CITES, they came to a pessimistic conclusion regarding the possibility of conducting a more thorough assessment:

> *The combination of needing to consider confounding factors that may affect the effectiveness of trade measures, and the difficult issue of achieving a measure of effectiveness for each species, makes the task of providing an independent evaluation of the trade measures* impossible at this time (IUCN, 2001, emphasis added).

As the reference to 'confounding factors' indicates, a major obstacle in the way of assessing the effectiveness of trade measures is the many different factors, of which trade measures are just one, that can affect what is happening to a species. These factors can include changes in the extent and quality of the habitat; the type of management regime that the species is subject to; the ownership rights (de facto and de jure) over the species; the level of harvesting for domestic consumption; the costs of harvesting and the price received for harvested species; the level of consumer demand; and the socio-economic circumstances of the harvesters. Moreover, not only may each of these factors affect what is happening to the species, but there can also be complex interactions among the different factors themselves. When this causal complexity is combined with the frequent absence of information about many of these factors, isolating, by means of empirical analysis, the causal contribution that trade measures have or have not made to determining the fate of a species becomes very difficult if not, as in the view of the IUCN study, impossible.

To show that it is difficult to establish whether trade measures are effective conservation tools is not, of course, the same as establishing that they are not effective tools. However, there are some grounds for thinking that trade measures may not be a universal remedy for species threatened by trade.

Faced with the difficulty of establishing, through empirical analysis, the presence or absence of a causal relationship between different factors, one response is to try to get a better understanding of the underlying causal mechanisms by elaborating a theoretical model of the important causal relationships. This is the route embarked on by the authors of the IUCN study and they outline what they call an economic analytic framework that will identify the key economic factors that influence the effectiveness of trade measures. A not dissimilar piece of work was carried out by Swanson (1994). While the IUCN authors acknowledge that the framework that they sketch is incomplete and although Swanson's work has been subject to criticism (Dickson, 2000), some conclusions can be drawn from this theoretical work. One is that there is no necessary reason why trade measures will contribute to the conservation of a species threatened by trade. The measures may be ineffective if their effect is to drive the legal trade underground. In some circumstances they may actually be counterproductive if, by reducing the returns to those engaged in the trade, they reduce the incentives to conserve the species and its habitat. A second conclusion is that for species threatened by trade there may be a range of other measures, besides trade regulations, which may be effective in contributing to the conservation of the species, either in conjunction with trade regulation, or in place of it.

The empirical difficulties in determining the efficacy of trade measures, combined with the theoretical reasons for thinking that in some cases they will not be effective and that resources might be better deployed elsewhere, challenge the basic assumption, identified earlier, that underlies the operation of CITES. Not surprisingly, then, there are lessons for the functioning of CITES. Three can be mentioned here. First, decisions about whether to introduce trade regulation should be made in the light of whether it is likely to be an effective tool in addressing the conservation problem. This, in turn, implies that either the criteria for listing species on the appendices should be amended to include this additional criterion, or the automatic link between listing and the introduction of trade regulation should be broken. Second, there is a case for integrating decisions about trade regulation with other decisions that may be taken to promote the conservation of the species, so that overall the most effective measures (or combination of measures) are adopted. Third, once the decision has been made to introduce trade measures, there should be a requirement to monitor the consequences of this decision for the conservation of the species.

Interestingly, CITES has already taken on board, albeit in a piecemeal way, the second and third of these lessons, if not the first. This has probably happened more as a result of practical experience with CITES measures than as a response to the theoretical work just mentioned. A brief look at the Significant Trade Review process, together with one group of species, sturgeons, which have been subject to it, can be used to illustrate this point.

The Significant Trade Review process

The Significant Trade Review process is designed to improve the functioning of Appendix II. If a species is listed on Appendix II it can only be exported if the range state issues an export permit. The treaty states that an export permit should only be granted if a scientific authority of the state of export has advised that the export will not be detrimental to the survival of the species. In practice, exporting states do not always adhere to this requirement, and export permits are issued even when species are being over-exploited. The aim of the Significant Trade Review process, introduced by Resolution Conf 8.9, was to close this loophole. Complex in its operation and subject to ongoing review and refinement, the process consists of three main steps. It begins with the identification of Appendix II species that are being traded at significant levels and are of concern. This is followed by a process of consultation and review, in which the situation is assessed in detail. Finally, recommendations to improve the situation are developed and implemented.

Two features of the Significant Trade Review process are worth noting in the present context. First, it involves a review of the efficacy of (some) CITES trade measures. As has already been suggested, if there are grounds for thinking that trade measures will not always be successful, then there is good reason to assess the success of those measures that are adopted. Of course, the original motivation for the Significant Trade Review process did not lie in scepticism about the universal efficacy of trade measures. It was simply intended to assess (and then to improve) the implementation of existing trade measures. Nevertheless, once the review mechanism is in place, the distinction between assessing the implementation of trade measures and assessing the efficacy of the measures themselves is quickly blurred.

Second, under the guise of issuing recommendations to improve the implementation of Appendix II trade measures, CITES bodies have, not infrequently, provided recommendations that are concerned more with the management regime that is applied to the species within the range states, than they are with the trade measures themselves. This, again, is consistent with the point made earlier that, in the light of the many different factors in addition to international trade that affect wild species, it makes sense for conservation bodies not to focus on trade measures alone if other actions will be more effective. The original resolution establishing the Significant Trade Review process opened the way for recommendations to address these other issues because, while it lists examples of what recommendations can deal with, the list is not put forward as an exhaustive one. The opportunity to make recommendations relating to the management of the species will be codified if a proposal currently being considered is accepted at the next conference of the parties. This proposal states that recommendations can include 'the application of adaptive management procedures' (CITES Secretariat, 2002).

In any case, whether or not this particular wording is adopted, there already exist examples where, at least partly under the framework of the Significant Trade Review process, CITES has moved beyond a simple focus on trade regulations and their enforcement, and towards encouraging, assisting and pressurizing states into a variety of actions that relate primarily to the way in which a wild species is conserved and managed within and by the range states. Sturgeons provide a good example of this.

Sturgeons are harvested for caviar and for their meat. The trade in caviar is of considerable economic significance. In 1998, for example, the EU, Japan and US imported caviar valued at just over US$60 million. More than 90 per cent of the legal caviar trade originates from the Caspian Sea. However, the numbers of sturgeon in the wild and the volumes of caviar traded have declined significantly in recent years. Sturgeons have a complex biology and their status in the wild has been affected by a range of socio-economic and political changes. While some of these processes have become better known, partly as a result of the involvement of CITES, our understanding of them is still far from complete. Nevertheless, the following factors appear to be implicated in the decline in the species: degradation and loss of spawning grounds, in part because of industrial developments, including hydroelectric schemes; pollution in the Caspian Sea; weakening of management institutions (and coordination between them), following the break-up of the Soviet Union; increase in domestic trade and consumption; overharvesting for international trade; and the rise of illegal harvesting, linked to the loss of alternative livelihoods.

A few sturgeon species were listed on CITES appendices in 1975, but the involvement of CITES was significantly increased in 1997, when the remaining 23 of the existing 27 species of Acipenseriformes were listed on Appendix II. A Significant Trade Review was initiated in 2000 and at its meeting in Paris in June 2001 the CITES standing committee reached an agreement with the key range states on a list of recommendations that had to be adopted according to a strict timetable. These recommendations were backed up with the threat of a complete suspension in trade if the agreed measures were not implemented.

Some of the recommendations relate to the implementation of the trade measures consequent upon the Appendix II listing, but a significant number do not. Among other recommendations, the range states are required, by specified deadlines, to:

- establish a long-term survey programme as the basis for future management of sturgeon stocks in the Caspian Sea;
- seek expert advice on the operation of regional fisheries management organizations, the management of shared fish resources and ways of dealing with unregulated fisheries;
- adopt a collaborative basin-level management system for sturgeon fisheries in the Caspian Sea as the basis for sustainable commercial exports of sturgeon;
- significantly increase their efforts to combat illegal harvesting and illegal trade, and to regulate domestic trade; and
- seek funding for the rehabilitation of sturgeon stocks, hatcheries and restocking programmes, and for stock assessments, marking systems, identification of specimens in trade, public awareness and enforcement (drawn from CITES Secretariat, 2001)

The complete set of standing committee recommendations constitute a multifaceted response to what is agreed on all sides to be a complicated problem. It is not yet obvious that this will turn out to be a success story for CITES. There are a multitude of factors contributing to the decline of sturgeon stocks and these recommendations may not be sufficient or may not be implemented with sufficient rigour. Nevertheless, the case illustrates the recognition by CITES that successful conservation of these species will depend not just on controlling exports and imports, but on a host of other measures relating to the management of the species within and by the range states.

One corollary of the point that there will often be a strong case for integrating trade regulations with other conservation measures is that when trade regulations alone are failing to conserve species, attempts to improve compliance and to strengthen the enforcement of those measures may not be a sufficient or even a particularly helpful strategy to adopt. It puts the emphasis in the wrong place. Rather than simply stressing better compliance with existing trade regulations, what is needed is the recognition of the importance of a more holistic approach to conservation problems, where it is acknowledged that trade regulations may not always be the most effective conservation tool and that, in many cases, they will at best constitute only one part of a more comprehensive package of measures.

Conclusions

Three concluding points can be made. First, the differences over the goal of regulating the wildlife trade are unlikely to go away. The view that trade in certain animal species is wrong and should be stopped is one that now has strong roots in many Western societies, even if it does not find expression in the CITES treaty. It is probably one reason why trade measures have continued to be applied within CITES as a universal remedy, even when the case for so regarding them has gradually been undermined. In contrast, the view that the conservationist goals of CITES need to be pursued in a way that is at least consistent with the overall goal of sustainable development is one that, through its incorporation in the Strategic Vision, now has some grounding within CITES. It gains legitimacy from the recognition that many range states for CITES species are also developing countries and that those most directly affected by conservation policies are often the rural poor. Nevertheless, the practical implications of this view have yet to be determined.

Second, CITES is founded on the misconception that whenever a wild species is threatened by trade, then trade measures will constitute an effective policy response. There is little empirical evidence to support this view, and theoretical reasons for thinking that trade measures will, at best, only be effective in some cases. In other cases, alternative measures are likely to constitute more effective tools for realizing conservationist goals. In the light of this, there is a need for parties to CITES to assess the likely efficacy of trade measures *before* they are adopted, to engage in a regular review of the efficacy of those trade measures that are adopted (Appendix I as well as Appendix II), and to integrate policies more closely with the management of species within range states. There are signs that, implicitly at least, CITES recognizes these needs.

Third, the progressively greater involvement of CITES in issues relating to the management of species within range states, provides a route by which it might be able to go some way to integrate its conservation goals with sustainable development. If the question 'Is CITES as an institution, well equipped to carry out this integration?' is posed, the answer is probably 'No'. But it may be better equipped than any other international institution that currently exists.

REFERENCES

CITES Secretariat (2000) *Strategic Vision Through 2005*, CITES Secretariat, Geneva

CITES Secretariat (2001) *Summary Report of Forty-fifth meeting of the Standing Committee, Paris 19–22 June 2001 (SC45 Summary Report)*, CITES Secretariat, Geneva

CITES Secretariat (2002)*Problems and Inconsistencies in Resolution Conf 8.9 (Rev) and Decision 11.117 (PC12 Doc 11.1 (Rev1))*, CITES Secretariat, Geneva

Dickson, B (2000) Global Regulation and Communal Management, in Hutton, J and Dickson, B (eds) *Endangered Species: Threatened Convention, The Past, Present and Future of CITES,* Earthscan, London

Environmental Resources Management (1996) *Study on How to Improve the Effectiveness of CITES*, Final Report to the Standing Committee of CITES, Lausanne

IUCN (2001) *A Report Prepared by IUCN – The World Conservation Union on the Effectiveness of Trade Measures Contained in The Convention on International Trade in Endangered Species of Wild Fauna and Flora (CITES)*, Prepared for the Economics, and Trade and Environment Unit, United Nations Environment Programme, Geneva

Martin, R B (2000) When CITES Works and When it Does Not, in Hutton, J and Dickson, B (eds) *Endangered Species: Threatened Convention, The Past, Present and Future of CITES,* Earthscan, London

Swanson, T (1994) *The International Regulation of Extinction*, Macmillan, Basingstoke

Chapter 3

Regulatory Design

Nick Sinclair-Brown

Introduction

As individuals the quality of our lives depends on the quality of our relationships with others, both in meeting our needs and deploying our talents. It is our relationships with others that enrich or impoverish our lives. However, although this is equally true in our public life, the problem we immediately confront is how to maintain relationships with those whom we don't know and whose conditions of existence are often beyond our own experience, or even imagination. It is here that we look for guidance so that the interests of the few and the interests of the many can be integrated in a way that serves as far as possible the interests of all. In providing guidance to the resolution of global issues, regulations matter. As a reservoir of accumulated informed thought, they are one of the most powerful tools we have yet created in building a secure and better future. The design of the regulatory context within which policy is fashioned and rendered into reality is of paramount importance.

International regulatory design is a big subject and here one can do little but reflect on a few aspects. In doing so the focus will be on international regulation as broadly conceived. By their nature measures concerning international trade in wildlife exert a strong influence on the domestic policy preferences of other states and within this context should be judged like any other strand of regulatory regime. I have taken for my model a simple grid set by a vertical and horizontal axis. This is by no means the only model, nor even necessarily the best. However, it is well suited to the points I wish to make. The horizontal axis comprises the allocation of authority and competencies to those tasked with the development of policy while the vertical axis comprises the mechanisms by which such policies are transmitted between the abstract international level and the concrete local level. Each intersection of the grid provides a political nexus where different groups of intellectual, ethical, and material interests and values are exchanged and, hopefully, engaged.

Constraints of time, money, and knowledge will always conspire to ensure regulatory regimes are essentially untidy. However, it is these 'loose ends' that ensure the opportunity for parties to engage each other in further development. Although CITES is far from perfect, and would not be the chosen starting place today, its parties have been able to remain engaged in a set of relationships that have at times transcended the limitations of the originating intent. The investment of time, money and knowledge accumulated to date in calibrating the operation of CITES to the conservation needs of endangered species indicates a robust regime capable of accommodating continual reform. Bill Adams, Reader in the Geography of Conservation and Development and Fellow of Downing College at the University of Cambridge, has commented that conservation is not about preserving the past but about handling change and the transition between past and future, not about trying to stop human impact on nature but about negotiating that impact. To this end language is crucial in setting the trajectory of future possibilities. The language with which regulatory regimes are built is drawn from an expressive palette ranging from the immediate power of exactitude to the latent possibilities of 'constructive ambiguity' by which opposing views can be ring-fenced for development in the light of subsequent experience and knowledge. If we are to avoid the grip of dead ideas over changing circumstances, loose ends are our lifeline and the words we choose to use are more than just the loose change of international negotiation.

Language however is not enough. Without a system to take what is written and enable it to be replicated in action, words would be writ in dust. In providing the guide rules by which societies can build on the past to prepare the future, the rule of law is fundamental. By rule of law we refer to the structure of rules and conventions that stand over the individual preferences of participating parties and derive their legitimacy from the recognition of those who are bound. This is to be distinguished from rule by law, a perverted doppelganger by which dictators impose their will, and only at its margins features the discipline of litigation as a means of determining disputes and clarifying expectations. The rule of law is constructed by two types of rules: those substantive, or primary, rules that embody social policies and those organizational, or secondary, rules by which substantive rules can be brought into being and evolve. It is these 'secondary' rules that dominate the vertical axis of our grid and to which we will now turn.

The Vertical Axis – Implementation of International Policy

The principle of subsidiarity is essential in making sense of the vertical axis and is of central importance in the devolution of policy implementation to levels of optimal efficiency. It enables policy design and financial resources to be managed at the level where they can be most accountable and transparent. The main objectives and principles to which they give rise are often best set at the international level. The design of action plans and main policy tools tend to be best handled at regional level where scales of economy can be achieved by coordination of resources, experience, and best practice in response to common problems. The ordering of priorities and the tailoring of incentives and disincentives to the context of particular circumstances are best done at national level. Increasingly the local level has become important both in effective implementation and also in providing the experience and reflections needed to fine-tune best practice and identify dysfunctional policies. Insights gained can then be fed back to other decision-making levels either directly by way of political representatives, or informally by sectoral groups often aided by non-governmental organizations (NGOs). The quality of this learning loop is an essential part of any regulatory mechanism and is one reason why the participation of civil society, although problematic in terms of decision-making, is crucial in setting plenary agendas and raising difficult or unwelcome issues.

The absence of a legislature in international affairs has tended to displace organizational rules with diplomacy and substantive rules with the fruits of diplomacy. Additionally, international negotiations are very expensive to hold and requisite levels of knowledge, expertise and authority are relatively scarce. Too much detail prolongs debate, too little pre-empts any hope of progressing consensus: both can cause frustration leading to uncoordinated domestic regulation and attendant fragmentation of policy. Under these conditions, the skill in establishing organizational rules is to provide a mechanism enabling shared expectations as to substantive rules to be leveraged through thresholds of increasing normative intensity. The realization of such processes was greatly facilitated by the collapse of the cold war and transition into globalization that enabled states to escape from the politics of coexistence to the politics of collective issue management. Formation of international legal regimes are now being achieved with increasing sophistication by managing agendas progressively through framework documents that specify and justify objectives, leading to more detailed policy protocols, and concluding in schedules of specific commitments. The process is one that cannot be rushed, as it is necessary for states to assure themselves that commitments are sustainable against unforeseen adverse consequences. Success depends on galvanizing consensus and recharacterizing dissent as an opportunity to address specific problems, generally by matching phased commitment with material assistance. This gradual stabilization of commitment enables regulatory regimes to move under collective discipline along lines of increasing determinacy from the rules of soft law to the 'hard' rules on which tribunals rely in deciding disputes between states.

The setting of agendas capable of moving complex objectives through to resolution is greatly helped by establishing composite principles to seed progressive development. A good example is 'sustainable development' incorporated into the strategic plan adopted by CITES in 2000. Sustainable development is often criticized as being a collision of incompatible concepts, an oxymoron, a representation of a reality that has never existed and is beyond our capacity to create. Although definitions are available – not least that offered by the Brundtland Commission in 1987 which defined sustainable development as 'development which meets the needs of the present without compromising the ability of future generations to meet their own needs' – they invariably serve to replace one paradox with another. An alternative way to regard these terms is that they have no inherent meaning but are designed to establish the terms of debate. The debate, however, needs to be handled with care if it is to be accepted as legitimate. Although negotiated by the representatives of participating states, such representatives are accountable only within the constitutional framework of the states they represent. Given disparities of power and development among states, any drift from consensus to unilateralism will lead to an increasing gap in legitimacy that will undermine the normative strength of the rule of law as well as weaken implementation of policy at the point of delivery.

The fact that habitat and species cross borders makes regional coordination essential rather than merely producing beneficial scales of economy. Although centralization of standards may make some aspects of implementation easier, the trade focus of CITES can distort implementation by focusing resources on policing common external borders at the expense of supervising internal movements. Valuable lessons can be learnt from the experience of the EU concerning cooperation within common borders as well as the more problematic experience of cross-border cooperation under the Lusaka Agreement on Cooperative Enforcement Operations Directed at Illegal Trade in Wild Fauna and Flora (1994).

The national level is able to provide authority for public expenditure and other resources necessary for policy objectives to be achieved. However, governments cannot solve problems alone. Without cooperation of those constituencies whose interests are affected or who are in a position to assist, resources and effort applied at other levels will be wasted. Marshall Murphree, Emeritus Professor at the University of Zimbabwe, has identified four phases in the attempt to find a formula for local implementation of policy: policies against the people, for the people, with the people, and by the people. Conservation against the people involved the use of protected areas and failed because without proper funding protection proved illusory and removal of communities merely created conflicts as to resource priorities. Conservation for the people saw a move to government agencies and was undermined by a lack of capacity as 'reach always exceeded grasp'. Conservation with the people became fashionable as donors adopted bottom-up rural development strategies but lacked sustainability as community projects were externally initiated and heavily subsidized. Conservation by the people is currently assuming increasing support and encourages the use and development of accumulated local knowledge into local strategies in the belief that a diversity of 'resourcefulness' will overcome a deficit of resources. With results difficult to monitor and reconcile with formal reporting, the emphasis has moved to establishing accountability of individuals and groups to the community rather than the prior strategy of placing accountability with the community. Essentially the difference is one of devolution rather than decentralization and as such can change the emphasis from implementation of specific conservation policies to pragmatically negotiating change in a way that provides a place for endangered species.

Successful implementation is essential at all levels and with it the means to deal with those who fail to comply. To this end a distinction exists between compliance and enforcement each of which is approached in a different way. Compliance is aimed at ensuring policies are properly adopted and work efficiently. It requires constant political engagement by those involved in conservation to ensure problems are identified and resolved as they arise. By contrast the emphasis of enforcement is on ensuring that regulatory evasion is detected and deterred. Here problems are invariably hidden and require the assistance of external agencies with other priorities. Although both compliance and enforcement consume considerable resources, enforcement is unlikely to be productive in the absence of severe sanctions and criminal definitions capable of catching those in possession of fraudulent documentation without having to establish accompanying intent.

The Horizontal Axis – Cohesion of International Policy

While the impact of implementation is felt mainly along the vertical axis, it is along the horizontal axis that matters of policy are invariably decided. Of the many issues involved with policy, two stand out: how technical groups tasked with overlapping policy formation relate to each other, and how broader interests are reconciled. The first of these issues concerns the notion of integration introduced by Chapter 8 of Agenda 21, which calls for the integration of environment and development at policy, planning and management levels. The second issue concerns the nature of responsibility and accountability and its relationship with consultation, participation and access to justice – principles which are increasingly considered an important part of any regime.

Integration is a bridging notion aimed at reconciling the views of different groups each of whose views are constrained by their sectoral experience and related interpretative frame of reference. It relies on a belief that a single goal can be established from which a policy programme can be developed capable of delivering simultaneous benefits across sectoral boundaries. This is a huge challenge and difficult to achieve if participants see accommodation of others' interests as concessions. It requires considerable political skills to ensure that policy goals converge as the goals of each participating group are rendered increasingly sensitive to the goals of others. One method often used is to adopt the triple bottom line of economic, social, and environmental impacts as cross-sectoral assessment criteria. However, even here without political leadership, differences in priorities can relegate the criteria to mere checklists as participants cease to listen to each other.

At an international level cross-sectoral integration is not easy given the procedural difficulties of varying the institutional mandates set by states. The design of a convention will inevitably influence the regime to which it gives birth and even where aims are broadly sympathetic, such as in the case of CITES and the Convention on Biological Diversity (CBD), there will be scope for overlapping mandates and divergent context and norms. Here integration is assisted by negotiation of memoranda of understanding, exploration of synergies, such as the report commissioned to identify synergies between CITES and the CBD, and the creation of 'early warning' strategies between secretariats to manage potential inconsistencies, of particular relevance to the World Trade Organization (WTO). These measures involve significant resources that can be seen as inflating overheads at the expense of operational concerns. Thus while secretariats themselves can achieve a lot, the continued efforts of the United Nations Environment Programme (UNEP) and the Global Biodiversity Forum are essential to maintain momentum and stimulate political will. Problems will also come under more control as states increase the range of international conventions to which they belong.

At regional and national levels political decisions tend to be taken on a portfolio basis and notions such as sustainable development can be seen merely as the grudging accommodation that has to be made to conservation and other environmental concerns. To overcome this, two techniques – merger and mainstreaming – have gained acceptance. Portfolio merger can be seen at a national level in the establishment of the Department for Environment, Food and Rural Affairs in the UK. However, at a regional level merger is more difficult due to sovereign sensitivities and integration such as that required by Article 103R of the Single European Act, and Articles 3 and 6 of the Treaty of Amsterdam and tends to be pursued by mainstreaming of agendas across sectors.

Unless sectoral walls are preserved, for example by memoranda of understandings or concordats, merger can lead to a dominant consensus establishing itself at the expense of divergent opinions which become viewed as dissent. Although this problem is avoided with mainstreaming, as each portfolio will tend to produce different views, difficult decisions will still need to be taken and are merely displaced to a level where they are more visible. Ultimately decisions will depend on the quality of analysis available. Here, the use of economic analysis is often criticized as unable to capture the diversity of real life, spiritual values, and synergies. Economic modelling is of course essentially reductionist. However, nothing can inform our thinking as powerfully as a good economic model. The focus on money as a fungible resource that can be applied to provide the time, effort, and materials necessary for policy development and implementation, forces a range of issues to be confronted. It demands clarity both as to means and ends and it forces contemplation of consequences, of what can be afforded and what must be forgone. It is this latter aspect that ensures decision-makers cannot escape an awareness of their responsibility to those who may be affected by their decisions and who need to be taken into account. While people are more than numbers, it is far worse to remain invisible.

In the making of any policy decision a distinction can be made between consultation, denoting an assessment of the potential consequences of the decision, and participation, denoting an involvement in the decision itself. To these may be added a third aspect, access to justice, a residuary right to ensure that decisions are taken with due regard to the interests of those affected. The distinction between consultation and participation is not always clear as participation is often used to denote a right to be informed and consulted. However, in the absence of such a distinction assignment of responsibility can be obscured and with it the accountability provided by access to justice. Those in positions of responsibility are usually wary of accountability as it has traditionally entailed liability. However, without accountability there is little opportunity to learn from the oversights of those responsible.

The responsibility that arises from consultation is to ensure that stakeholders likely to be affected are identified, informed, and their views taken into account. Two broad constituencies can be distinguished, those adversely affected by a policy being withheld, and those adversely affected by it proceeding. Consultation among the former invariably takes place during policy evolution while consultation among the latter will usually take place when considering the feasibility of implementation. As certain policies will invariably advance some interests and impede others, political judgement and leadership is essential and with it the responsibility to take account of all interests so that a strategy is in place to minimize known adverse impacts and the occurrence of unintended consequences. The nature of participation, and thus responsibility, will vary at every level of subsidiarity depending on constitutional arrangements and the extent they allow some constituencies direct or indirect influence to capture policy to the detriment of other constituencies.

There is particular concern where decisions are taken by majority vote and minority interests may thereby be ignored. At a national level, human rights regimes have come to be seen as an essential counterweight to the power of the majority. However, at an international level, even unilateralism, such as can occur by way of stricter domestic measures under Article XIV of CITES, remains an option and has traditionally been the cause of much distrust and bitterness between states. The issue here has been one of *de facto* participation in the policy priorities of range states without those adversely affected having either been consulted or having access to justice. It is one of the unfortunate consequences of sovereignty that it serves to insulate national legislation from taking into account the interests of constituencies in other countries. National politicians are neither representative of, nor responsible or accountable to, affected communities in other states but understandably respond to domestic policy chains and constituencies whose own knowledge of the likely impact on those affected is invariably limited. This can sit uneasily with the consultation requirements implicit in the *chapeau* of Article 20 of the General Agreement on Tariffs and Trade (GATT) particularly where, as in the US, executive discretion can be held hostage to judicial intervention. Somewhat softer is the shadow non-detriment findings used by the EU to negotiate changes in policy where measures are preceded by consultation and often underpinned by support in the design and implementation of local strategies. The multilateralism of the CITES Significant Trade Process moves this type of exercise to a more legitimate basis and is a stride towards maturity that hopefully will create a more receptive context for effective conservation strategies.

The distinction between participation and consultation is one that is particularly important to lobby groups. It is, of course, the hope of every group to influence decisions. However, the more one moves from rights of consultation to rights of participation, the more one takes political responsibility for ensuring that outcomes take into account broader ranges of interests. This can be difficult to square with the limited mandates by which lobby groups are usually established.

Conclusion

In concluding, CITES has done much to remove the pressures of illegal trade and has generated rich reserves of information and technical expertise. However, there is a need to continue working on the 'loose ends' recognizing that species listing and seizures are not conservation, listings without linkages to local communities are weak, and that the division into Appendix I and Appendix II listings may itself be problematic. Commercial depletion of certain species within 'open access' hardwood forests and marine fisheries is of serious concern, not fully addressed by CITES, incentives for sustainability are weak, the costs of structural adjustment politically sensitive, and identification of species from derivative products such as oils impossible outside a laboratory.

Although no generation will ever hope to resolve the problems with which it is faced, each generation can make its own significant contribution. Since the 1990s recognition has increasingly been given to the transfer of technological and financial assistance to developing states and the recognition of the differentiated obligations that flow from their lack of capacity. From this arise two challenges: the political challenge of ensuring that necessary assistance is given, and the intellectual challenge of ensuring that such resources are deployed in a manner that engages clear lines of responsibility and accountability. We started by considering the importance of relationships in the world in which we wish to live. By finishing on the challenges of assistance and accountability we have identified two elements which form the heart of any relationship.

Chapter 4

Regulation, Conservation and Incentives

Brendan Moyle

INTRODUCTION

Wildlife regulations are common in many countries. The aim of such regulations is to limit the depletion of wildlife by directly controlling access (harvest limits) or by indirect means (for instance, suppressing trade activity in threatened wildlife). These regulations are typically backed by legislation. The legislation may stem from domestic concerns about species loss such as the US Endangered Species Act or the requirements of international treaties such as CITES.

Regulations that stem from an authorized statutory body are the principal focus of this chapter. This means we will ignore the role of customary measures to regulate harvest. Such regulations occur in indigenous communities, such as the Murihiku Mäori of New Zealand and their titi (sooty shearwater) harvests. We will also ignore market-based approaches to regulate harvest. These basically include the use of hunting or access fees and other related instruments to ration harvest levels.

The consequence of wildlife regulations is to reallocate the costs of conservation effort. All conservation programmes involve some measure of costs. If such costs were not relevant, then regulations would become irrelevant. Regulators for instance, could simply purchase all the reserves required to safeguard wildlife regarded as threatened.

Regulations exist to control behaviour. Such controls have their basis in the threat of sanctions. If people are detected violating such rules, sanctions against them are applied. This does not eliminate the cost of providing, say, habitat for wildlife to society. Costs will have to be borne whether private individuals are compelled to provide reserves on their land or the state purchases and manages the reserve. What regulations do is simply reallocate the costs of conservation effort. Often this is away from public sector agencies towards private individuals or communities.

This may be efficient at some level. For instance, it may be that private individuals or communities have lower costs of managing wildlife than state agencies. Thus costs to society would be minimized if responsibility for protecting the wildlife were shifted to private individuals or communities. While some may find this hypothesis intriguing, it is not obvious that this is true. Indeed if it were true, then there would be little point in having any national reserves or any public sector organizations as conservation could be more readily provided on private land by non-specialists!

Nonetheless, while regulations may conceal the actual costs of providing conservation, these costs are real. Some of these costs will be borne by the public sector agency that administers the regulation. Resources will need to be committed towards the enforcement of these regulations. Likewise some costs will be borne by other parties. Landowners may find that their land values fall, that management costs rise and they have to forgo income to insulate wildlife from some land-use practices. Indigenous communities may resent such regulations as inimical to their culture and their aspirations to use traditional resources.

Hence all parties have an incentive to avoid or minimize the cost of regulations on them. Naturally, an easy way to avoid the cost of such regulations is not to comply with them. In this sense regulations convert a conservation problem into a law-enforcement problem. To prevent non-compliance becoming a problem, wildlife agencies have to devote resources to the detection and prosecution of wildlife crimes.

COMPLEXITY

The second challenge is the complexity of the systems which regulations are expected to influence. Biological systems are of course, complex. The same is also true for social and economic systems. Complex systems have a number of defining characteristics, which have a powerful effect on the success of regulations. Complexity also creates incentives for decision-makers and lobbyists to adopt simplifying rules. The Nobel laureate Simon elaborated this practice of simplifying a complex problem. This tendency to simplify problems is the logical outcome of two factors. The first is that information about a complex system is difficult to collect, and often requires specialized analytical skills. Simplifying rules thus economize on the amount of information that needs to be collected. When information is costly to obtain, people have an incentive to economize on how much they collect. The second factor is the limited ability of people to deal with complex problems. This led Simon to argue that people will tend to adopt simpler decision rules that seem to produce satisfactory outcomes.

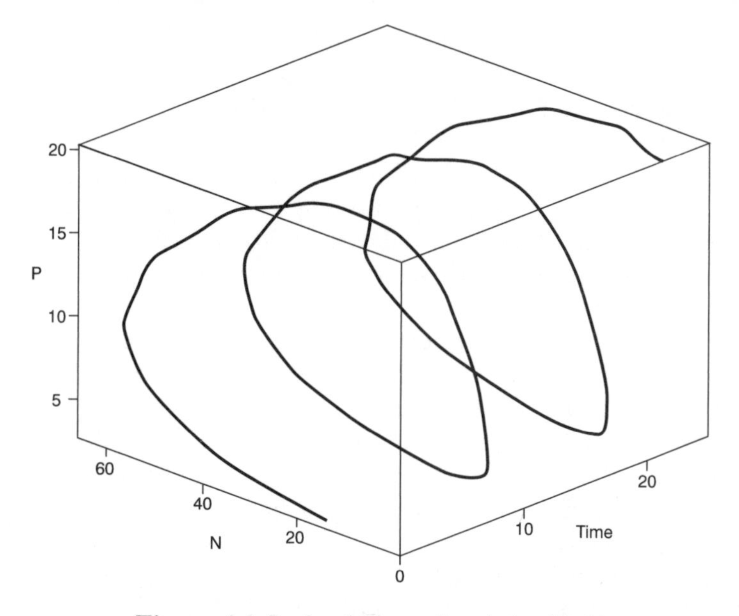

Figure 4.1 *Lotka–Volterra Population Model*

What then are the characteristics of a complex system? The first characteristic is that simple, linear trends don't persist in complex systems. This is what makes forecasting from ecological or economic data difficult beyond the short term. Turning points and thresholds are notoriously hard to predict. Complex systems have their paths influenced by feedback and spillovers, which create turning points and thresholds in the system's path. These turning points and threshold effects are notoriously hard to predict. These feedbacks in economic systems gave rise to Adam Smith's metaphor of the 'invisible hand' for the market. Such feedback gave rise to the complexity of the simple population models developed by Lotka and Volterra (Figure 4.1).

For instance, in the predator-prey model, rises in prey numbers (N) prompt a rise in predator numbers (P) and a decline in resources. These cause the prey numbers to decline. With the fall in prey numbers, resources recover while predator numbers decline. A rise in resources and less predators allows the prey to rebound in numbers. Population numbers thus oscillate rather than follow a straight line. Complex systems have many interacting components. These interactions lead to spillovers from one part of the system to another. For example, rats are a serious threat to many native New Zealand birds. As a consequence of this threat, rat-eradication programmes are often initiated. In some cases, rat suppression has not led to an increase in bird numbers. The problem here is that feral cats switch from the now less-abundant rats to the relatively more abundant birds. The change in feral cat predation patterns is a spillover caused by the rat control.

Spillovers are also common in economic systems and may be the result of consumption, production or government decisions. For instance, the European Common Agricultural Policy (CAP) intensifies agricultural output in Europe and in the past, agricultural surpluses have simply been dumped in world markets. For developing countries, dumped produce combined with limited market access to Europe limits exports and prosperity. The intensification of agriculture in Europe also has had adverse environmental effects. Declines in wildlife have been caused by the land use, and associated pesticide and fertilizer practices prompted by the CAP.

The second characteristic of complex systems is that they cannot be fully described. Complex systems include many components that are in the first instance unknown. Most wildlife is after all invertebrate and for these species, most are unknown even at a taxonomic level. That means we don't even have a name to start with. Aspects of the biology (such as distribution, status, life-history) of described species are also largely unknown. An ecosystem is at a very rudimentary level, unknowable. Similarly, an economy is driven by the actions, values and beliefs of its participants. Such information is not only not being recorded, it is incapable of being recorded.

The third characteristic is that observations are the result of underlying processes. Consider for instance, a species. Earlier 'creationist' thought considered that such a complex thing must be the product of conscious design. In short, by considering only the outcome of evolution, creationists were able to discount completely the evolutionary paths that generate species. Species are a consequence of the processes of natural selection, chance mutations and genetic drift. It is this emphasis on the underlying processes that represents the remarkable achievement of Charles Darwin.

Likewise, a market price is a consequence of many underlying processes. A price is a way of economizing on information within a society. It communicates the relative scarcity of the good to consumers and suppliers. The market price reflects many different factors. These include customary factors and demand factors (for example, the price of substitute and complementary goods, incomes and time of the year). It also embodies supply factors, such as input prices. Stock factors also exert an influence on prices as if stocks tend to accumulate, prices tend to fall to eliminate excess stocks. Finally, the expectation of future price changes can also influence current prices. Consumers who expect prices to rise in the future, may increase demand now to escape the expected price increase. Such behaviour may have occurred with elephant ivory as Asian carvers keen to avoid stock shortages, started a bidding war that set prices rising during the 1980s. Conservationists that treat market prices as largely indicative of current demand are frequently in error.

Complex living systems are also dynamic. The underlying processes have a kind of momentum that keeps the system changing or evolving. As a result of the many feedbacks and spillovers that are part of the system, changes to one part of the system must also affect other parts.

Complexity has a number of implications on policy. For instance, it may be that a policy has a short shelf life. That is, it starts off being effective but when the system changes (as a consequence of the dynamic nature of complex systems), the effectiveness of the policy changes. For instance, Keynesian macroeconomic management proved reasonably effective in the 1960s. In the next decade however, high inflationary expectations combined with Keynesian policies contributed to recessions.

Policies implemented in complex systems may also fail through the unexpected. Complex systems are incapable of being fully described. As a result, the full impact of a policy can never be determined with certainty. Without complete knowledge of the system, managers and policy-makers may be easily surprised when the unexpected occurs. For instance, the introduction of mustelids into New Zealand as a biological control agent was a conservation disaster. These new introduced species decimated native birds and contributed to the extinction of many ground-dwelling bird species. Likewise the resumption of trade in the Australian salt-water crocodile surprised many policy-makers by neither encouraging poaching nor over-harvesting.

Similarly, many economic policies adopted in the late 1970s and early 1980s were based on certain presumptions about the oil prices. Mexico for instance, borrowed heavily on the basis of oil export receipts, presuming that they would stay high and/or continue to rise. The fall in oil price in the early to mid-1980s surprised many policy-makers and the decline in oil income for Mexico, led to its defaulting on its loans in 1983.

People may also respond in ways that frustrate regulations and policy. For instance, fishery policy in many countries is associated with regulations designed to make fishing effort more costly. These regulations include restrictions on boat size, fishing season or gear and net restrictions. Many of these regulations have a short shelf life. For instance, restrictions on the size of boats in the American Pacific North West salmon fishery were overcome when the smaller boats were redesigned to take the fishing gear previously associated with larger boats.

Consequences of Ignoring Complexity.

The incentive to treat complex systems as simple is often manifested in wildlife use. Simple 'rules-of-thumb' are applied to a wide variety of circumstances, often by articulate and influential lobbyists. The attraction of policy-making in simple systems is that a particular action (like a policy or regulation) has a straightforward and immediate effect. There are no uncertainties, no spillovers and no interactions. With the presumption of simplicity, it is not surprising that the rigorous application of a single policy instrument is often advocated.

Fundamentally, this usually confuses the actual observations – what is happening – with the underlying causes and processes. In short, the symptoms of the problem get attacked. This is often seen in attempts to maximize the legal protection of wildlife. For instance, many attempts to get species listed on Appendix I of CITES reflect this attitude. Such an attempt was graphically illustrated in the 1994 proposal by New Zealand to get all kiwi species listed on Appendix I. These species already attract high levels of regulatory protection and, in terms of threats, international trade does not merit mention. The fact that possession of such species is so highly circumscribed and regulated, means that there is little possibility that such a trade could emerge. It was largely in the face of such strict domestic measures and an inability to show the feasibility of a trade emerging that the proposal was rejected.

The actual problem facing the kiwi is predation by exotic pests (mustelids and feral dogs and cats). This level of decline occurs despite the very degree of legal protection awarded to the species and substantial public nature reserves (32 per cent of New Zealand's terrestrial area is reserved for conservation). The kiwi is expected to be extinct over almost its entire range within 20 years. The fear that trade, whether domestic or international, represents a threat to the wildlife, also prevents private conservationists from covering their management costs. The history of captive breeding of kiwis in New Zealand is characterized by the break-up of successful breeding pairs and the permitting of very few bird transfers at low, set prices.

The root problem is treating the social and economic system in which private breeding takes place as 'simple'. Simple systems follow (in principle) linear trends. If policy-makers believe that commercial captive breeding necessarily leads to poaching and over-harvest, then steps to pre-empt a market in wildlife forming will be taken. The consequences for such wildlife can be grim. Such policies do nothing to address the underlying causes of decline. In the case of the kiwi, it is control of exotic predators that is necessary to guarantee survival.

Imposed limitations on wildlife harvests may appear to address the problem of decline. In complex systems, this is not at all certain. Limiting harvests can perversely reduce the value of wildlife to local communities. Reductions in the value of such wildlife cause spillovers. In the face of such reductions in value, poachers may take over-harvest from locals as black market prices rise relative to legal prices. Poachers often have different and less prudent harvest methods. Local communities may change management practices in response to the drop in wildlife values. They may now seek to expand domesticated livestock or agricultural lands and assist or tolerate poachers. In such a case, the native wildlife is moved to another extinction path as a response to the regulations.

The reliance on regulations to suppress market activity to discourage poaching has been a spectacular failure in many instances. Regulations need to be enforced and poachers can, by adjusting harvest strategies, minimize the risk of being caught. If the risk of being caught is not credible, then a single-policy approach of banning trade can promote wildlife decline. The salient lesson from complex systems is that relying upon a single policy instrument to achieve a policy goal carries the risk of perverse failure. Such a stance is intended to work in simple systems where wildlife is not subject to multiple threats and is largely isolated from the economic or social systems that bound it.

If the presumption of simplicity is made, regulatory bodies may be encouraged to do little management. The attraction of doing nothing is that it minimizes the costs for the conservation body. The presumption is that the agency has correctly diagnosed the problem and that individuals and organizations will conform to the regulations when passed. These are the hallmarks of treating a complex system as simple. Such logic discounts completely the lack of incentives facing individuals and organizations to conform to regulations.

This problem was aptly illustrated with the case of the red-tailed black cockatoo in the Northern Territory of Australia. The species is subject to legal protection which, in theory, protects both the adult population from harvest and the nesting sites from destruction. The costs of monitoring the population, conducting research and enforcing the regulations were minimized by not doing any of the above. This reflected the position that the regulations had dealt with the problem, obviating any need to take on a more active management role.

This was similar to the case of the little spotted kiwi in New Zealand. This species was extinct over much of its natural range by the 1970s, except for a natural population on the west coast and translocated populations on a handful of small offshore islands. The presumption that the regulatory stance had somehow dealt with the threats facing the species, deterred any active management decisions. The sudden discovery that the species was actually extinct on the west coast resulted in a catastrophic revision of the status of the species.

The perception that regulations are an effective management tool changes the incentives facing conservation bodies. The two major risks associated with this are first, it encourages a passive, do-nothing approach. The second risk is that it biases regulations towards measures that have low management costs for the agency. Typically this is evidence in support of bans as a policy instrument. Bans have the convenient property of very low management costs (if enforcement is avoided). The salient lesson is that regulatory bodies are not immune to the pressure to minimize their costs.

The challenge of generating policy in complex systems makes simplifying decision rules attractive. With this comes the danger that policy-makers lose sight of the complexity of the system and treat it as simple. The ability of simple decision rules to generate satisfactory conservation outcomes is contingent on time and place. Once the system changes, then satisfactory rules can quickly become unsatisfactory.

This is manifested in the temptation to advocate doing 'more of the same'. Thus the same policy solutions are endlessly recycled to cover all variations in the actual conservation problem. The inability to adopt different policy measures is often handicapped by the satisfactory performance of these measures in the past.

The ability to update knowledge about the system is deterred by several factors. The first is that the cost of obtaining specialized analysis of neglected components of the system may be high. Policy-makers may prefer a 'do-it-yourself' analysis, despite the lack of any specialized knowledge on the component. Thus biologists can instantly become 'experts' on economics and bureaucrats instant 'experts' on economics and biology – without the cost of obtaining a formal background in these disciplines! Unfortunately the requisite specialized knowledge often lies in the skill at discerning the underlying processes of the system. The do-it-yourself approach to analysis lends itself to attacking symptoms rather than addressing the real problem.

This do-it-yourself approach to analysis also contributes to doing 'more of the same'. Not only did simplifying rules get adopted to select the preferred strategy, such simplifying rules get adopted to discount alternative approaches. Where these are not properly tested, policy-makers and lobbyists may get locked into an approach of simply doing more of the same.

This was illustrated at the last CITES meeting with the proposals to up-list the Southern African elephant populations to Appendix I. The proposal originated was put forward by the governments of Kenya and India. Its background in fact, went back to the 1980s when poaching in Africa was decimating populations in many regions. At the 1989 meeting of CITES, a ban on trade in elephant ivory was agreed to.

The rationale for the ban was straightforward. The legal trade in ivory was providing poachers with a means of smuggling ivory into final markets in Europe, North America and Asia. Authorities and consumers were unable to distinguish poached ivory from legally obtained ivory. This gave poachers the least-cost way to market their product in overseas markets. Hence, if the legal trade was sacrificed, poachers would not have this smuggling route available. This sacrifice did, however, give elephant populations a chance to recover.

The disturbing factor was the largely intact populations of Southern Africa. Later three such countries from the region would succeed in getting the populations down-listed to permit a limited trade with Japan. On the basis of allegations of this trade prompting an increase in poaching effort, Kenya and India proposed that the Southern African populations again be up-listed to Appendix I.

Contributing to this were two simplifying decision rules. The first was that the legal market in ivory contributed to the demand in the illegal market. The second was that bans work by eliminating demand in consumption markets. These simplifying rules both share an important characteristic. They are wrong.

The legal market in ivory did not cause demand for illegal ivory. Rather it provided a vehicle for the illegal traffic to take place. Smugglers and poachers face the same incentives as any economic enterprise. Black-marketeers are just as interested in finding low-cost distribution networks as any other business. For a while, the legal market in elephant ivory gave them this network.

In economic terms, goods can be usefully classified as complements and substitutes. Complementary goods are ones where an increase in demand in one good leads to an increase in demand for another. For instance, an increase in demand for motor cars is likely to lead to an increase in demand for tyres. Hamburgers, soft drinks and fries may exhibit such characteristics, which is why fast food chains try to bundle such goods together as special 'deals'.

Substitute goods are those where an increase in demand for one good, leads to a decrease in demand for the other. Such goods often share similar characteristics. For instance, Pepsi and Coke are substitute cola drinks. Given their similar characteristics, poached and legally sourced elephant ivory are also substitutes. The problem is not that legal trade in ivory creates demand for the illegal, it is that consumers could not distinguish the two products. Illegally sourced ivory was the classic market 'lemon'. Poached ivory had an undesirable characteristic (its illegal origin) that was unable to be detected by discerning customers.

In the face of the perception that poaching was on the rise again, Kenya and India wished to repeat the success of the earlier ban on ivory trade. Part of the rationale was that the ban restricted the demand for ivory, rather than restricting supply. The absence of ivory in Asian markets following the ban was, attributed to a fall-off in demand in the Kenya–India proposal. This was followed by the completely contrary argument that demand in Asia remained high after the ban! It may be more reasonably presumed that the lack of ivory for sale reflected the supply shortage created by the commercial ban.

Trade bans in fact limit supply. In doing so, consumption of the product is limited as some consumers get priced out of the market. The trade regulations ideally drive up the cost of supplying the product. Some of these costs get passed on to consumers in the form of higher prices. Some of these costs must be absorbed by smugglers. If smugglers cannot absorb these costs, then they may drop out of this particular industry.

There were two obstacles facing the Kenya–India proposal. The first was that the perception that poaching had decreased and then was on the rise was not supported by credible observations. Appropriate monitoring of elephant populations and poaching levels had not occurred since the ban. The second was that the evidence on poaching no longer confirmed any legal-market link. Rather ivory was now being smuggled from the source country to the final market. Ivory was being discovered in containers that ostensibly carried machine parts. Smugglers had achieved independence from the legal market. They had also developed new markets in Asia and the Middle East to replace the lost European and North American markets.

This change in smuggling behaviour is what happens in complex systems. Faced with a sudden rise in distribution costs, smugglers patiently developed alternative routes that were independent of the legal traffic. Instead of simply waiting and hoping for the ban in ivory to be lifted, new routes and new markets were developed. This meant that renewed attempts to close down the legal trade in ivory (noting that on the evidence provided, the legal exporting African countries had the least problem with poaching) was doomed to failure. Doing more of the same could not work because the characteristics of this illegal market had changed. However, policy-makers locked into using 'simple decision rules' were unable to perceive these changes nor vary their policy approach.

This illustrates a point associated with complex systems. Simple policy measures may work for a time but they end up being circumvented. Regulations rearrange costs and have flow-through effects into final markets. These market spillovers spur participants to circumvent these costs – or take advantage of opportunities that are created. This is illustrated with the case of the black market in Australian parrots.

Despite the existence of a legal market in Australian parrots, the commercial export of live Australian parrots is banned by domestic legislation. However, Australian parrots are in high demand overseas. The ban in effect, creates an artificial shortage of parrots in foreign markets. Foreign markets are legally supplied from stock imported prior to the ban and from excess birds supplied by zoos. This is not enough to make up the shortage, and foreign prices of Australian parrots are much higher than domestic prices. The Australian galah is a prolific cockatoo that often becomes an agricultural pest. Its domestic price is around AU$50 (US$29) a pair. In the US, galahs can sell for US$3000–4,000. Other Australian parrots command even higher prices. The red-tailed black cockatoo is very rare overseas and has sold for almost AU$30,000 (US$17,115) a bird on occasion.

This price difference creates a business opportunity for smugglers. Parrots can be bought cheaply in Australia and sold dearly in foreign markets. Best of all, there is little competition with the legal exporters excluded from the market. Exacerbating the illegal export of parrots are insufficient resources for the detection of smugglers and the weak sanctions applied to convicted smugglers. The conservation problem has simply been turned into a law enforcement problem, rather than being solved by the trade ban. It still requires a large investment in law enforcement activity. In the absence of such effort, smugglers have shown they have been able to operate for years without detection.

One novel smuggling method is the egg-vest. Rather than live birds being exported, the eggs are harvested from nesting sites and put into a special vest, which is concealed under ordinary clothing by the smuggler whose body temperature keeps the eggs viable for the trip. The eggs can then be incubated in aviaries in the foreign country and passed off as legally bred within that market. This method of export was also expedited by the introduction of the long distance air-carrier which minimized delays and border crossings.

Another expedient in the Australian black market is to export the birds to New Zealand where again they are 'laundered'. New Zealand is the largest legal exporter of Australian parrots worldwide and this trade can conceal the activities of smugglers. In one known case the birds were purchased in Australian pet-stores and flown illegally to small unsupervised airfields in New Zealand. It is worth noting that the most prolifically traded Australian parrot is the galah. While they do not command the premium prices of some cockatoos, procurement costs are significantly lower. The rate of profitability on galahs exceeds that of red-tailed black cockatoos.

The Australian experience confirms that bans do not reduce demand for wildlife products. Perversely, it shows that the trade ban has had the unexpected consequence of perpetuating and sustaining a black market in native parrots. This is an expected outcome of narrow policy adopted in a complex system. The principal effect of a ban is to reduce supply to foreign markets and change expectations about future supply. For instance, the expectation of a contraction in supply during the 1980s led to Japanese seal carvers collecting a stockpile of elephant ivory sufficient for ten years supply.

CONCLUSION

The chief effect of regulations is to reallocate the costs of conservation effort and convert conservation problems into law enforcement problems. The widespread failure to invest in a level of law enforcement that would deter poaching is understandable. It saves on costs and it is not even clear that high levels of law enforcement activity are feasible. Where this is fed by the perception that individuals will conform to regulations irrespective of personal costs or absence of sanctions, policy-makers can be biased towards bans. Perversely, this can encourage wildlife losses that the regulations were intended to overcome.

Complex systems require the use of several integrated policy measures. These can test assumptions about how the system works, and gives policy-makers more scope for switching into more effective strategies. The use of a single policy instrument – like a trade ban – does not test even poorly grounded assumptions about the economic behaviour of poachers and smugglers. Without any ability to revise knowledge, policy-makers have fewer options to employ when surprises occur or their favoured policy reaches its expiry date.

Chapter 5

Control and the Holy Grail

Marshall Murphree

Introduction

In their book *The Lessons of History*, Will and Ariel Durant (quoted in Kurlansky, 1998) have this to say:

> *So the first biological lesson of history is that life is competition. Competition is not only the life of trade, it is the trade of life – peaceful when food abounds, violent when the mouths outrun the food. Animals eat one another without qualm: civilized men consume one another by due process of law.*

This extract mentions several key aspects of our exploitation of the natural world. It speaks of supply, it speaks of demand, and it speaks of competition and control. Humankind's use of species and ecosystems is critically determined by these three variables. And it is in the relationships between the three that the clues are to be found as to whether our use of natural resources is likely to be sustainable or not. This chapter considers the issue of control, which is a necessary (if not sufficient) condition for sustainability in use and unless we get this condition right exploitation will result in resource depletion. If we get it right, we may well find the Holy Grail of 'sustainable use'.

All forms of environmental management are essentially regulative in function. They are, of course, more than this and are usually also directed at improving environmental productivity. But as they are, being above the level of individual management, systems of collective action for collective good, they must have the institutional means to induce collective conformity if they are to work.

All of this may sound commonplace and it is an assumption which runs through the international environmental culture, including the plethora of environmental conventions with which we interact, such as CITES and the

Convention on Biological Diversity (CBD). Thus Article II of CITES in describing its appendix listings speaks of 'particularly strict regulation' (Appendix I), 'strict regulation' (Appendix II) and 'effective control' (Appendix III). The CBD uses similar vocabulary, and in Article 8 we find, for instance, the words 'regulate', 'manage', 'control' and 'prevent'.

What is unfortunately not so commonplace, however, is the recognition by this international environmental culture that effective regulation is far more than a matter of proscriptive legislation. We only grasp this when we understand a central sociological insight, that regulation is comprised of a set of incentives, both negative and positive. Incentive is thus the fulcrum of regulation. Regulation almost invariably requires an element of negative incentive, proscriptions backed by powers to enforce them. But any regulatory system which relies primarily on negative incentives is – in the long term – in trouble. Enforcement costs are high and the legitimacy of the system in the eyes of the enforced is called into question. History shows that such systems are unstable and that sustainable systems of regulation are those that rely primarily on positive incentives – economic, cultural and institutional – which are affordable.

If we take this lesson from social history seriously and apply it to environmental governance, we must conclude that one of the main reasons our efforts have, if we are honest, not generally produced the results we seek lies in the fact that they have the balance wrong between negative and positive incentives. They emphasize negative and expensive proscriptions which are beyond their capacities of enforcement. They give insufficient attention to positive inducements, which are more powerful and more cost-effective. This balance must be redressed. The issue is not one of negative or positive incentives per se, but one of finding the right mix of these ingredients in specific systemic contexts. We need to re-profile our approaches so that they represent incentive packages of regulatory compliance in which negative sanctions can be enforced because they are held to affordable levels and in which the burden of compliance is shifted to positive, more viable and implementable incentives.

Incentives and Scale

If we accept the need to find the right mix of negative and positive incentives, which work in specific systemic contexts, the next question is to ask whether the incentive regimes which we advocate are congruent with the characteristics of the resource or ecosystem concerned and with the profile of management dynamics involved. We cannot begin to answer the first part of this question until we disaggregate resources and ecosystems into categories determined by their management requirements rather than by Linnaean or other typologies. When we do so we discover that the required regime varies widely. What is required for 'locally' migrant sand grouse and what is required for the globally migratory arctic terns are likely to be vastly different in scale.

We cannot answer the second part of the question unless we also grasp the importance of scale on institutional efficiency. Generally, the smaller a regime, the more effective and efficient it will be. Increases in scale complicate communication and decision-making and beyond certain levels regimes must bureaucratize with attendant costs. Compliance inducement shifts from low-cost modes of moral and peer-pressure to the high-cost methods of policing and formal coercion. Beyond this, increase in scale erodes the sense of individual responsibility. These insights led Garrett Hardin to once remark that in environmental affairs 'globalization favours evasion'. He than went on to advocate a simple rule: 'Never globalize a problem if it can possibly be dealt with locally' (Hardin, 1985).

Thus our search for effective incentive regimes must reconcile scale effects on institutional dynamics with the regime requirements of specific environmental problems. There are global environmental problems requiring collective international incentives to control them. The level of greenhouse gases continues to rise, with climatic effects which are hotly debated in their specifics but are nevertheless likely to significantly alter the extent and configurations of biological diversity. Toxic pollutants seep through aquifers or spread through the atmosphere, inhibiting ecosystem resilience and negatively impacting on populations far from their source. Issues of this type are truly global and require collective international controls. And, indeed, there has been no lack of international response to these issues. To date, nearly 200 multilateral environmental agreements have been produced. Many of these are 'soft' agreements, statements of mutual concern and voluntary intent to carry out remedial action. But, as Douglass points out, 'voluntary agreements tend to have little direct behaviour-modifying effect on nations'. Thus 'soft' agreements become largely 'an intermediate step to a "hard" agreement which will bind the parties to a common, enforceable goal' (Douglass, 1998).

So far, so good. But, when we examine 'hard' multilateral agreements and conventions, we find that the incentives for compliance they contain are almost exclusively punitive and negative. Furthermore, punitive mechanisms which are politically viable are limited. In fact 'non-compliance protocols' usually boil down to one measure: trade sanctions against the offending state. 'Economic sanctions have become the policy enforcement tool of choice for international enforcement' (Douglass, 1998). Leaving aside any discussion of the costs involved in using this instrument, and the conflict between it and another major global trend – the dismantling of protectionist barriers and the encouragement of free trade – we can note that little if anything by way of positive incentive is offered in these treaties and conventions.[1] There is, of course, one important exception to this. National and international environmental bureaucracies 'become both the benefactors and beneficiaries of environmental treaty development' (Douglass, 1998). As Wiener observes, 'The diplomats negotiating the treaty often come from the very government agencies and elite cliques which would be enlarged and enriched by the task of handling these resource transfers' (Wiener, 1997).

This profile of incentive packages in our global efforts to address global problems – heavily skewed towards negative and expensive sanctions of questionable impact – constitutes a prescription for stasis and inefficiency, for discord and disillusion. The world is understandably becoming impatient with the noise of our solemn assemblies, with expensive gatherings which turn into choirs singing hymns of pious environmental rectitude, strong in proscriptive resolutions reflecting intent but weak in approaches which link intent and consequence through incentive regimes which work.

Returning for the moment to the issue of scale, we need to recognize that most of the problems involving the sustainable use of natural resources will be determined by the policies and actions of people at a smaller scale, at national and sub-national levels. The further down the hierarchy of scale we go the closer we get to hands-on management and use and it is here that the determinative decisions on use are made. At these levels decisions are personal rather than abstract, operational rather than propositional, emphasize positive effort rather than passive compliance and their implementation is direct, carried out by those who make them. Because they are generally made in contexts distanced from any effective instruments of international or state coercion they are relatively autonomous, responsive to private or local agendas rather than those set by the abstractions of international conservation discourse.

Two important points arise. Firstly, since these determinative decisions are taken in contexts insulated from, and indeed often hostile to, externally imposed regulatory proscription, incentives for sustainable use at this level must give particular attention to positive inducements. Secondly, since these contexts represent a myriad number of specific situations, no single incentive profile can be universally applicable. As it has been put rather colourfully:

> *Sustainable use is not an exercise in colouring by numbers. Instead what you have is an identification of the social, economic and biological factors that always need to be considered, and which sometimes enhance, or not, the sustainability of resource use. And the sustainability lies not in the factors themselves but the interaction between the factors* (Robinson, 1998).

This complexity and variability should serve as a warning against our reductionist proclivity to search for polyvalent 'guidelines' rather than principles.

Incentives in Socio-economic Context

Let us turn now to the importance of values and goals in constructing effective incentive packages for sustainable use. Socio-economic and socio-cultural location importantly shape what these values and goals are. For those located in urban and industrialized society wildlife and habitat have little direct economic significance and emphasis is placed on the intrinsic or recreational values derived from these resources. Our definitions of conservation are couched in abstract terms such as 'biodiversity' and 'ecosystem maintenance' and our objectives become those of the maintenance of species and habitats for aesthetic, recreational or scientific purposes. Incentive packages for sustainability responsive to these objectives are likely to emphasize the role of the state, the guidance of science and the compliance of the citizenry in preserving the little of what urbanization and technology has left of 'the natural'.

For rural farmers and pastoralists, where the presence of wild land and wildlife has important economic implications, conservation incentives take a different, more instrumental form. While they, too, hold profound and powerful intrinsic valuations of nature, conservation is for them an investment for present and future value, the goal being the maintenance or enhancement of their livelihoods. Sustainable use is conservation; whether it involves regulated off-take of biological productivity or the designation of areas for tourism enterprises.

There is nothing intrinsically incompatible in the two incentive profiles just described. The difference is over what is regarded as the ultimate goal and what is simply the means to that goal. One stance treats conservation as the ultimate goal and sustainable use initiatives that enhance livelihoods are the means to that end. The other stance treats human well-being as the goal and conservation as the means to that goal. Dissonance arises when the two are brought together in one arena of action and where one stance is accorded what Hirschman has called 'privileged problem' status (Hirschman, 1963). At present the tendency is for intrinsic and existence valuations to be accorded higher-order-level status and to regard local and instrumental conservation incentives as lower-level factors to be co-opted in the pursuit of these values. This produces an impasse. Allied to international and state coercive instruments, intrinsic and existence valuations impose proscriptions which inhibit the implementation of local, instrumental incentives. However, local incentives also have a powerful veto dimension. Unless they are accommodated, international and national values and goals will be subverted by local responses ranging from defiance to covert non-compliance.

Incentive Compatibility and Conflict

To get around this impasse, one approach is to identify the congruent aspects of incentives which operate at different levels of scale and bind them together in structures and processes which enhance their potential for synergy. Bromley (1994) refers to this as 'incentive compatibility' which, he says:

> *is established when local inhabitants acquire an economic interest in the long-run viability of an ecosystem that is important to people situated elsewhere... Such ecosystems represent benefit streams for both parties; those ... who seek to preserve biodiversity and those who must make a living amid this genetic resource.*

There is a great deal that can be said in support of strategies of incentive compatibility. Conflicts over the environment are not necessarily zero-sum games, where if one party benefits the other must lose. It is possible to structure incentives so that the interests of both the larger collective whole and those of the people who use and manage the constituent elements of the natural environment are satisfied. This is the implicit assumption which lies behind the many programmes that flourish today under such titles as 'integrated conservation and development' and 'community conservation'.

But we should not allow our enthusiasm for 'win–win' solutions and for incentive-compatibility to cloud our grasp of politico-economic realities. Providing effective incentive packages for sustainability at local levels usually will require significant transfers of power, of rights and resources. There will be losers as well as winners. This is an unpalatable fact, but unless we face it, our prescriptions will continue to deal with symptoms rather than causes.

Consider the case of 'community conservation' projects mentioned above. In a recent comparative study of such projects in Eastern and Southern Africa (AWF et al, no date) it was found that performance rarely approximates promise and is sometimes abysmal. There are a number of reasons for this. Some of them relate to planning and implementation. Some are demographic or ecological and involve resource/demand ratios. Some, importantly, are institutional and organizational. But the single most important reason for failure is aborted devolution; the failure to confer the necessary level of rights and responsibilities required to achieve efficient localized control regimes enhancing sustainability. The incentive package, in both its negative and positive dimensions, is incomplete and inadequate.

Why this aborted devolution, in spite of all the rhetoric by governments and funding agencies about 'community-based management' and 'decentralized control' over natural resources? The answer lies fundamentally in the value of natural resources and the importance of power to control and benefit from them. The history of colonial Africa is a history of the appropriation of this power and benefit by the state from those who live with and use natural resources. This was done largely by claiming the *de facto* and often *de jure* ownership of natural resources for the state and conferring only weak, usufructural rights to the land on which these communities live. This condition has persisted into the modern post-colonial state almost without exception. As in colonial times, 'communal lands' continue to be in varying degrees the fiefdoms of state bureaucracies, political elites and their private-sector entrepreneurial partners.

This example has been from Africa, but its characteristics can be found in a multitude of examples from around the world – not only the developing but the developed world as well. Devolution in tenure, responsibility, rights and access to benefit streams is a fundamental allocative and political issue. Power structures at the political and economic centre are not disposed to surrender their privileges and will use their power, including their abilities to shape policy and law, to maintain the monopolies of their position.

All this is not new in essence. An anonymous 18th century rhyme put the issue succinctly for that period of English history:

The law doth punish man or woman,
That steals the goose from off the common.
But lets the greater felon loose,
That steals the common from the goose.

And so we are back to the observation of the opening quote of this chapter. In the competition which is the trade of life, 'civilized men consume one another by due process of law.' It is not being suggested here that we dispense with law, with socially legitimated proscriptions against deviance which form an important negative incentive in our search for sustainability. What is being suggested is that the processes which lead to policy and law be further democratized and made more responsive to the incentives for sustainability which lie with those who are the primary users, producers and managers of our natural resources. To put it differently, good civil governance is an indispensable component in the search for sustainability.

SCIENCE AND THE DEVOLUTION OF IDEAS

The robust devolutionism that incentives for sustainability require involves not only a fundamental reallocation of rights to resources and benefit streams. It also involves a reallocation of the roles and rules in cognitive discourse, a new configuration of scholarship more pluralist, more inductive, more experimental in its approaches and more contingent in its conclusions. It involves the 'mainstreaming' of adaptive management in environmental science. It requires, in a phrase, cognitive devolution.

A move in this direction is evident among environmental scientists concerned with evolutionary biology and system approaches to ecology which extend the scope of investigation beyond physical and biotic data to include the structures and dynamics of human activity. Scientists in this school recognize the inherently contingent nature of scientific knowledge and emphasize its role, with policy and management, in social experiment (Holling, 1993). They recognize that sustainability is a social goal, not a 'fixed end-point to be reached but a direction that guides constructive change' (Lee, 1993).

This perspective on professional science's epistemology and role, in its applied form, has 'emerged regionally in new forms of resource and environmental management where uncertainty and surprises became an integral part of an anticipated set of adaptive responses' (Holling, 1993). Dissonance remains, however, where bureaucracies retain the expectation that science can provide *a priori* certainties. As Constanza remarks, '... most environmental regulations ... *demand certainty* and when scientists are pressured to supply this non-existent commodity there is not only frustration and poor communication, but mixed messages in the media as well' (Constanza, 1993). One can also add that this pressure is a perverse incentive for the integrity of science itself, since it carries with it the temptation to assert as definitive that which is tentative.

Unfortunately, there remains a strain in our scholarship where science is still regarded as a specialized domain outside the realm and mandate of local people. Our language often betrays this, as when for instance we read the following criterion for sustainable use: 'Governments involve local people in decisions affecting the use *while continuing to base management decisions on science*' (Species Survival Network, 1996. Emphasis added.) That last phrase is the tell-tale clause. We can 'involve' and 'consult' local users and managers, but the decision-making base for management must remain ultimately with a professional scientific establishment separate from them.

A frank examination of our record must conclude that there is an epistemic environmental establishment located at an international scale distanced from the levels where most of the operational decisions on sustainability are made. It is fed by professional and bureaucratic self-interest, with their imperatives of centralized control. It acts as a magnet for recidivism, drawing the reality of our scholarship back from the rhetoric of our policy.

These assertions will be vigorously denied by many. There are significant advances in cognitive devolution and these should not be discounted. But if we candidly examine our stratagems of knowledge production with their reliance on paid professionals and glossy publications; if we review our allocations of programmatic and administrative budgets in terms of the locus of control and direction of scholarship, a persistent profile emerges. The world of on-the-ground use and management remains largely the intellectual fiefdom of an entrenched professional-cum-bureaucratic elite.

NOTES

1 The Convention on Biological Diversity, with its emphasis on the sustainable use of biodiversity and the equitable sharing of the benefits of such use, is a notable exception

ACKNOWLEDGEMENT

This chapter is an edited version of the keynote address prepared for the symposium workshop on conservation (Topic 1d) 'Sustaining Use of Species and Ecosystems', held during the 50th anniversary celebration of IUCN, Fontainbleau, 3–5 November 1998.

The author thanks Rowan Martin for drawing his attention to the 18th century rhyme quoted above.

REFERENCES

AWF, CASS and IDPM (no date) *Study on Community Conservation in Africa: Principles and comparative practice,* funded by the Economic and Social Research Council, UK

Bromley, D (1994) Economic Dimensions of Community-based Conservation in Western, D and Wright, R M (eds) *Natural Connections: Perspectives in community-based conservation,* Island Press, Washington DC

Constanza, R (1993) Developing Ecological Research that is Relevant for Achieving Sustainability, *Ecological Applications,* 3(4)

Douglass, C (1998) *Environmental Crossing Guards: International environmental treaties and US foreign policy*, Policy Brief no 168, Center for the Study of American Business, Washington University, St Louis

Hardin, G (1985) *Filters Against Folly*, Penguin Books, New York

Hirschman, AO (1963) *Journeys Towards Progress*, Twentieth Century Fund

Holling, C S (1993) Investing in Research for Sustainability, *Ecological Applications,* 3(4)

Kurlansky, M (1998) *Cod: A biography of the fish that changed the world*, Jonathan Cape, London

Lee, K N (1993) Greed, Scale Mismatch, and Learning, *Ecological Applications,* 3(4)

Robinson, J (1998) Evolving Understanding of Sustainable Use, in van der Linde, J and Danskin, M (eds) *Enhancing Sustainability: Resources for Our Future*, SUI Technical Series vol 1, IUCN, Gland

Species Survival Network (1996) *Criteria for Assessing the Sustainability of Trade in Wild Fauna and Flora,* Wildlife Use Working Group of the Species Survival Network, Humane Society of the United States, Washington DC

Weiner, J B (1997) *Designing Global Climate Policy: Efficient Markets Versus Political Markets*, Policy Study 143, Weidenbaum Center, Washington University in St Louis, Missouri

Part 2

Systems of Regulation and Enforcement

Chapter 6

Compliance and Enforcement Mechanisms of CITES

Juan Carlos Vasquez

Introduction

This chapter provides reflections on compliance and enforcement mechanisms of CITES.[1] It focuses on the need for a multifaceted approach to successfully address the relationship between regulation and enforcement within the context of the convention.

In order to have a common starting point, it is useful to look at some provisional definitions for implementation, compliance and enforcement as elements of such a multifaceted approach. 'Implementation' is usually interpreted as a generic term covering all the measures taken by governments to fulfil their obligations under the convention, including for example enacting national legislation. States implement their CITES obligations in three distinct phases. First, by adopting national implementing measures which include legislative and economic provisions, information systems, management plans and enforcement units; second, by ensuring that national measures are complied with by those subject to their jurisdiction and control; and third, by fulfilling obligations to the CITES Secretariat, such as reporting the volume of trade and the measures taken to give effect to international obligations.

'Compliance' means to act in accordance with, and in fulfilment of, the measures that have been adopted. Without compliance, requirements will not achieve the desired results. Compliance, like implementation, does not happen automatically once requirements are established, since the convention is not a self-executing treaty.

Compliance has two dimensions: at international level, measures taken by parties to comply with the obligations of the convention; and, at national level, it refers to actions taken by individuals or legal entities such as corporations or government agencies to comply with domestic legislation. 'Non-compliance' can include a failure to give effect to substantive norms, for example failure to prohibit trade in all CITES-listed species in violation of Article VIII of the convention; failure to fulfil procedural requirements, for example to carry out a non-detrimental finding assessment, as required by Articles III and IV; or failure to fulfil an institutional obligation such as submission of the annual report.

'Enforcement' is a term which originated in the Anglo-Saxon legal culture and has become a key element in the legal structure of Multilateral Environmental Agreements (MEAs). It is hard to find a proper translation of this word in other languages but comparable terms can be found in countries of all the six regions that compose the CITES world. Enforcement is the formal response of the regulatory system and institutions either to a finding of non-compliance or to encourage compliance.

In the CITES context, enforcement is the set of actions that parties take to correct or halt illegal trade. This includes inspections to determine the compliance status of the legislation and to detect violations; and legal action, where necessary, to compel compliance and to impose sanctions for violating the convention (or national law). The need for enforcement arises from non-compliance.

These definitions have to be harmonized with the underlying structures of the respective legal and administrative systems around the world which are evolving out of different traditions and cultures. These different systems are all converging in the acknowledgement of the necessity to combat illegal wildlife trade and comply with the provisions of CITES.

Effective Law Enforcement

CITES is known as a convention which possesses effective decision-making and enforcement mechanisms. The effectiveness of CITES listing depends on the ability to control illegal trade and to give local people economic and social incentives for maintaining wildlife. Consequently, improving enforcement, increasing funding and public awareness need to be accompanied by social and economic incentives. Otherwise, enforcement will only play a minor role in preventing illegal trade.

We cannot talk about 'law enforcement' without a regulatory framework being in place. A solid legal basis is essential for effective enforcement. However, approaches that focus on repressive and punitive policies to control poaching and to protect listed species are incomplete. The listing itself does not eliminate the demand and even optimal enforcement levels are unable to eliminate black markets.

The debate on enforcement, referring to national as well as international regulatory frameworks for wildlife trade, has to tackle the crucial question as to what degree national legislation implementing CITES is adequate and enforceable. The parties to CITES have generally found a way to adapt the convention to new changes and to address enforcement problems in a practical way.

In order to evaluate the effectiveness of national legislation as the basis for CITES law enforcement, the National Legislation Project, was initiated in 1992. Through this initiative the parties have defined an approach for reviewing and evaluating the legal basis to implement the convention. Four criteria and three categories are used to assess a party's legislation. The criteria, as set out in Resolution Conf 8.4, are provision to designate management and scientific authorities; provision to prohibit trade in specimens in violation of the convention; provision to penalize prohibited trade; and provision to provide for the confiscation of unlawfully traded or possessed specimens.

After analysis, based on the four requirements, national legislation for implementing CITES is placed in one of three categories:

1. Category 1: legislation generally meets requirements for implementation of CITES;
2. Category 2: legislation generally does not meet all requirements for implementation of CITES;
3. Category 3: legislation generally does not meet requirements for implementation of CITES.

The National Legislation Project, is currently in its fourth phase. By June 2002, legislative analyses had been prepared for 148 out of 158 parties. These show that approximately 70 per cent of the parties reviewed did not have the full range of national legislative and administrative measures needed to give effect to all aspects of the convention and related resolutions of the conference of the parties.

These findings show clearly that the majority of parties still need to adopt or strengthen their legislative, regulatory and institutional measures if a global regulatory framework is to be made effective. For CITES to work correctly, all countries must put adequate implementation and enforcement measures in place to avoid loopholes and weak links.

Currently, a majority of parties rely on their general wildlife legislation, and sometimes on customs legislation or foreign trade legislation, to control trade in specimens of CITES-listed species. The use of such legislation can give rise to a variety of enforcement problems. Existing sector-based legislation is rarely suited to the specific requirements of the convention.

An important priority for domestic law enforcement is the coordination between the key actors involved in compliance and enforcement, namely CITES authorities, police and customs, judiciary bodies and NGOs.

CITES enforcement officers like many other law enforcement agents, exercise a significant amount of discretion. They are often confronted with unprecedented or unanticipated situations. If the situations encountered are not adequately addressed in the legislation, the agency and the enforcement officers must outline a course of action they believe to be consistent with the legislative intent. Because this determination is subjective and open to question, an affected individual might disagree with the agency actions. For this reason, the powers of enforcement officers should be clearly defined, preferably in the CITES implementation legislation. They should be as extensive as possible, while remaining consistent with constitutional requirements and established rules of criminal procedure.

Such powers typically include powers to search persons, baggage and other property and vehicles; powers to search premises or, where the law requires the prior grant of a search warrant by a magistrate, to apply for such a warrant; powers to request information, to inspect documents and to take samples of specimens for identification purposes; powers of arrest; and powers to seize specimens when there are grounds to believe that they are being or have been illegally imported or otherwise obtained.

WILDLIFE CRIME AS A LEGAL CONCEPT

The term wildlife crime is presently used without a specific definition or identification of the activities to which the term refers. Popular journals, magazines and even enforcement officers use the term to describe acts that cause harm to wildlife. What does it mean to refer to something as a wildlife crime?

There is a need for a 'legal definition' of wildlife crime in the context of CITES. Crime is usually defined as an act punishable by law, as being forbidden by statute or injurious to the public welfare (properly including all offences punishable by law, but commonly used only for grave offences). Some authors propose to define wildlife crimes as 'violations of criminal law designed to protect wildlife' and they classify wildlife crime as a subcategory of white-collar and organized crime.

When establishing definitional criteria for wildlife crime in the context of CITES, at least five different elements may be considered: the type of activity, the specific act, the actor, the social status of the actor, and the sanction applied. The categorization of CITES offences as crimes endeavours to encompass all problems posed by illegal trade in CITES-listed species and to provide sanctions for all acts and offences conducive to the trafficking of these species.

First, consider the type of activity. There are a wide variety of activities casually referred to in the popular media and academic literature as wildlife crimes. As an example, consider international trafficking in CITES species. The importation, exportation, re-exportation, introduction from the sea or transport, of any specimen of a species listed in the CITES Appendices without a valid permit or certificate, or with a forged permit or certificate, or a permit or certificate that has been modified by anyone other than the management authority, or with a permit or certificate that is invalid for any other reason shall be liable to imprisonment and/or a fine.

Consider another activity, poaching. There is a difference between the type of crime (poaching) and the act (killing an animal). Poaching is defined as the taking of a game animal out of season or through illegal means. Certainly the law allows hunters to kill animals, but hunting is closely regulated. The taking of single species happens in the wild, regardless of granted authorizations or designated hunting seasons. If an animal is killed without authorization or out of season, would this be a wildlife crime? If only one animal was taken, rather than, say, 20 animals, would that be a wildlife crime? It is undetermined whether all violations should be considered wildlife crimes or whether wildlife crimes are restricted to activities for which criminal remedies are sought.

Wildlife crime can be divided into three basic categories:

1. violations of a permit condition;
2. violations committed outside the regulatory scheme; and
3. acts that would be illegal regardless of the regulatory provisions.

The Role of Criminal Sanctions

For the most part, wildlife law consists of 'heavy administrative orders'. The legal response to CITES violations includes administrative, civil, and criminal remedies. Criminal penalties for illegal wildlife trade may, however, offer the most potent legal deterrent effect on potential violators. Some law enforcement officials also put the case this way: 'Criminal enforcement is an essential strategy for stemming wildlife wrongdoing'.

When offenders are not in compliance with regulations, criminal law has been sought as a tool to force compliance. Although criminal prosecution of wildlife-crime cases is still used sparingly, many criminologists argue that wrongful behaviour 'is generally deterred more by criminal prosecution than by civil or administrative action'.

The traditional reasons for imposing the criminal law on convicted offenders is summarized in the four goals of punishment: deterrance, incapacitation, rehabilitation and retribution. Prison takes criminals out of society and therefore prevents them from committing other violations. In addition, society might have a more basic reason for making an offence criminal – to impose a moral stigma on certain activities.

Although criminal sanctions for CITES offences are outlined in the national legislation of a few countries, the more severe criminal sanctions are rarely used, and the majority of CITES violations are addressed through regulatory or civil remedies. However, in some cases wildlife legislation has been aggressively enforced. Enforcement agents use wildlife legislation to prosecute violators to the fullest extent allowed by law (zero tolerance). Take the example of China. A total of 12 criminals have been sentenced to death and already executed in China for wildlife cases, including 7 individuals for poaching giant pandas and smuggling the skins during the period 1985–1996, and 5 individuals for poaching Asian elephants and smuggling their tusks in Yunnan Province in 1994. Taking another example, the bald eagle *Haliaeetus leucocephalus* is a CITES Appendix I species. The fine for the illegal killing, possession, or sale of a bald eagle can run as high as US$500,000, and the accused violator can be sentenced for up to five years in prison for each offence in the US.

Should criminal sanctions be used to enforce CITES provisions that are now generally enforced by regulatory agencies?

Effective law enforcement efforts should include strong sanctions against offenders accompanied with institutional, economic and social incentives. The criminalization of illegal wildlife trade can help to deter violators and the use of economic instruments can help to remove economic benefit of non-compliance.

On the other hand, poachers harvesting CITES species under open-access conditions can make a lot of money with a minimum investment. The profit margin can be so high that it doesn't matter what effort they have to make to elude enforcement controls. Consequently, the effectiveness of CITES enforcement depends also on the ability to remove perverse incentives for poaching and to create economic and social incentives for maintaining wildlife in its natural form.

For instance, the assignment of property and use rights could be granted to the local communities or the private sector, including self-administration of resource use and the right to sell hunting licenses. It can help to reduce enforcement costs by providing resource owners with an incentive to protect 'their' resources.

Organized Crime

In the new global age, borders have opened up, trade barriers have fallen and information speeds around the world at the touch of a button. Business is booming – and so is transnational organized crime. Fortunes are being made from illegal wildlife trade. Wildlife crime does not really differ from other forms of crime. Large criminal groups often mimic legitimate business by forming multinational alliances to extend their reach and push up profits. The modern approach to fighting organized crime is through intelligence-led targeting of smuggling, but also targeting the initial illegal taking of specimens in producing countries and then targeting the dealers in consuming countries.

Criminal groups have established international networks to carry out their activities more effectively through sophisticated technology and by exploiting today's open borders. The Secretariat, in cooperation with the CITES authorities, Interpol, World Customs Organization (WCO), NGOs and other enforcement agencies tries to map the latest trends among organized criminal groups, highlighting their potential worldwide danger so that preventive measures can take place.

CONCLUSION

In any regulatory system some people will comply voluntarily, some will not comply, and some will comply only if they see others receive a sanction for non-compliance. To illustrate this, let me use an interesting ratio presented by TRAFFIC South America in a recent meeting on enforcement and wildlife crime: the '25–50–25 formula' under which 25 per cent always follow the law, 25 per cent always break the law and 50 per cent could go either way depending on the extent of regulation, opportunity and greed. This phenomenon – that people will change their behaviour to avoid a sanction – may also be motivated by economic incentives.

All too often, enforcement agencies deploy their resources to spend time looking at people who are actually already in compliance: the first 25 per cent. They sit and examine CITES documents to see if they have been completed properly, while the smuggler who does not bother with documents slides past behind their backs. There is a need for enforcement agencies to think more about what we are doing and to focus on the real problems.

NOTES

1 The views expressed in this chapter are strictly those of the author and do not bind the CITES secretariat or the parties.

ACKNOWLEDGEMENT

The author would like to thank John Sellar for his valuable insights and comments.

Chapter 7

The European Community Wildlife Trade Regulations

David Morgan

INTRODUCTION

At its root, trade in wildlife products is a commercial activity like any other and under the treaties establishing the European Community (EC)[1] such matters are subject to community competence. This means that common rules need to be established which apply to traders in all 15 of the current member states.

Trade in wildlife indigenous to the EC is regulated by the Birds Directive[2] and the Habitats & Species Directive[3]. The provisions of these measures largely prohibit trade in all European threatened native species. Trade in wildlife products originating from outside the EC mostly concerns imports from developing countries and is regulated by other community law[4]. This law is applied by the national authorities in each EC member state who are responsible for issuing the necessary permits and certificates. Its application is coordinated and harmonized by the European Commission.

The EC sought to gain membership of CITES in 1983 and in that year the CITES parties agreed an amendment to the text of the convention to allow regional economic integration organizations such as the EC to join. However, this amendment cannot come into force until two-thirds of the CITES parties who were members at the time have ratified the change. Nearly 20 years later this target has still not been reached. Nevertheless, given the legal realities, the EC developed its own legislation on the subject in 1984. This legislation was substantially expanded and updated in 1997 to take account of, among other things, the abolition of internal customs borders inside the community.

The legislation, which takes the form of Regulations which have the direct effect of law in all member states, implements virtually all of the provisions of

CITES and the many resolutions of the conference of the CITES parties. However, as the EC has not yet been allowed to join CITES, it does so on an entirely voluntary basis. As a non-party, the EC cannot be held accountable to CITES for any actions it takes in this field.

Such a situation is paradoxical as the EC provides one of the largest and most diverse market for CITES species, estimated to represent around one-third of the world market for CITES-listed goods. The scale of trade in various groups of CITES species is given in Table 7.1.

Table 7.1 *Approximate legal EC CITES imports in recent years*

Species group or product	*Quantity*	*Percentage of global total*
Primates	7000	30
Live birds	850,000	65
Live reptiles	55,000	15
Plants	800,000	75
Caviar	15 tons	50

Source: TRAFFIC Europe

Stricter Domestic Measures

The EC legislation on wildlife trade not only provides for the comprehensive implementation of all CITES requirements but includes some stricter domestic measures. The first of these is that extra species are subject to controls, that is species not currently covered by CITES. Secondly import permits are required for specimens of all CITES Appendix II species whereas under CITES, only export permits are required before international trade in these can be allowed. Thirdly there are stricter biological sustainability tests that must be applied before specimens are imported or exported. This feature is of considerable practical significance. Before any import of specimens of species listed in CITES Appendix II, the importing scientific authority must, after examining available data, be able to confirm that:

> *the introduction into the EC would not have a harmful effect on the conservation status of the species or on the extent of the territory occupied by the relevant population of the species, taking account of current or anticipated trade.*

Under the terms of CITES it is the duty of the exporting country to make such a 'non-detriment finding' before allowing international trade. EC legislation requires such a finding before import as well. Furthermore, the terms of the EC legislation apply a reversal of the burden of proof in that it has to be clear that no detriment will accrue from any trade. Given that the inclusion of a species in the CITES appendices implies some degree of concern for the sustainability of its use in trade, such action may be considered a precautionary approach. For practical purposes the term 'relevant population' of the species in the clause above has been taken to mean the population in the exporting country. This might make little biogeographical sense, but it does reflect the way the species are managed in the CITES context.

When the scientific authorities from the EC member states are agreed that it is not possible to confirm that the status of the species will be unharmed by current or expected trade, an import suspension may be established by the European Commission. In late 2001 there were import suspensions applied to about 375 taxa, from a combined total of around 900 source locations (by country). Most of these were established because it could not be demonstrated that the trade would be harmless to the conservation of the species. A small number were based on other features of the legislation: the import of 16 taxa was suspended on the grounds that any specimens imported to the EC would be unlikely to survive for a substantial part of their potential lifespan and the import of two taxa was suspended on the grounds that the species pose an ecological threat to native species of fauna and flora.

In order to assess the effectiveness of the EC stricter domestic measures, the European Commission financed two independent reviews in the mid-1990s; one by TRAFFIC Europe and one by the United Nations Environment Programme–World Conservation Monitoring Centre (UNEP–WCMC). The reviewers were asked to address the following questions:

1. Were agreed import suspensions fully implemented by the member states?
2. Was the international trade in the species concerned affected by the suspensions?
3. Did the action result in a more sustainable use of the species concerned?

Impact of EC Import Suspensions

After examining several case studies, the reviewers concluded broadly that there was an overall reduction in international trade in the species concerned, but that there were some other effects which might not have had a positive impact on the conservation of the species. The following case studies illustrate some of the scenarios encountered.

The EC instituted a complete import suspension for Asian giant tortoises from all countries of origin in 1989. As can be seen from Figure 7.1 this was largely effectively applied, but after certain disruption to the trade new markets seem to have been found in Japan and the US.

In another case, an EC import suspension on reticulated pythons from Indonesia was applied between 1992 and 1994. As can be seen in Figure 7.2,

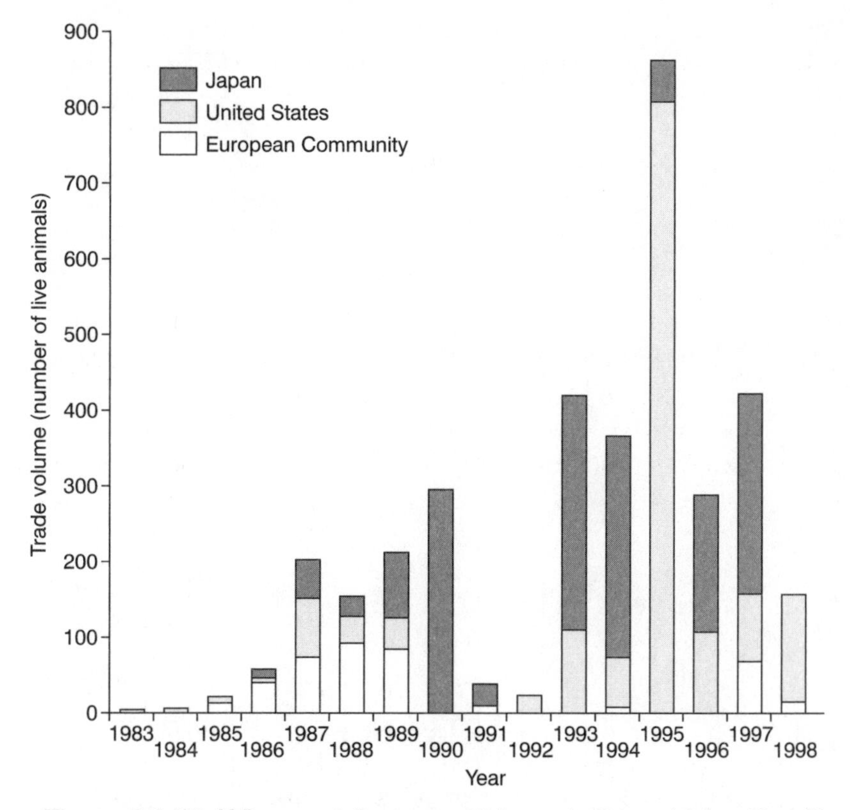

Figure 7.1 *World Imports of Specimens of* Manouria Emys *(Asian Giant Tortoise) (1983–1998)*

direct imports from Indonesia stopped but importation into the EC via other countries, especially Singapore, continued such that the overall level of trade was largely unchanged. This situation was perhaps due to inadequate instructions about the application of the suspension or the declaration of imported products as 'old stock'. Procedures have now been made clearer and the import of 'old stock' in similar circumstances is not allowed. There are some signs of a reduction in the overall trade levels after EC stricter measures were applied but in such cases it is difficult to link cause and effect.

Poicephalus senegalus is a small parrot popular in the pet trade. Following concerns expressed by the scientific authorities of the EC member states a temporary suspension on imports from Mali was agreed in 1987. Some import permits were still valid for use in 1988 but as can be seen from Figure 7.3 legal imports of specimens of this species from Mali ceased for several years after this. However in 1995 imports suddenly resumed again from this country. Most of the specimens concerned were claimed to have originated in other countries – either Guinea or Senegal (they will have been accompanied by documentary evidence to support this claim). Other specimens were declared as having

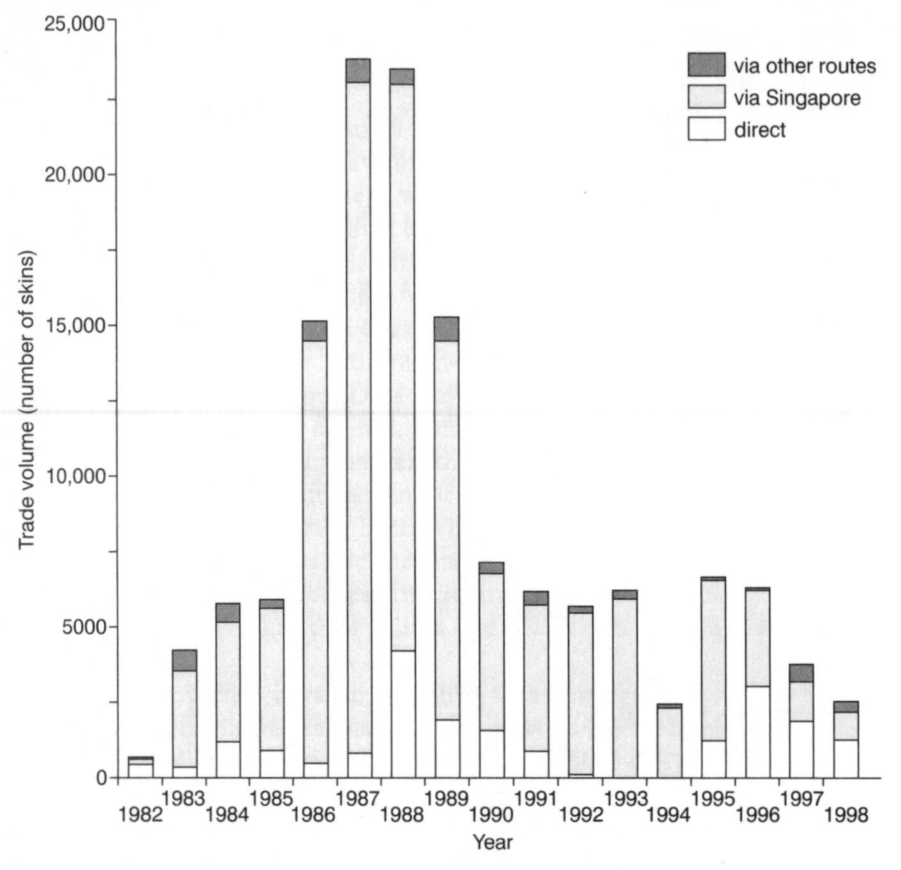

Figure 7.2 *EC Imports of* Python Reticulatus *(Reticulated Python) from Indonesia (1982–1998)*

originated in Mali itself and were allowed into the EC in error, presumably because it was such a long time since the initial import suspension was agreed and officials had consequently overlooked its continued existence. It is not clear why exports from Mali suddenly resumed but it is obvious that EC import controls were not the factor that was driving trade patterns.

In 1992, the EC decided on a temporary import suspension for all imports of CITES wildlife from Indonesia in response to serious concerns about non-detriment findings for a host of species. At the same time consultants were engaged by the European Commission to offer any assistance required by the Indonesian authorities to address the perceived problems with non-detriment findings and other aspects of wildlife trade control. A multi-stakeholder workshop was held in Jakarta and extensive discussions undertaken at all levels. These resulted in changes in the way wildlife trade controls were applied in Indonesia. Following these actions there was a significant and sustained drop in the levels of international trade for a large number of species.

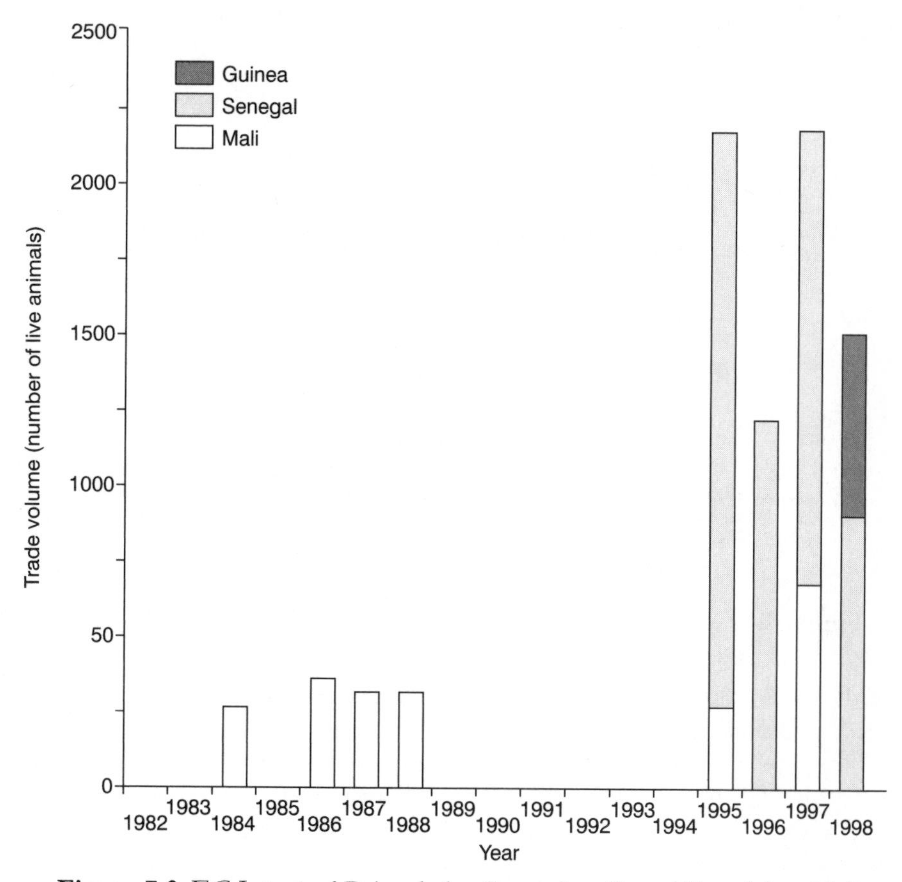

Figure 7.3 *EC Imports of* Poicephalus Senegalus *(Senegal Parrot) from Mali*

Figure 7.4 shows some examples of this from CITES Appendix II members of the parrot family. At the time that this action was taking place there was widespread concern about the level of exports of parrots from Indonesia – several proposals were being made to list Indonesian parrot species in Appendix I of CITES. Since then these fears have subsided. Although the trade impact of this EC action varied from species to species, the reduction in parrot exports from Indonesia did appear to be a favourable outcome.

Conclusions

From the examination of individual cases undertaken on behalf of the European Commission, it does appear that in general member states respected EC decisions well. There were isolated problems, which are perhaps inevitable when collective decisions have to be implemented by 15 countries, working in 11 different languages and issuing some 100,000 documents per year. In many

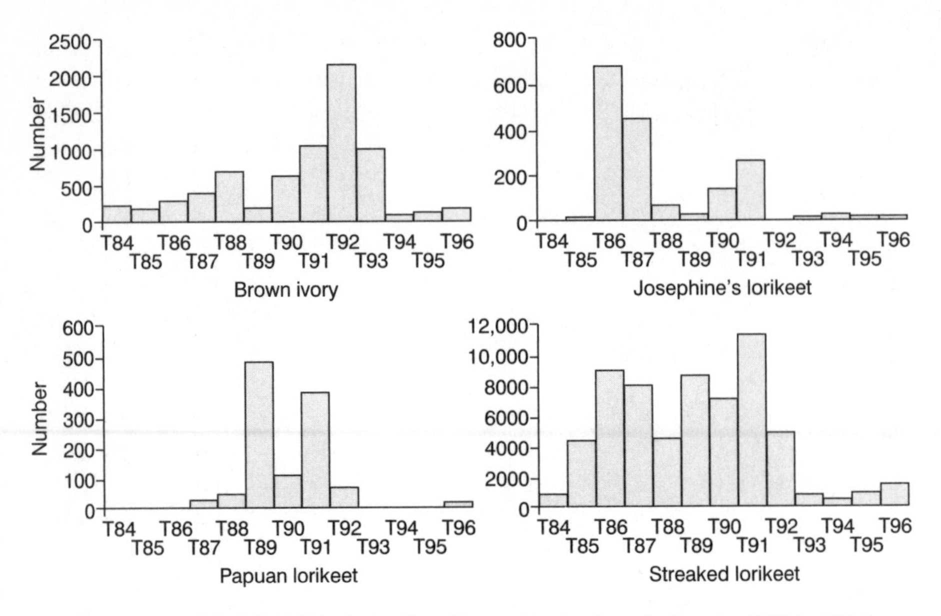

Figure 7.4 *Net World Trade in Four Parrot Species from Indonesia (1984–1996)*

of the cases examined it also appeared that the import suspensions applied did result in changes in the pattern of international trade in the species concerned. It should be stressed however that because of logistical problems in gathering and analysing global wildlife trade statistics there is an element of uncertainty in determining whether this has happened. Among the changes to trade patterns that have been observed are:

- changes in the countries of origin supplying the global markets;
- changes in the markets for specimens being exported in response to the temporary closure of the EC market; and
- changes in the source of specimens in international trade. In West Africa for instance, reptile exporters responded to import suspensions for wild specimens by developing various farming systems to produce the specimens required by the market.

While there are signs that the pattern of international trade was altered, the question of whether the actions resulted in more biologically sustainable use of the species concerned is much more difficult to demonstrate. In some cases there is evidence of a significant and sustained reduction in international trade levels. In these instances, to the extent that trade levels prior to the prohibition were indeed unsustainable, the stricter domestic measures applied did work. However, because of the number of variables involved and the lack of ground-truthing undertaken, it is very difficult to separate cause and effect. The effects on trade patterns seemed to be greater and more durable when the EC temporary import suspensions were accompanied by dialogue or negotiation with the countries affected. This dialogue involved a variety of local stakeholders and supports the notion that encompassing social and economic factors as well as purely environmental or biological ones in the decision-making process encourages full sustainability.

Since 1989, CITES itself has been engaged in an evaluation of non-detriment findings made by parties exporting specimens of CITES species. This action, known as the Significant Trade Process was modelled on procedures already in operation in the EC. It seems likely that in a global market, global initiatives such as the Significant Trade Process are more likely to lead towards sustainability than stricter domestic measures taken by any one country or group of countries. The continued failure of the CITES parties to enact their decision of 1983 to permit the EC to become a party to the convention has perpetuated a fragmented approach in this regard. When the EC becomes a party to CITES, it will certainly be able to play a more active part in developing global solutions aimed at sustainable use of wildlife.

Notes

1 For the sake of clarity the term 'European Community' is used throughout this chapter although it is only one of the pillars of the European Union.
2 Council Directive 79/409/EEC of 2 April 1979 on the conservation of wild birds.
3 Council Directive 92/43/EEC of 21 May 1992 on the conservation of natural habitats and of wild fauna and flora.
4 Council Regulation 338/97 of 9 December 1996 on the protection of species of wild fauna and flora by regulating trade therein.
Full details of the provisions of EC law on wildlife trade and how it is applied can be found on http://europa.eu.int/comm/environment/cites/home_en.htm

Chapter 8

Evolution, Impact and Effectiveness of Domestic Wildlife Trade Bans in India

Manoj Misra

Introduction

India is one of the ten richest countries in the world in terms of biodiversity. It comprises 16 forest types (Champion and Seth, 1968) ranging from arid scrub to alpine forests in 10 bio-zones (Rodgers and Panwar, 1988). India has 45,000 plant species (7 per cent of the world's known flora) and 81,000 animal species (6.4 per cent of the world's known fauna), and is situated at the crossroads between east and west in biogeographic terms.

In addition to being the dominant geographic entity in the region, India has, on account of historical and cultural factors, porous international borders with its immediate neighbours like Nepal, Bhutan, Myanmar, Bangladesh and Sri Lanka. Porosity of the borders facilitates easy movement of people between countries and it also helps in a rampant informal trade in wildlife across the borders. Such trade is often in clear violation of the domestic laws of different countries in the region as well as in contravention of international regulations like CITES. It is notable that India is as much a consumer of wildlife and wildlife products as it is a producer. India has taken major steps to control the trade in wildlife and these are discussed further in this chapter.

EVOLUTION OF THE WILDLIFE TRADE REGULATIONS IN INDIA

Traditionally, India has played a key role in national and international trade in wildlife and wildlife items. 'Shikar' was, in former times, a way of life for the royalty and the wealthy. Big-game sport like tiger hunts, and activities such as falconry, duck shooting, ivory carving and taxidermy were much respected pastimes and trades. The royalty employed hunter-gatherer tribesmen for shikar purposes. A forester was not considered 'blue-blooded' until he had bagged his first big game. Regular shikar parties were de rigeur for senior government officials from the revenue, judiciary and the police departments. Nevertheless, as shikar was a pastime only of the rich and influential, with strictly enforced prohibitions for others, and as there were vast forested tracts in most parts of the country, wildlife continued to flourish. There were, however, signs of things to come, reflected for example by the near extinction of cheetah in the country by the time of independence in 1947.

The post-independence decades of the 1950s and 1960s saw a large-scale decimation of forests as well as wildlife in different parts of the country. 'Nature conservation' as a government policy was yet to take root at the national or the state level and regulatory mechanisms to prevent wildlife harvest and trade were conspicuous by their absence. Until 1972, when the national Wildlife (Protection) Act came into being, India was a major player in international wildlife trade markets. Exports included reptile skins (snakes, turtles, crocodilians), cat skins (tiger, leopard and lesser cats), ivory products (originating from both African and Indian elephants), musk, live birds, rhino horns, frog legs, and live mammals such as elephants, tigers, rhesus macaque and lesser cats.

Table 8.1 *Examples of Indian Wildlife Exports*

Product	*Quantity*	*Year*
Cobra and rat-snake skins	4 million	1977
Python skins	10,000	1977
Lizard skins	1 million	1977
Frog legs	995,789	1979
Furs	7313	1982
Whale shark meat	200 tonnes	1995–96
Sea-horses	9 tonnes	1996–97
Sea shells	668 tonnes	1996–97

Source: Hanfee, 1998; Jain Pushp, 2001

Salient features of the Wildlife (Protection) Act, 1972

The Wildlife (Protection) Act, 1972 (WPA) is a pioneering and comprehensive law relating to protection of wildlife. Since being passed by the Indian Parliament in 1972, it has been amended in 1982, 1986, 1991 and 1993 and is currently undergoing a further major revision. There is currently a proposal to include a special chapter dealing with CITES as a part of the WPA, and also proposals to tighten up loopholes in the legislation.

The WPA provides for the appointment of authorities; the creation and management of national parks and sanctuaries; the regulation of zoos; the protection of wild plants; the prohibition of hunting of wild animals; the prohibition of trade in wild animals, animal articles and trophies; and the prevention and detection of offences. There are six schedules appended to the text of the act which contain lists of species covered by the provisions of the legislation. Schedules I and II give the key endangered and threatened wild animal species within the country. Schedules III and IV list other wild animal species requiring legal protection. In 1991, a new Schedule VI was included to provide protection to certain threatened plant species. A recent notification dated 5 December 2001 has added nine shark and ray species and nine mollusc species to Schedule I together with 15 additional mollusc species in Schedule IV. This indicates the resolve of the government to take legal measures for the protection of marine wildlife, which was hitherto little protected by the law.

Specific prohibitions relating to trade in wildlife are provided by Chapter VA of the WPA: as follows:

No person shall:

- *commence or carry on the business as –*
  1. *a manufacturer of, or dealer in scheduled animal or articles; or (1a) a dealer in ivory imported into India or articles made therefrom or a manufacturer of such articles; or*
  2. *a taxidermist with respect to any scheduled animals or any parts of such animals; or*
  3. *a dealer in trophy or uncured trophy derived from any scheduled animal; or*
  4. *a dealer in any captive animals being scheduled animals; or*
  5. *a dealer in meat derived from any scheduled animal; or*
- *cook or serve meat derived from any scheduled animal in eating-house.*

A 'scheduled animal ' means an animal specified in Schedule I or part II of Schedule II. As mentioned above these are the endangered or threatened animals of India.

An offence under the WPA carries maximum punishment for violation of provisions of Chapter VA as follows:

> *any person who contravenes any provisions of Chapter VA, shall be punishable with imprisonment for a term which shall not be less than one year but which may extend to seven years and also with a fine which shall not be less than five thousand rupees.*

Other Wildlife Trade Regulations

India has also used other regulatory mechanisms to regulate international wildlife trade. The EXIM (Export Import) Policy and the Foreign Trade (Development and Regulation) Act 1992, specify the restricted list of imports and exports with information on the nature of prohibitions and restrictions. Accordingly, while 'wild animals including their parts and products and ivory' are prohibited for import, 'all forms of wild animals including their parts and products' are prohibited for export. All plant items included in Appendix I of CITES, as well as plants specified in Public Notice No. 47 (PN)/92–97 dated 30 March 1994 issued by the Director General of Foreign Trade are prohibited for export.

CITES and the Indian Domestic Wildlife Trade Bans

It is interesting to note that domestic Indian law has sometimes followed regulations and prohibitions made by CITES and in other cases Indian law has been stricter than that mandated by the convention. For example, India banned all trade in ivory in 1991 after its prohibition by CITES in 1989. In 1994, India prohibited exports in raw form, of a number of medicinal plants listed in various appendices of CITES.

In 2000, India banned all exports of wildlife from the country, irrespective of its status in the CITES appendices, so now national legislation employs 'stricter domestic measures' than the convention.

Effectiveness of Measures

The legal prohibition on hunting and trade in wild animals and their parts and products is now well known in India as a result of frequent media coverage and spread of information by word of mouth. Taxidermy as a craft and an art has generally lost its relevance and popularity in the country. Wildlife articles such as ivory products, cat-skin garments, reptile-skin products, fur items, and musk are no longer freely available in Indian markets and seizures of illegal wildlife items together with arrests of offenders have notably increased. Some traditional as well as emerging wildlife trade items of concern in India remain, however, as highlighted below.

Some Enforcement-related Shortcomings

Although public awareness has increased, the exact provisions and prohibitions of the WPA are not yet well known to the public as the state has made little effort to disseminate information or educate the public about the legislation.

In terms of enforcement, there is little inter-agency communication, consultation or joint action against illegal wildlife traders, for example between forestry, police, customs, judiciary and paramilitary personnel. Enforcement is hindered by a major lack of availability or access to identification material as well as a lack of relevant skills within the enforcement agencies. Consequently smugglers are often able to get away with misdeclarations and misrepresentations. Wildlife forensic science is still in its infancy in the country.

Although the Director General of Foreign Trade (DGFT) has taken cognizance of a need to control trade in endangered wildlife out of India, there is little understanding of the real issues as the matter does not seem to be high on the list of priorities. Cross-international border-agency dialogue and exchange of information leaves much to be desired and harmonization of legal provisions between neighbouring countries is still a pipe dream.

The criminals are well aware of the difficulties faced by the state (for various reasons) in enforcing its laws and the long-winded legal procedures that can be misused to offset any effective enforcement action. There are also some shortcomings in the WPA which although being addressed by the current revision of the legislation, continue to provide loopholes which are misused by unscrupulous dealers. Seizures of wildlife items and arrests of alleged offenders are common but rarely result in convictions in the court of law. A big gap between seizures, arrests and conviction rates remains.

There is little enforcement focus on inconspicuous but high volume wildlife-traded species such as the pangolin *Manis crassicaudata*, monitor lizard *Varanus bengalensis*, otter *Lutra* spp, mongoose *Herpestis* spp and other smaller species and nocturnal mammals like the small Indian civet *Viverricula indica*. Enforcement is also weak for marine species. Plant species like sandalwood *Santalum album*, red sanders *Pterocarpus santalinus* and agarwood *Aquilaria malaccensis* continue to be illegally felled for trade purposes. Also there is continuing unregulated and destructive extraction of medicinal plants of commercial importance. There are still species or wildlife items in trade which are either not covered by the WPA or the regulation of trade in them has proved to be intractable, for example with edible swiftlet nests and shahtoosh.

Role of NGOs and the Media

NGOs like the WWF, in particular TRAFFIC India and the Wildlife Protection Society of India, (WPSI) have played a key role in highlighting the issue of illegal wildlife trade in the country. The 'Say NO to Shahtoosh' campaign by TRAFFIC India can be cited as a media success of recent times. NGOs have also provided enforcement assistance in the form of intelligence on wildlife criminals, as well as identification tools and publicity materials. The NGOs have also, through field studies and the publication of their results, highlighted little-known issues related to wildlife trade in the country and consequently engendered suitable action by the state. Legal activism by the NGOs has also facilitated legal and field action by the state. The listing of agarwood in CITES Appendix II, the ban on ivory and snake skin trade, the implementation of the ban on trade in shahtoosh, and the listing of whale shark in the WPA schedule are some of the actions taken by the state on initiatives from the NGOs.

The media has consistently played a very important role in pointing out lapses by the state and also in highlighting issues that deserve urgent action. But the media has also sometimes acted irresponsibly by quoting figures that bear no relation to the actual figures for the wildlife items in trade. The media is also not very scrupulous while deciding which advertisements to carry and hence may directly or indirectly promote use of banned wildlife.

Improving Enforcement Action

In January 2000, following a large-scale seizure of wildlife items at Khaga, Uttar Pradesh, North India, the Ministry of Environment and Forests (MOEF) authorized the CBI (Central Bureau of Investigation) to proactively deal with the wildlife offences. This is the first time that a police organization has been invested with this authority.

Other positive ways forward include the steps taken by the Government of India (GOI) to form a national 'Wildlife Crime Bureau' for a systematic collection of intelligence and action against wildlife criminals. GOI has also established an inter-agency consultative body for periodic review of the wildlife crime situation especially as it pertains to control of illegal trade in wildlife in the country. This high-level body is headed by the secretary of MOEF and includes representatives of all relevant agencies and ministries at the union level. There is generally a growing amount of interest among the functionaries of various agencies, for wildlife trade control measures.

India and Nepal have taken a serious view of cross-border wildlife trade and have started a formal high-level dialogue process for joint action. Two such meetings took place in 1998 and 2000. Dialogue has begun for such meetings with Bangladesh and Bhutan.

Presumptions in Government Policy

The following are some of the presumptions held by the state, which remain matters for debate:

- *Opening even an experimental trade will open the floodgates?* There is a fear that any reopening of legal trade in wildlife and wildlife products within the country or from the country will lead again to large-scale use and ultimate decimation of the country's wildlife.
- *Blanket bans work better than regulation in the long run?* It is believed that bans are effective.
- *The enforcement of laws will improve with time.* It is believed that with time and better training, enforcers of laws will become more effective.
- *The law will continue to keep pace with the changing times.* As the WPA has seen frequent amendments it is believed that it will continue to evolve with changing requirements.

Conclusions and the Challenges Ahead

India has comprehensive legislation covering wildlife trade as part of its biodiversity conservation legislation. At present all exports of wildlife and wildlife products from the country are banned. Enforcement is improving but remains weak in some areas. There is an urgent need for capacity building within the various enforcement agencies. Revision of the legislation is needed with public debate and dissemination of information forming part of this process.

One specific challenge will be to design policy with regard to management of animal species whose populations have recovered satisfactorily (at least in some parts of the country) so that they are beginning to cause problems in terms of human–animal conflict in areas where the carrying capacity of the habitat has been surpassed. Some such examples are blackbuck *Antelope cervicapra*, nilgai *Boselaphus tragocamelus*, wild boar *Sus scrofa*, sloth bear *Melursus ursinus*, and rhesus macaque *Macaca muletta*. Solutions may include culling and trade in wildlife items from such species. Elephant *Elephas maximus* and leopard *Panthera pardus* are special cases in that while they are problem animals in some parts of the country they also continue to be significantly hunted for trade in their parts and products. Release or use of crocodilians in captive facilities also needs urgent attention.

At the same time the challenge remains with enforcement of controls for such species as the tiger *Panthera tigris*, snow leopard *Panthera uncia*, musk deer *Moschus moschiferus*, one-horned rhinoceros *Rhinoceros unicornis* and several small mammals which continue to be adversely affected by illegal trade in their parts and products.

Improvements in international trade controls are needed for these and other species. As a priority a mechanism is required to facilitate active dialogue and joint action plans between countries in the region for the effective regulation of legal trade and control of illegal trade across international borders.

REFERENCES

Champion, H and Seth, S K (1968) *A Revised Forest Classification of India,* Government of India

Hanfee, F (1998) *Wildlife Trade – A Handbook for Enforcement Staff,* TRAFFIC India/WWF India

Jain Pushp (2001) *CITES and India,* MOEF, TRAFFIC India and WWF India

Rodgers, WA and Panwar, H S (1988) *Planning a Protected Area Network in India,* 2 vols, FAO, Dehra Dun, pp267 and 339

Part 3

Case Studies

Chapter 9

Regulation and Protection: Successes and Failures in Rhinoceros Conservation

Nigel Leader-Williams

Living Rhinos and Uses of their Horns

There are five living species of rhino, but only just. Three species, Sumatran, Javan and Indian rhinos, occur in Asia while two species, black and white rhinos, occur in Africa. Rhinos are now among the world's most endangered large mammals. Two Asian species, the Javan and Sumatran, and one African species, the black rhino, are critically endangered (Table 9.1). Several sub-species, including both sub-species of Javan rhino, the northern white rhino and the western black rhino, occur at such low numbers that they teeter on the edge of extinction. By contrast, the southern white rhino is currently well conserved in limited areas of its range in southern Africa, as is the Indian rhino in even more limited areas in India and Nepal. However, the total world populations of southern white and Indian rhinos are still only in the low thousands, and their continued long-term survival is by no means guaranteed (Foose and van Strien, 1997; Emslie and Brooks, 1999).

In global terms, the population of all species of rhino has probably declined from some hundreds of thousands in the early 1900s, to perhaps 75,000 in the early 1970s, and to some 13,000 based on the most recent published estimates (Table 9.1).

Historically, rhino numbers have declined for three main reasons. First, much habitat has been lost in the rainforests and flood plains of Asia, and in the grasslands of southern Africa. Second, legal hunting of rhinos, both to clear land and for sport, greatly reduced numbers of Indian, Javan, black and southern white rhinos early in the 20th century. Because of increasing moves to

Table 9.1 *Estimates of Numbers of Different Rhino Taxa Alive in the Wild and an Assessment of their Status*

Species	*Status of species*	*Sub-species*	*Number in wild*	*Status of sub-species*
White rhino		*C.s. cottoni*	25	CR
Ceratotherium simum		*C.s. simum*	8440	LR (cd)
Black rhino	CR	*D.b. michaeli*	485	CR
Diceros bicornis		*D.b. minor*	1365	CR
		D.b. bicornis	740	VU
		D.b. longipes	10	CR
Indian rhino	EN		2095	
Rhinoceros unicornis				
Javan rhino	CR	*R.s. sondaicus*	<60	CR
Rhinoceros sondaicus		*R.s. annamiticus*	<15	CR
Sumatran rhino	CR	*D.s. sumatrensis*	<230	CR
Dicerorhinus sumatrensis		*D.s. lasiotis*	?	EX
		D.s. harrisoni	<70	CR

Key to status
CR: critically endangered
EN: endangered
EX: extinct
LR(cd): lower risk (conservation dependent)
VU: vulnerable
Source: Foose and van Strien, 1997; Emslie and Brooks, 1999. Assessment of status according to the IUCN Red List Categories (Hilton-Taylor, 2000).
The Javan rhino sub-species R.s. inermis is now almost certainly extinct, and is not included

establish protected areas and to ban the hunting of rhinos, these are not now so important for rhinos in Africa. However, habitat loss is still an important issue for Asian rhinos, given the high human population densities in many areas of the continent. Third, as a result of high demand for rhino horns, unprotected populations of rhinos have been exploited unsustainably. The trade in their horn has largely been responsible for reducing them to their presently threatened status (Leader-Williams, 1992).

The international trade in rhino horn has a long history. The Chinese were recorded as using rhino horn as a medicine between 200 BC and 200 AD (Martin and Martin, 1982). During the Ming and Ching dynasties, the Chinese also carved rhino horns into beautiful cups, plates, bowls and figurines. However, westerners long believed that the main use of rhino horn was as an aphrodisiac, but this myth was debunked in the early 1980s (Martin and Martin, 1982). Some rhino horn might indeed be consumed as an aphrodisiac, but this is limited to use by the Gujaratis in India. Rhino horn has had two far more important uses in terms of volumes traded in recent times.

Horn and other rhino products such as blood, skin and urine, are important constituents in traditional medicines and potions used to reduce fevers, headaches and other illnesses in the Far East. Such medicines are used primarily by the Chinese, but also by Burmese, Thais and Nepalis. In contrast, the Japanese and Koreans also learned to use rhino horn in medicines through early cultural links with the Chinese, but do not use other rhino products. Rhino horn is generally sold in the Far East in one of two forms, first as 'raw' horn by traditional pharmacists who make up the medicine for individual customers in their shops, and second as a constituent in manufactured medicines. Furthermore, 'Fire' (Asian) horn is believed more efficacious than 'Water' (African) horn and therefore Asian horn is considerably more expensive (Martin and Martin, 1982; Nowell et al, 1992). Thus both African and Asian rhino horn are used widely throughout the Far East both by indigenous people but particularly by the resident Chinese communities found in most Far Eastern countries (Martin, 1983). In addition, confiscations in Los Angeles, San Francisco and Brussels show that Chinese communities use rhino horn in medicines in Western countries.

Yemenis, by contrast, have used African rhino horn since at least the 8th century to make handles for traditional daggers, known as *jambias*. Daggers are important status symbols in the cultural life of Yemeni men. The advantage of rhino horn over other materials used for dagger handles such as water buffalo horn, is that rhino horn improves in appearance and lustre with age (Martin et al, 1997). However, the demand for horn in the Yemen varies greatly depending on the economic status of the country, which in turn is linked to oil prices, and on the availability of substitutes (Vigne and Martin, 2001).

Approaches to Conserving Rhinos

Two main approaches have been followed over the past quarter century to prevent rhinos from being killed for their horns. The first approach has been the attempt to close or halt the international trade in rhino horn through regulation. The second approach has been the attempt to improve the protection of rhinos in situ (Foose and van Strien, 1997; Emslie and Brooks, 1999).

Regulation of International Trade in Rhino Horn

When CITES entered into force in 1975, rhinos and their products were among the first species to be placed on the CITES Appendices (Table 9.2). By 1977, all *Rhinocerotidae* were placed on Appendix I, therefore banning international trade in the whole family of rhinos and their products from that date.

Nevertheless, a large illegal trade in rhino horn continued during the 1980s and early 1990s (Leader-Williams, 1992). This is well illustrated for the more accurately estimated and formerly numerous black rhino, which continued to decline following its listing on CITES appendices (Figure 9.1). Indeed, its numbers plummeted from an estimated 65,000 in the 1970s, to a low of 2400,

Table 9.2 *Changes in Listing of the Rhinos on Appendices I and II*

Year	*Appendix I*	*Appendix II*
1975	Sumatran rhino, *Dicerorhinus sumatrensis* Javan rhino, *Rhinoceros sondaicus* Indian rhino, *R. unicornis* Northern white rhino, *Ceratotherium simum cottoni*	Black rhino, *Diceros bicornis*
1977	Black rhino, *Diceros bicornis* Southern white rhino, *C.s. simum*	
1994		Southern white rhino, *C.s. simum*[1]

Note: 1 South African population for trade in live specimens and in hunting trophies only

over a period of 25 years. During this period, the species became locally extinct within at least 18 range states in Africa. The once numerous and wide-ranging Sumatran rhinoceros has probably undergone no less spectacular a rate of decline, but this has been less well documented due to the difficulty of counting this species in rainforest habitats. Nevertheless, even considering more recent estimates, it is suggested that Sumatran rhinos have declined from an estimated 600–1000 in the early 1990s, to perhaps 300 in 1995 (Foose and van Strien, 1997).

The failure of the Appendix I listing to prevent the decline of the global stock of rhinos stimulated further efforts from the parties through the adoption of resolutions (Wijnstekers, 1995). This series of resolutions (Table 9.3) plots a gradually changing philosophy to the international ban on trade in rhino products. Initial concern centred on the various major markets for rhino horn that occurred in countries such as Taiwan and Yemen that were not parties to CITES (Wijnstekers, 1995). As such, these countries were outside the controls operating on international trade in rhino horn. Furthermore, certain parties continued to sell stocks of rhino horn held by relevant government and parastatal wildlife authorities. Therefore, Resolution Conf 3.11 was approved in 1981 (Table 9.3) and called on nations that were not parties to CITES also to take measures to prevent the international trade in rhino products. Furthermore, the resolution called for a moratorium on the sale of all government and parastatal stocks of rhino horn, and required that any stocks should be recorded in annual reports to the convention. Subsequent to the adoption of this resolution, the illegal killing of black rhinos in Africa, and of Sumatran rhinos in Asia, continued unabated.

The obvious failure of Resolution Conf 3.11 prompted the adoption of Resolution Conf 6.10 in 1987 (Table 9.3). This resolution called for immediate, drastic and even stricter measures to be taken by parties to curb an illegal trade in rhino horn that had no respect for international boundaries. Furthermore, concern was also expressed at stockpiles of rhino horn held by respective authorities, which had stimulated theft and further horn entering illegal markets.

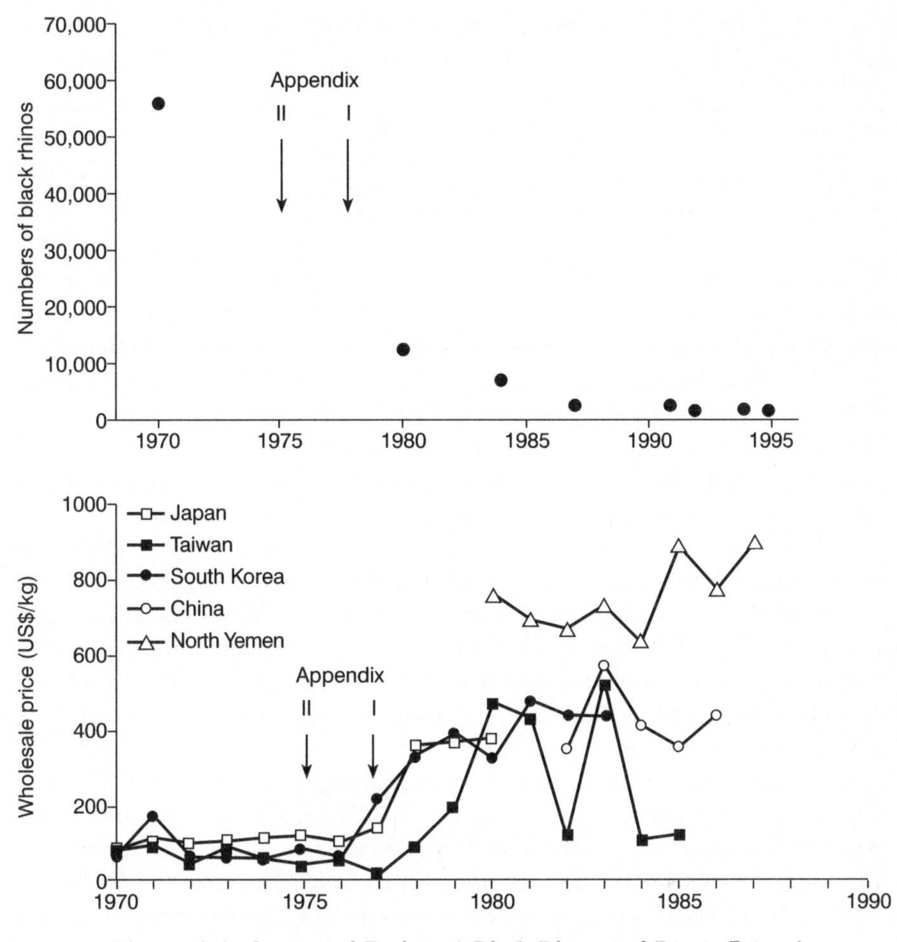

Figure 9.1 *Continental Decline of Black Rhinos and Rise in Price of Horn in Consuming Nations*

Therefore, Resolution Conf 6.10 urged all parties to completely prohibit all sales and trade, whether internal or international, in rhino parts and derivatives, particularly horn, excluding non-commercial movement of hunting trophies. Furthermore, all parties were urged to destroy all government and parastatal stock of rhino horn with supporting contributory funds from external aid sources to be used for rhino conservation in the state concerned. Other measures that were urged comprised: issuing instructions to all law enforcement agencies to be particularly alert to smuggling of rhino horn; to increase penalties for individuals and companies convicted of relevant offences; and, to take firm action against middlemen and poachers involved in cross-border poaching and trafficking of horn.

Because the 1981 resolution was being ignored by several countries, Resolution Conf 6.10 also recommended that parties use all appropriate means,

Table 9.3 *Resolutions Adopted to Prevent further Loss of Rhinos*

Resolution	*Title*
Resolution Conf 3.11	Trade in rhino horn
Resolution Conf 6.10	Trade in rhino products
Resolution Conf 9.14	Conservation of rhino in Asia and Africa

including economic, political and diplomatic, to exert pressure on countries continuing to allow trade in rhino horn. In other words, this resolution broke new ground by urging and recommending actions that were well outside the remit of the convention to regulate international trade. Nevertheless, many range states again ignored Resolution Conf 6.10, and did not destroy their stockpiles of rhino horn. Nor indeed was any compensation forthcoming to promote the destruction of stockpiles. Furthermore, several key consuming nations failed to implement domestic legislation to curb the rhino horn trade. Losses of black rhinos in Africa continued (Milliken et al, 1993), while illegal horn continued to be available in the market place (Leader-Williams, 1992).

By 1992, the governments of South Africa, Zimbabwe and Namibia began to express dissatisfaction with the international ban on trade in rhino products, and concluded that a controlled legal trade in rhino horn might be a better option. Both Zimbabwe and South Africa held considerable stocks of horn attained through seizures from traders, through collection of horn from dead animals, and in the case of Zimbabwe through dehorning operations undertaken to enhance the protection of rhinos. At the 1992 Conference of the Parties, South Africa proposed to down-list its white rhino population to Appendix II and Zimbabwe proposed to down-list both its black and white populations to Appendix II. These proposals were rejected. The dissatisfaction with the Appendix I listings generated further contradictory actions between the 1992 and 1994 Conferences of the Parties, and several major changes in direction at the 1994 Conference of the Parties.

Three main actions were undertaken between the 1992 and 1994 Conference of the Parties. First, the US government threatened four consuming nations with sanctions under a piece of domestic legislation known as the Pelly Amendment. This legislation empowers the US president to suspend any wildlife and fisheries trade between the US and any country considered responsible for diminishing the effectiveness of an international treaty designed to protect any threatened or endangered species. Governments of consumer nations responded to this pressure from the US by passing some domestic laws and intensifying efforts to control illegal trade, but this served only to drive trade further underground and to raise the illegal prices charged for rhino horn (Mills, 1993). The second action was that the United Nations Environment Programme (UNEP) held a meeting in Nairobi in 1993 to raise funds for rhino conservation, there having been no external aid for rhino conservation in response to Resolution Conf 6.10. At this meeting, some US$60 million was requested in emergency funds over the next three years, but only some US$5 million was pledged. At this meeting, South Africa again expressed its belief that a controlled legal trade in rhino horn offered a potential solution, because sales of legally held stockpiles could provide a substantial source of revenue to conservation agencies that the international community was patently unwilling to provide. The third action was that efforts were finally made to seek the views of the traditional Chinese medicine community about how they viewed their healing role relative to the threat posed to rhinos and other endangered species included in their medicines.

At the 1994 Conference of the Parties, South Africa again proposed to down-list its white rhino population to Appendix II. However, even though the down-listing was agreed, an annotation confined this to trade in live specimens and in hunting trophies only (Table 9.2). Therefore, the international ban on trade in rhino horn and other products remained in place, even though one rhino population was down-listed to Appendix II. Nevertheless, a more far-reaching resolution was adopted at this meeting that resulted in the repeal of Resolution Confs 3.11 and 6.10. Resolution Conf 9.14 recognized many of the problems in rhino conservation, and urges the following:

- those parties that have legal stocks of rhino horn to identify, mark, register and secure all such stocks;
- all parties to implement adequate legislation including internal trade restrictions, aimed at reducing illegal trade in rhino products;
- range states to be vigilant in their law enforcement efforts and to place increased emphasis on the prevention of illegal hunting and early detection of offenders;
- that law enforcement cooperation between states be increased in order to curtail trafficking in rhino horn;
- the consumer states to work with traditional-medicine communities and industries to develop strategies for eliminating the use and consumption of rhino parts and derivatives.

Resolution Conf 9.14 also directed the standing committee to continue to pursue actions aimed at reducing illegal trade, ensuring that all such actions are accompanied by evaluations of their effectiveness, through the use of standardized indicators, and that policies guiding interventions are responsive to the outcomes of evaluations and modified accordingly. The resolution also recommends that each range state develop for its rhino population a recovery plan that inter alia: is appropriate for the situation in that country; will not adversely affect rhino conservation in other range states; and, includes provisions for the reinvestment of revenues derived from use of rhinos that is consistent with the convention, in order to offset the high costs of their conservation. Finally, Resolution Conf 9.14 urges potential donors to assist with funding the efforts of range states to implement their recovery plans, and the Global Environment Facility to fund the protection of rhino populations within the context of broadly-based projects for the conservation of biological diversity.

At the 1997 Conference of the Parties, South Africa yet again attempted to set in motion measures that would lead eventually to a controlled legal trade in rhino horn, but this proposal was again rejected. South Africa, conserving as it does some 70 to 80 per cent of the global population of rhino, remains concerned about incentives for rhino conservation, particularly for private land owners who conserve some 15 per cent of South Africa's rhinos. Meanwhile, black rhino numbers in Africa appear to have stabilized, and indeed to have increased slightly, at a continental population of around 2600 (Table 9.1). Hence, a sense of cautious optimism seems to have pervaded the cause of rhino conservation internationally. Indeed, rhinos hardly featured at the 2000 Conference of the Parties, apart from some revisions that were made to Resolution Conf 9.14 (Rosser et al, 2001). These revisions recognized both ongoing and recent successes, but in particular called for better reporting by the range states, so that the effectiveness of different measures to conserve rhinos could be assessed.

Taken overall, the Appendix I listing has failed to stop either trade or poaching within the rhino family. Indeed, the raised stakes caused by making international trade in rhino horn illegal was evidenced by soaring prices for rhino horn in consumer markets (Figure 9.1). In turn, this may have stimulated poaching in range states where rhinos were inadequately protected and where the incentive structure favoured poachers rather than conservationists (Milner-Gulland and Leader-Williams, 1992). However, even an intuitively obvious comparison of data on population decline and rising prices of horn (Figure 9.1) masks a number of complexities that need to be addressed in evaluating the Appendix I listing for the rhino family. The most obvious question is whether the decline in black rhino numbers, the start of which pre-dated the Appendix listings (Figure 9.1), would have been faster or slower without the listings. This question cannot be adequately answered with the available data. Nevertheless, economists believe that the convention has been responsible for regulating the extinction process in rhinos (Swanson, 1994; t'Sas Rolfes, 1995). Another issue is that certain important consuming nations like Taiwan and Yemen were not parties to the convention at the time many rhinos were being lost in the late-1970s and the 1980s. Hence, the role that this might have played cannot be determined with any certainty.

Whatever the answer to these imponderable questions, the rhino family has certainly played an important role in developing thinking within the workings of the convention. As a result, the convention has extended its mandate to roles other than purely dealing with issues of regulation of international trade. Indeed, the latest resolutions on rhinos consider wider issues of conservation in situ, many of which fall within the purview of responsibility of the range states rather than of the convention.

IN SITU PROTECTION OF RHINOS

The in situ protection of rhinos has almost been a game played on two fronts, one of failure and the other of success. On the failure front, high priority was given in the 1980s to protecting large populations of rhinos within extensive protected areas. As noted already, it has been hard to monitor the situation accurately for the widely distributed Sumatran rhino in its rainforest habitats. However, the fate of the black rhino is better known (Figure 9.1). The focus of poaching moved from Kenya and northern Tanzania in the 1970s, southwards to southern Tanzania and Zambia in the early 1980s and thence to Zimbabwe in the late 1980s and early 1990s. A shortage of resources and political commitment, resulting in de facto open access, saw large populations of black rhinos decline rapidly in one country after another. Under this ongoing illegal regime, with its increasingly high rewards, the costs of poaching escalated. The bows and arrows that were used in Kenya in the 1970s were replaced by automatic rifles. Poachers increasingly risked death through shoot-to-kill policies, while the costs of effective policing rose considerably in real terms.

Nevertheless, there have been considerable successes in rhino conservation in both Africa and Asia. Over the course of the 20th century, numbers of southern white rhinos have increased dramatically in Southern Africa, as to a more limited extent have Indian rhinos in India and Nepal (Foose and van Strien, 1997; Emslie and Brooks, 1999). Indian rhinos have increased from the low hundreds in the early 1900s to 2500 today (Table 9.1). Southern white rhinos have likewise increased from the low hundreds in the 1900s to more than 10,000 today. Equally, these increases continue trends that had been set in motion in the early 1900s, when small and well-protected reserves were established in India and South Africa to prevent the then remnant populations from going extinct. Hence, these spectacular successes are quite unrelated to actions taken under the convention. Nevertheless, the down-listing of South Africa's white rhinos to Appendix II (Table 9.2) provides international recognition of a national success with that sub-species. Furthermore, the spectacular increase of southern white rhinos has occurred where limited use is allowed, through sport hunting and live sales, in a system whose regulation has now been reduced from an Appendix I to an Appendix II listing. In turn, this change in listing has removed the requirement that the prior grant of an import permit is required before a hunting trophy or a live sale can be exported internationally. Southern white rhinos continue to increase, largely through incentives to private land owners as carrying capacity has been reached in state protected areas (Emslie and Brooks, 1999).

WHICH DIRECTIONS IN FUTURE?

As noted already, a sense of cautious optimism now pervades the cause of rhino conservation. Black rhinos have begun to recover in Kenya, South Africa and

Namibia. This has been largely achieved by following a similar formula to the ongoing successes with Indian and southern white rhinos, of providing good protection, usually in small areas attracting high protection budgets. In the case of the black and southern white rhinos, this has included protection on both state and private land, and strong biological management through monitoring, translocation and the seeding of new populations. Furthermore, with southern white rhinos, an incentive-based and slightly deregulated system is firmly in place to underpin the most impressive success of all. This all amounts to better news than for many a year.

Is this sense of cautious optimism justified? The revised Resolution Conf 9.14 concludes that the decline of all rhino populations has not been halted. The Sumatran rhino appears to be continuing its slide towards extinction. Furthermore, only small remnant populations remain of Javan rhino in two locations, one in Java and another in Vietnam. Likewise, northern white rhinos remain in only one location in the Democratic Republic of Congo, while western black rhinos remain in only one location in Cameroon. In addition, Indian rhinos are no longer increasing as rapidly because carrying capacity has been reached in the available state-protected areas.

Different approaches are being explored in the conservation of particular populations and species of rhinos in situ (Foose and van Strien, 1997; Emslie and Brooks, 1999). Tactics include translocation to unoccupied habitats in areas of former range; concentration of resources and conventional law enforcement efforts in small areas; use of fencing; involvement of local communities in conserving rhinos on communal land; and, more recently, the dehorning of rhinos to reduce their attractiveness to poachers. To offset the costs of rhino conservation some countries have investigated tourist viewing and consumptive activities, such as live sales and limited trophy hunting of surplus males, as sources of income. By realizing the full economic potential of rhinos some countries hope to encourage further cooperation of both the private sector and local communities in conserving rhinos. As the plight of some taxa of rhinos has worsened and the cost of policing has risen, conservation organizations have received increasing demands on their limited funds.

The revised Resolution Conf 9.14 recognizes that the illegal trade in rhino horn remains a global law enforcement problem. A key question remains, and that is whether the horn trade should be deregulated and legalized. A considerable diversity of opinion exists as to the most effective approach. On the one hand, even when horn trade was legal, rhinos lost ground in terms of their distribution, and presumably of their numbers. Furthermore, much trade in horn was not legally declared in customs statistics. Equally, a number of interlinked issues still remain, including:

- How best to deal with stockpiled horn?
- How best to reduce rewards for poaching illegal products?
- How best to reduce policing costs, particularly on state land?

- How best to reduce abuse of human rights?
- How best to provide incentives to ensure that strong ownership remains or is encouraged on communal and private land outside state-protected areas?

These issues require serious consideration over the next few years, as the fate of Sumatran, Javan and northern white rhinos continues to hang in the balance. There are five living species of rhino, but even after all the effort spent on regulation and protection, still only just.

REFERENCES

Emslie, R H and Brooks, M (1999) *African Rhino: Status survey and conservation action plan,* IUCN, Gland and Cambridge

Foose, T J and van Strien, N (1997) *Asian Rhinos: Status survey and conservation action plan,* IUCN, Gland and Cambridge

Hilton-Taylor, C (compiler) (2000) *IUCN Red List of Threatened Species*, IUCN, Gland, Switzerland and Cambridge

Leader-Williams, N (1992) *The World Trade in Rhino Horn: A review,* TRAFFIC International, Cambridge

Martin, E B (1983) *Rhino Exploitation: The trade in rhino products in India, Indonesia, Malaysia, Burma, Japan and South Korea,* World Wildlife Fund, Hong Kong

Martin, E B and Martin, C B (1982) *Run Rhino Run,* Chatto and Windus, London.

Martin, E B, Vigne, L and Allan, C (1997) *On a Knife's Edge: The rhinoceros horn trade in Yemen*, TRAFFIC International, Cambridge

Milliken, T, Nowell, K and Thomsen, J B (1993) *The Decline of the Black Rhino in Zimbabwe: Implications for future rhino conservation,* TRAFFIC International, Cambridge

Mills, J A (1993) *Market under Cover: The rhinoceros horn trade in South Korea,* TRAFFIC International, Cambridge

Milner-Gulland, E J and Leader-Williams, N (1992) A model of incentives for the illegal exploitation of black rhinos and elephants: poaching pays in Luangwa Valley, Zambia, *Journal of Applied Ecology*, 29, pp388–401.

Nowell, K, Chyi, W W L and Pei, K C J (1992) *The Horns of a Dilemma: The market for rhino horn in Taiwan,* TRAFFIC International, Cambridge

Rosser, A, Haywood, M and Harris, D (2001) *CITES: A conservation tool. A Guide to Amending the Appendices to the Convention on International Trade in Endangered Species of Wild Fauna and Flora,* Seventh Edition, IUCN Species Survival Commission, Cambridge

Swanson, T M (1994) *The International Regulation of Extinction,* Macmillan, London

t'Sas-Rolfes, M J (1995) *Rhinos: Conservation, Economics and Trade-Offs,* Institute of Economic Affairs, London

Vigne, L and Martin, E B (2001) Closing down the illegal trade in rhino horn in Yemen. *Pachyderm*, 30, pp87–95.

Wijnstekers, W (1995) *The Evolution of CITES: A reference to the Convention on International Trade in Endangered Species of Wild Fauna and Flora,* CITES Secretariat, Geneva

Chapter 10

Elephant Poaching and Resource Allocation for Law Enforcement

Hugo Jachmann

INTRODUCTION

After a long period of illegal unsustainable off-take, the African elephant (*Loxodonta africana*) was transferred to Appendix I of CITES, leading to the international ivory trade ban that came into effect in early 1990. Since 1990, two attempts have been made to assess the impact of the ban on illegal off-take of elephant (Dublin and Jachmann, 1992; Dublin et al, 1995). The results of these studies, however, were for the most part statistically inconclusive due to a lack of reliable data from the majority of sites in the six target countries covered.

This chapter focuses on the enforcement of elephant conservation legislation in Zambia and considers this in relation to the Appendix I listing. The relationship between the levels of resources allocated to law enforcement in the Luangwa Valley, eastern Zambia, and the numbers of elephants killed illegally between 1979 and 1995 (Jachmann and Billiouw, 1997; Jachmann, 1998) is identified. It is shown that variation in poaching levels can be attributed to differences in resource allocation alone.

METHODS

The South Luangwa Area Management Unit (SLAMU), formerly known as the Luangwa Integrated Resource Development Project (LIRDP), operated in the South Luangwa National Park (9050 km^2) and the Lupande Game Management Area (4950 km^2), situated in the central Luangwa Valley. The project area contained more than half of Zambia's national elephant population. From its inception in 1988 to 1995, LIRDP collected accurate in-depth information on elephant trends, law enforcement input and levels of illegal activity. This information is supplemented by some additional information from the period from 1979 to 1986 when the Save the Rhino Trust (SRT) was operating in the area.

In the LIRDP area, conventional aerial sample counts were carried out from the early 1970s to 1995 (Caughley and Goddard, 1975; Leader-Williams et al, 1990; Bell et al, 1992; Jachmann, 1995; Jachmann et al, 1995; Jachmann, 1998). For the period from 1973 to 1988, numbers of elephants killed illegally were estimated from carcasses observed during aerial counts and a modelling procedure (Bell et al, 1992). For the LIRDP operational period from 1988 to 1995, nearly all of the elephants found killed illegally were detected by foot patrols, although some were reported by tour operators and later confirmed by wildlife personnel. A series of aerial surveys carried out during this period detected no unknown fresh carcasses (Jachmann, 1998).

For the period from 1979 to 1986, resource allocation, in terms of patrol days and financial input, relate to SRT operations alone.

Law-enforcement methods used under LIRDP fell into two classes: conventional foot patrols within the project area, and investigation operations following up information supplied through a system of informers outside the project area. Foot patrols from each of the scout camps covered the entire project area, divided into six patrol sectors, on a regular basis. A patrol consisted of between six and ten scouts, while patrol duration was usually around ten days. Total patrol time was made up of 'placement days', that is days spent moving between base and the location where the patrol started or finished, and 'effective patrol days', that is days spent actively in pursuit of illegal activity (Bell, 1985). For the SRT period (1979–1986), only information on total patrol days was available, which includes 'placement time'. For the LIRDP period (1988–1995), information on both total patrol days and 'effective patrol days' was available. Up to 1994, for each patrol, most of the equipment was hauled by permanent carriers. In 1995, however, financial constraints forced the project to dismiss most of the permanent carriers, leaving a fluctuating small number of temporary carriers. Investigation operations were mainly carried out in the towns and villages surrounding the project area, while operation time was also made up of 'placement days' and 'effective days'. An essential feature of the law-enforcement programme was the bonus system, providing cash rewards for information obtained from informers or scouts that eventually led to an arrest or the confiscation of a firearm or a trophy.

Because the resource data for the period prior to 1988 is incomplete, it will be subjected to a crude analysis only, using elephant trends and projected elephant mortality as a measure of illegal activity, and total patrol days as a measure of resource allocation (Jachmann, 1998). The resource data from the LIRDP period are far more detailed and accurate, and modelling procedures will be used to investigate the relationship between resource allocation and illegal off-take of elephants (Jachmann and Billiouw, 1997; Jachmann, 1998). The number of elephants killed illegally was not corrected for numbers of live elephants, as poachers may focus on areas of known high elephant density, because this was found to have a minor, non-significant impact on the outcome of the analysis (Jachmann, 1998).

To investigate the relationship between resource allocation and illegal off-take for the LIRDP period, the logarithmic link function, specifying Poisson errors, in the GLIM statistical modelling package was used (Crawley, 1993). In our model, the *response variable* (Y) is the number of elephants found killed illegally per annum, while the *predictor variables* (X_1 to X_9), are the total law-enforcement budget per km^2 (US$), personal emoluments per scout per month (US$), transport expenditure per km^2, km^2 per scout, km^2 per carrier, effective patrol days per km^2, effective investigation days, numbers of bonuses paid, and the average bonus rates (US$). For a detailed description of the analysis procedure the reader is referred to Jachmann and Billiouw (1997), and Jachmann (1998). The ultimate goal was to produce a minimal adequate model with the easiest possible interpretation and the least number of terms, explaining the temporary variation in elephant poaching in the study area between 1988 and 1995.

Results

Elephant trends

In the early 1970s, the elephant population in the central Luangwa Valley was more or less stable at about 35,000 elephants. Elephant numbers began to decline sharply from about 1976 as a result of the wave of illegal off-take that spread southwards through Africa during the second half of the 1970s, peaking in Zambia in about 1977 (Figure 10.1). The wave of illegal off-take was caused by a number of factors acting in concert, starting with the collapse of the purchasing power of currencies and wages in many African countries. This led to the search for economic opportunities outside the formal economy, including commercialization of illegal hunting for ivory and rhino horn. As a result, elephant numbers dropped to about 15,000 in 1987 (Figure 10.1). In 1988, the population further declined to 2400, partly due to illegal off-take, and partly due to movement of elephants away from the project area (Jachmann, 1998). With the onset of an effective law-enforcement programme of LIRDP in 1988, illegal hunting of elephants dropped dramatically, and, mainly as a result of elephants moving back to the project area, the population increased to 5400 by 1989. From 1989 to 1995, elephant numbers gradually increased to about 9000 (Figure 10.1).

Resource allocation and elephant poaching

In the early 1970s, there may have been as many as 60 wildlife scouts stationed in the central Luangwa Valley. However, these scouts were not supported with allowances, transport, operational support or supervision, and consequently the

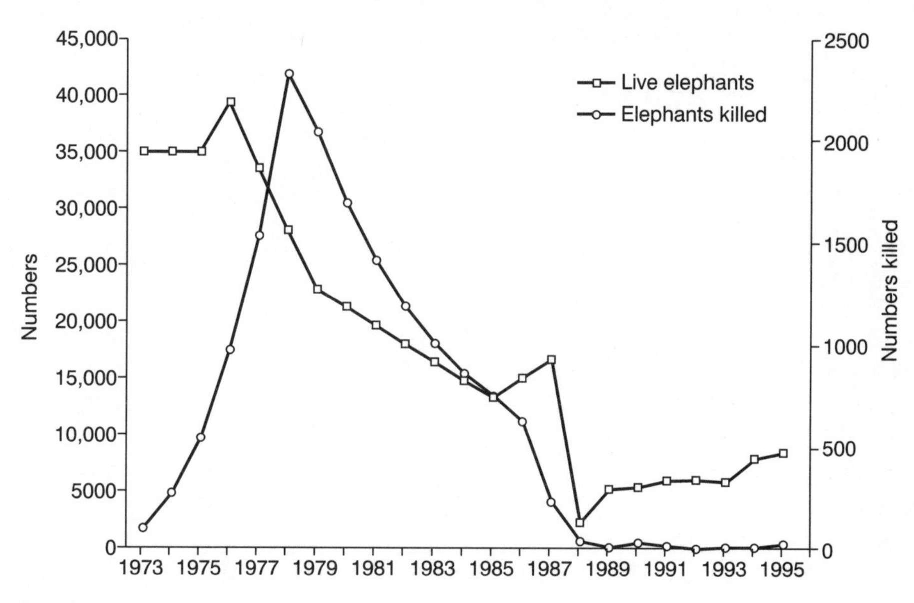

Source: Jachmann, 1998

Figure 10.1 *Elephant Population Estimates and Projected Elephants Killed for the LIRDP Area (1973–1995)*

law-enforcement effort of this scout force was negligible. As a result, illegal hunting of elephants was proceeding at will at a very high rate of approximately six elephants killed per day. For the period from 1979 to 1986, the numbers of effective wildlife personnel were confined to 22 SRT scouts. Total patrol days under SRT increased from 363 in 1979 to 4484 in 1983 (Leader-Williams et al, 1990). For the period from 1984 to 1987, information on total patrol days was lacking. The improved enforcement effort under SRT, even on a small scale, evidently had a major impact in reducing illegal off-take (Figure 10.2). With the initiation of LIRDP in 1988, effective scout numbers increased to 133, with a further increase to 286 in 1991, gradually declining to about 214 in 1995. Total patrol days increased from 11,462 in 1988 to about 30,000 in 1992, declining to about 10,000 in 1995. The vastly improved manpower input under LIRDP resulted in a massive reduction in elephant poaching two years before the international ivory ban came into effect (Figure 10.2).

The operational law-enforcement budget fluctuated between US$15 and $22 per km^2 per year between 1979 and 1988, which includes the operational budget for SRT of approximately US$11 per km^2 per year, increasing to nearly US$52 in 1991, declining to about US$24 in 1995.

During the LIRDP operational period (1988–1995), numbers of elephants found killed illegally declined from 39 in 1988 to 7 in 1992, and gradually increased to 23 in 1995 (Figure 10.3).

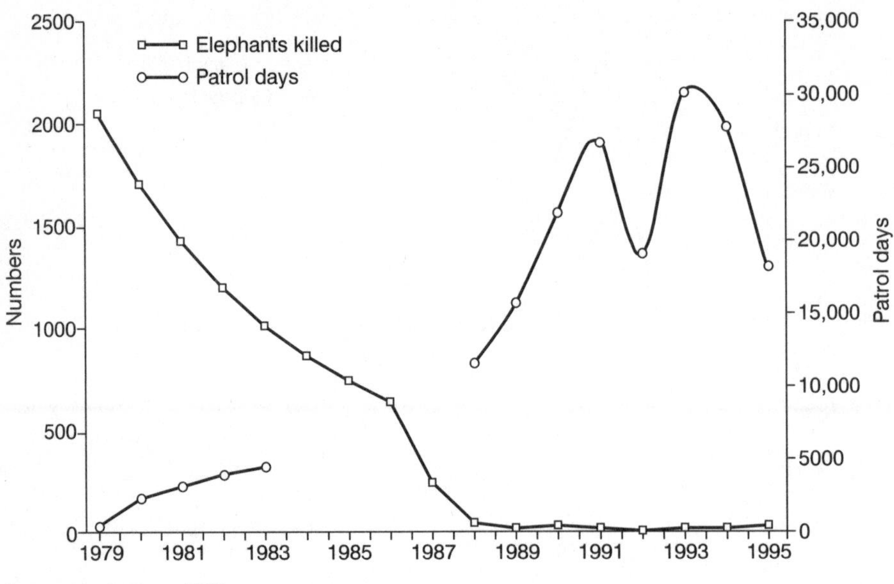

Source: Jachmann, 1998

Figure 10.2 *Projected Numbers of Elephants Killed and the Total Numbers of Patrol Days for the LIRDP Area (1979–1983 and 1988–1995)*

Resource allocation for this period follows the opposite pattern, with both financial and manpower input increasing to its highest level for the period in 1991–1992, then gradually declining to lower levels in 1995 (Table 10.1).

Univariate (Poisson) regressions show that all of the manpower predictor variables (Table 10.1) and two of the budgetary predictor variables (expenditure and emoluments), significantly influenced the numbers of elephants found killed illegally (Jachmann and Billiouw, 1997). However, the most important factor that influenced elephant poaching during this period was the incentive system (that is the predictor variable 'numbers of bonus claims paid'). Two-variable Poisson regression models, using log numbers of bonus claims paid and each of the other variables, showed that only one model was adequate and biologically plausible. The predictor variables bonus claims paid and effective investigation days together explained more than 95 per cent of the temporal variation in elephants found killed illegally between 1988 and 1995 (Fig 10.4). However, as a result of correlation between all the manpower variables and bonus claims paid, the latter incorporates the influence of the numbers of scouts and carriers employed as well as the numbers of effective patrol days (that is the entire manpower input).

Table 10.1 *The Response Variable, Numbers of Elephants found Killed, and Predictor Variables Relating to the Law-enforcement Input of LIRDP, used for the Modelling Procedure (1988–1995)*

Year	*1988*	*1989*	*1990*	*1991*	*1992*	*1993*	*1994*	*1995*
Response variable								
Elephants killed	39	16	27	16	7	9	12	23
Predictor variables Budget (US$)								
Expenditure/km^2	3.11	21.78	48.84	51.47	47.66	31.41	36.98	23.73
Emoluments/ scout/month	13.08	51.54	89.53	96.38	127.71	78.06	117.94	83.16
Transport expenditure/km^2	0.46	0.79	2.01	10.45	5.25	4.55	6.43	5.34
Average bonus rates	2.26	1.81	2.03	5.84	1.95	0.60	0.53	0.44
# Bonus claims paid	54	372	1189	2692	22537	9823	3483	557
Manpower								
km^2/scout	105.26	81.40	63.06	48.95	48.95	58.33	60.34	63.93
km^2/carrier	2000	2000	225.81	104.48	104.48	245.61	245.61	411.76
Effective patrol days/km^2	0.61	0.96	1.31	1.60	1.03	1.75	1.63	1.15
Effective investigation days	331	1554	250	2769	3110	661	1152	232

Source: Jachmann and Billiouw, 1997

DISCUSSION

In this case study it has been shown that the minor improvement in local enforcement during the SRT period (1979–1986) had a significant impact in reducing elephant poaching, while the effective law-enforcement programme of LIRDP reduced illegal off-take to acceptable levels in 1988, two years before the ivory ban came into effect. Furthermore, the analyses show that the temporal variation observed in the numbers of elephants found killed illegally between 1988 and 1995 can be explained by variation in resource allocation alone, without any contribution of external factors, which includes the international ivory ban. The success of LIRDP enforcement was due largely to a steep rise in the overall budget, an increase in manpower, but above all, the introduction of investigation operations and the incentive system. These were found to be the most important factors contributing to elephant conservation in the central Luangwa Valley. Thus, in the central Luangwa Valley, it was local enforcement effort, and not international regulation that was crucial to elephant conservation. As an example, during the early 1990s, the elephant population in the LIRDP area nearly doubled, whereas the population in the Kafue system in

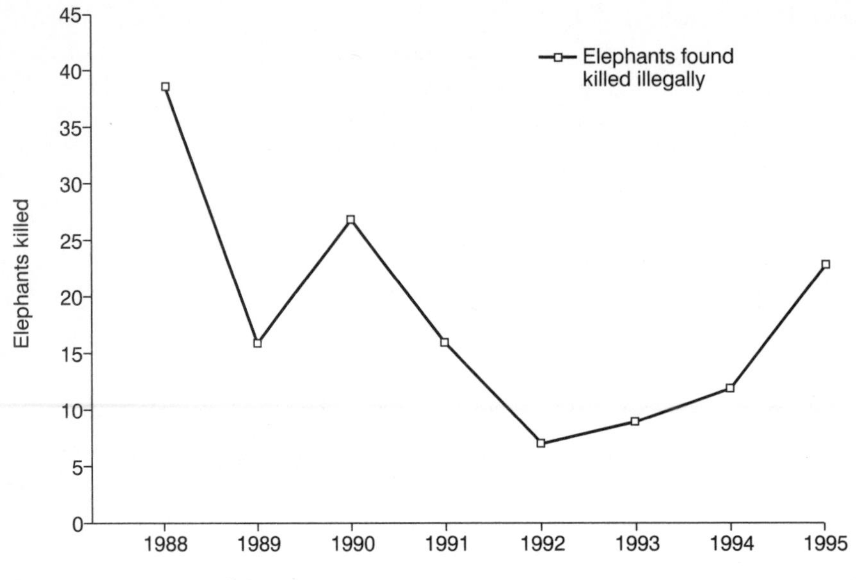

Source: Jachmann and Billiouw, 1997

Figure 10.3 *Numbers of Elephants found Killed Illegally in the LIRDP Area (1988–1995)*

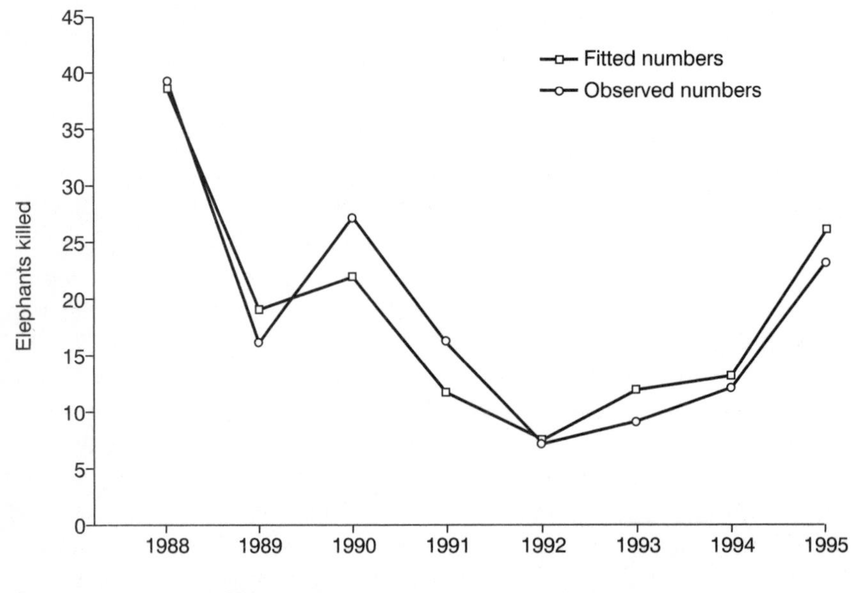

Source: Jachmann and Billiouw, 1997

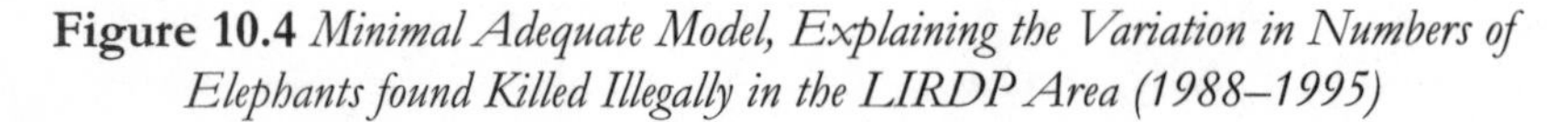

Figure 10.4 *Minimal Adequate Model, Explaining the Variation in Numbers of Elephants found Killed Illegally in the LIRDP Area (1988–1995)*

Zambia (56,600 km^2) was nearly halved (Jachmann, 1998). The only difference between the two areas was investment in local enforcement – about US$4 per km^2 per annum in the Kafue area compared to about US$30–50 per km^2 per annum in the central Luangwa Valley.

ACKNOWLEDGEMENT

The late Richard H V Bell introduced me to the subject of monitoring of law enforcement and of illegal activity when working in Malawi in the late 1970s. Richard was also instrumental in setting up the monitoring system in the central Luangwa Valley, when working as co-director for LIRDP. His sharp intellect and his friendship will be sadly missed.

REFERENCES

Bell, R H V (1985) Monitoring of illegal activity and law enforcement in African conservation areas, in Bell, R H V and McShane-Caluzi, E (eds), *Conservation and Wildlife Management in Africa,* US Peace Corps, Washington DC

Bell, R H V, Jachmann, H, Chimbali, D M and Mulonda, E Y (1992) *Illegal Activity and Law Enforcement in the Central Luangwa Valley, Zambia, from 1979 to 1992,* LIRDP, Chipata

Caughley, G and Goddard, J (1975) Abundance and distribution of elephants in the Luangwa Valley, Zambia, *East African Wildlife Journal*, 13, pp39–48

Crawley, M J (1993) *GLIM for Ecologists,* Blackwell Scientific Publications, Oxford

Dublin, H T and Jachmann, H (1992) *The Impact of the Ivory Ban on Illegal Hunting of Elephants in Six Range States,* World Wide Fund for Nature International Research Report, Gland

Dublin, H T, Milliken, T and Barnes, R F W (1995) *Four Years after the CITES Ban: Illegal killing of elephants, ivory trade and stockpiles,* IUCN/SSC African Elephant Specialist Group Report, Gland

Jachmann, H (1995) Survey experiments and aerial survey of elephants in the South Luangwa National Park and the Lupande Game Management Area, Zambia, 1993, *Pachyderm*, 19, pp81–86.

Jachmann, H (1998). *Monitoring Illegal Wildlife Use and Law Enforcement in African Savanna Rangelands,* Wildlife Resource Monitoring Unit Technical Handbook no 1, ECZ, Lusaka

Jachmann, H, Berry, P S M and Imae, H (1995) Tusklessness in African elephants: A future trend, *African Journal of Ecology*, 33, pp230–235

Jachmann, H and Billiouw, M (1997) Elephant poaching and law enforcement in the central Luangwa Valley, Zambia, *Journal of Applied Ecology*, 33, pp1241–1250

Leader-Williams, N, Albon, S D and Berry, P S M (1990) Illegal exploitation of black rhinoceros and elephant populations: patterns of decline, law enforcement and patrol effort in the Luangwa Valley, Zambia, *Journal of Applied Ecology*, 27, pp1055–1087

Chapter 11

Crocodiles: Legal Trade Snaps Back

Jon Hutton and Grahame Webb

INTRODUCTION

Using international trade in crocodilian hides as a case study, this chapter addresses two competing hypotheses:

1 that legal trade in wildlife can be used to displace illegal trade; and
2 that legal trade in wildlife will inevitably encourage illegal trade.

Both hypotheses have their adherents, and in most discussions of wildlife trade the relationship between legal trade and illegal trade will eventually become an issue. For example, the tension between the two competing hypotheses was neatly captured 25 years ago in debate on the conservation and trade in crocodilians:

> *Crocodile farmers have claimed that hides from captive stock, with their steady supply, and uniform size and quality, will replace wild hides in the international market. On the other hand some conservationists fear that the farmed hides will stimulate, but fail to satisfy, increased demands for crocodilian products* (Anon, 1976).

This chapter briefly addresses the two assumptions, highlighting some of their characteristics. It presents a case study of the crocodilians, and attempts to draw conclusions.

THE COMPETING HYPOTHESES

Legal trade displacing illegal trade

The idea that legal trade might be a useful tool to displace illegal trade is one commonly advocated by economists who promote market solutions to conservation problems. They seek to link the economic consumptive use of wild resources to incentives for sustainable harvesting. Discussion is usually couched in terms of property rights, the capture of economic rents, discount rates and institutions. For example, with respect to the African elephant it is claimed that:

> *It is not the mere existence of rents from ivory harvesting but who captures these rents which often determines the incentives for over-exploitation* (Barbier et al, 1990).

An alternative but related argument suggests that in some circumstances legal trade from species produced in captivity can directly substitute for illegal or unsustainable trade originating from wild harvests, as follows:

> *Where a wild population is being over-exploited for trade, it is possible that an alternative supply from captive sources could divert some of the trade and reduce pressure on the wild population ... increasing the supply so that the market becomes saturated and the price is driven downwards* (Luxmoore and Swanson, 1992).

It can be argued that this hypothesis has been supported by the Articles of CITES where the commercial trade in Appendix I species is allowed, provided the products come from captive breeding or artificial propagation of the species (Article VII (4)), but not if they come from sustainable harvesting from the wild.

Legal trade leading to illegal trade

Even if legal trade poses no direct threat to the survival of a species, it is widely recognized, including by the proponents of market solutions, that legal trade may provide increased opportunities for illegal trade. This situation has been well articulated as follows: 'giving wildlife commercial value is a double-edged sword. Poachers like wildlife with commercial value too' (Sutton, in Keller, 1992).

Illegal trade is rightly regarded as both difficult to control and more likely to lead to unsustainable harvesting than legal harvesting, and there are plenty of examples where illegal trade has flourished under the cover of legal trade. In the past, this was certainly a challenge with crocodilians:

> *'Laundering', poaching, and difficulties in identifying species and countries of origin are problems that perpetuate the [illegal] crocodilian trade and make it difficult to monitor* (Roeper, 1983).

However, an entirely reasonable concern has often been recast as an immutable assertion that legal trade inevitably leads to illegal trade and that this will, in turn, enhance rates of resource depletion. Support for this argument is based on acceptance of the following assumptions:

1. Any market will result in over-exploitation as the inevitable result of human greed combined with the opportunity for short-term financial gain.
2. Legal trade will stimulate demand which it is then unable to meet, leading to an escalation in price thus adding to the incentive for illegal harvesting and trade.
3. Attempts to counter or mitigate the threat to species resulting from trade will be ineffective. The force of markets, once unleashed, is so great that enforcement can never meet the challenge.

In the words of two adherents, Favre and Hoyt, to this axiom:

> *It is in the nature of individual economic decision-making to seek to maximize individual financial return even if it is at the cost of reducing the resource base being used* (Favre 1993).
>
> *Legal production tends to stimulate and perpetuate the markets for such products, thus* increasing, *or at least maintaining, the poaching pressure on wild populations* (Hoyt, 1994).
>
> *When luxury products from wildlife are legally traded in international commerce, the economic incentives for killing such animals are overwhelming* (Hoyt, 1994).

Over the years the notion that legal trade will inevitably lead to unsustainable, uncontrollable, illegal trade has been at the heart of a great deal of the opposition to proposals to transfer species from Appendix I to Appendix II of CITES. Thus:

> *WWF believes that resuming a legal trade in horn carries many risks. The move would perpetuate a demand that has caused the catastrophic fall in rhino numbers over the last 30 years* (WWF, 1992).
>
> *The history of trade in this species clearly indicates that illegal trade in sea turtle products flourishes under the cover of legal trade.... Any legal trade, particularly on a continuing basis, is likely to generate even more demand for illegal products* (IFAW, 2000).

In the CITES context, even the discussion of legal trade is sometimes held to be dangerous. Serious consideration of legal trade is said to send the 'wrong signals' to would-be poachers and illegal traders, encouraging their activities:

> *What will happen if the proposals (for elephants) are accepted? Poaching will resume. Indeed the very existence of the proposals has led to increased poaching* (Greenpeace, June 1997).

EXPLOITATION AND TRADE IN CROCODILIANS

Of the 23 crocodiles, alligators and caiman species (collectively known as crocodilians) generally recognized in more then 90 countries, 15 or more have commercially valuable hides. They have experienced remarkably similar histories of use, conservation and management, regardless of the countries in which they occur (Ross, 1998). From the 1800s onward, crocodilian skins became commercially valuable in some countries. In the US, for example, trading firms in New York were handling more than 60,000 American alligator *Alligator mississippiensis* skins a year in the late part of the 19th century (Fuchs et al, 1989).[1] The demand for many species appears to have increased exponentially after the Second World War. Thus, in the late 1940s it is reported that 120,000 Nile crocodile *Crocodylus niloticus* skins were being exported annually from Madagascar to tanneries in France (Games et al, 1997) while in the mid-1950s, nearly 60,000 Nile crocodile skins were exported from East Africa every year (Fuchs et al, 1989).

By the 1960s almost all wild populations of commercially important species were being exploited for trade to some degree and conventional wisdom holds that, as recently as the early 1970s, over two million crocodilian skins were to be found in trade. The vast majority, perhaps as many as 1.8 million, were from the South American caiman *Caiman crocodilus*[2] originating in a wide range of countries including Bolivia, Brazil, Colombia, Paraguay and Venezuela, with the balance made up of alligators from the US and crocodiles from many other parts of the world (eg Brazaitis, 1989).

There is strong anecdotal evidence that by the 1970s many wild crocodilian densities had fallen dramatically, sometimes to levels where populations were in danger of becoming extinct (eg Cott, 1961). Not unnaturally, conservationists concerned about this situation tended to advocate an end to harvesting and trade. It is thus not surprising that when CITES was introduced in 1975 all crocodilian species were listed on the Appendices, most[3] on Appendix I where commercial trade is completely prohibited.

There were, however, conservationists who saw the curtailing of trade only as a short-term management tool. Due to their influences, the late 1970s saw the growth of a nascent movement away from 'prohibition for ever' towards the development of programmes in which wild crocodilians could be harvested on a sustainable basis to generate ongoing economic and conservation benefits. This happened in several countries with diverse economic, social and cultural settings, notably Australia, Papua New Guinea, US, Venezuela and Zimbabwe, where the impetus for sustainable use often came from quite different directions (Webb et al, 1987).

The early success of these programmes led to a dramatic shift in the relationship between conservation, exploitation and trade. Initially seen only as a conservation problem, trade was increasingly co-opted as a conservation solution. Today, crocodilians are subject to biologically sustainable harvests in some 30 different nations (Table 11.1) in programmes that are widely considered to be models for market-led conservation (Fernandez and Luxmoore, 1996; Joanen et al, 1997; Loveridge, 1996; Thorbjarnarson and Velasco, 1998; Webb et al, 1987). There is no doubt that the unprecedented international scrutiny of the crocodilian skin trade through CITES has been a pivotal factor in this success.

CITES and Crocodilians

Because almost all exploitation feeds international trade, the harvesting of crocodilians has been particularly amenable to influence from CITES. On the face of it, the Appendix I listings in place when the convention came into force meant that legal trade in many traditionally important crocodilian species was technically impossible. In practice, however, trade often did continue through several different mechanisms. Firstly, in the 1970s a number of important producer and consumer nations were not parties to CITES (including Zimbabwe, France and Italy) and continued to trade. Secondly, when joining in the 1970s and 1980s many new parties lodged 'reservations'[4] against crocodilian species allowing them to maintain their harvesting and industry programmes (including, for example, Botswana, Zambia, Zimbabwe, France, Italy and Japan). Thirdly, CITES allowed specimens from Appendix I listed species that were bred in captivity for commercial purposes to be traded legally as if they were in Appendix II. In addition to legal trade through these mechanisms, a combination of continuing high demand for crocodilian hide, inappropriate regulation and poor national controls meant that considerable trade continued on illegally.

During the 1980s the possibility for legal trade between non-members was restricted as the majority of traditional producer and consumer countries joined the convention. In addition, even though it is perfectly legal to trade Appendix I crocodile skins under a reservation, member countries came under pressure to withdraw their reservations when it was argued that these allowed trade in skins taken illegally in their country of origin.[5] On the other hand, new possibilities for legal trade were created when, from 1981, it became possible to transfer some crocodilian populations from Appendix I to Appendix II if certain

Table 11.1 *List of Countries with Crocodilian Production Programmes*

Country	*Species*	*Mode of use*
United States	*A. mississippiensis*	Ranching, wild harvest and captive breeding
Mexico	*C. moreletii*	Captive breeding, ranching under development
Honduras	*C. acutus*	Captive breeding
Nicaragua	*Caiman crocodilus*	Wild harvest
Cuba	*C. rhombifer*	Captive breeding
Colombia	*Caiman crocodilus*	Captive breeding
Venezuela	*Caiman crocodilus*	Wild harvest and ranching
Guyana	*Caiman crocodilus*	Wild harvest
Brazil	*Caiman crocodilus*	Captive breeding, Ranching under development
Bolivia	*Caiman crocodilus*	Wild harvest
Paraguay	*Caiman crocodilus*	Wild harvest
Argentina	*Caiman latirostris*	Ranching
South Africa	*C. niloticus*	Captive breeding, ranching
Mozambique	*C. niloticus*	Ranching
Botswana	*C. niloticus*	Ranching
Malawi	*C. niloticus*	Ranching
Zimbabwe	*C. niloticus*	Ranching, captive breeding
Zambia	*C. niloticus*	Ranching
Uganda	*C. niloticus*	Ranching
Kenya	*C. niloticus*	Ranching, captive breeding
Tanzania	*C. niloticus*	Wild harvest, ranching
Ethiopia	*C. niloticus*	Ranching
Madagascar	*C. niloticus*	Ranching, captive breeding
Thailand	*C. siamensis*	Captive breeding
China	*Alligator sinensis*	Captive breeding
	C. porosus	Captive breeding
Cambodia	*C. siamensis*	Captive breeding
Indonesia	*C. porosus*	Captive breeding, wild harvest
	C. novaeguineae	Wild harvest
Malaysia	*C. porosus*	Captive breeding
Singapore	*C. porosus*	Captive breeding
Papua New Guinea	*C. porosus*	Ranching, wild harvest
	C. novaeguineae	Ranching, wild harvest
Australia	*C. porosus*	Ranching, captive breeding
	C. johnsoni	Ranching, captive breeding

Note: Wild harvest is direct harvest of adults from the wild. Ranching is collection of eggs from the wild that are raised in captivity, captive breeding is the production of eggs from adults held in captivity.

precautionary measures were adopted, including systems of production based on 'ranching'[6] or governed by strict quotas.

By 1989, as CITES began to close down illegal and unregulated sources of crocodilian skins, the number of skins in trade was reduced from an estimated

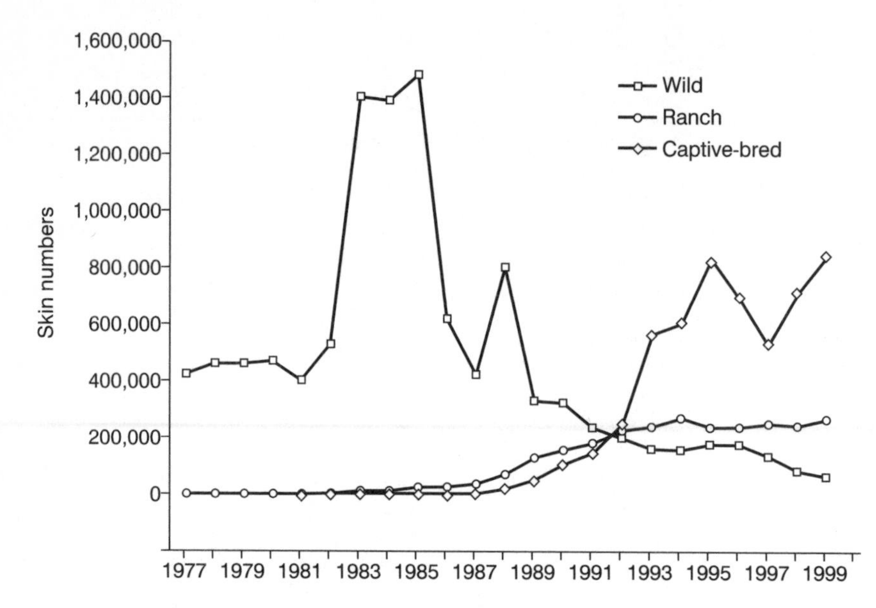

Figure 11.1 *Numbers of Crocodilian Skins Harvested (1977–1999)*

high of 1.5 million a year to a low of about 500,000. During the 1980s an increasing number of countries developed sustainable use programmes and turned their attention to ways in which their crocodilian populations could be transferred from Appendix I to Appendix II to allow legal, well-regulated trade to continue or recommence. Others focused on captive breeding that could benefit from the exemptions afforded to Appendix I species under such programmes. As a result, the number of crocodilian skins in trade began to rise again until it reached a new peak of almost 1.2 million skins in 1999 (Figure 11.1).

Trade before the 1980s was dominated by skins harvested from the wild. After the 1980s the vast majority originated from ranching and captive breeding. It is thought that about 300,000 classic[7] crocodile and alligator skins entered trade each year in the early 1970s (Ashley and David 1985), almost all originating from animals harvested in the wild. By 1983, under the influence of CITES, this number had fallen to 43,000 and the number of skins from the wild has hardly changed since then. In 1999 it is reported that 390,000 skins entered trade, but the increase reflects the bias of CITES towards ranching and captive breeding which together supplied 336,000 skins (Table 11.2). Over the same period the number of wild caiman skins in trade dramatically decreased from 1.4 million to 34,000 while the number of skins produced by captive breeding (principally in Colombia) increased from zero to over 770,000 (Table 11.2) (McGregor, 2001).

Table 11.2 *Classic and Caiman Skins in Global Trade by Method of Production (1977–1999)*

	Classics				Caiman			
	Captive-bred	Ranch	Wild	Total	Captive-bred	Wild	Total	TOTAL
1977	0	1258	38,831	40,089	0	388,322	388,322	422,013
1978	0	175	71,045	71,220	0	388,322	388,322	451,794
1979	0	991	67,902	68,893	0	388,322	388,322	458,954
1980	0	1039	81,869	82,908	0	388,322	388,322	514,429
1981	403	3193	66,306	69,902	0	338,265	338,265	435,219
1982	2	3339	39,839	43,180	0	223,300	223,300	288,319
1983	73	6523	63,557	70,153	0	1,349,426	1,349,426	1,439,978
1984	222	11,975	56,105	68,302	0	1,333,281	1,333,281	1,402,293
1985	640	18,473	64,653	83,766	0	1,428,145	1,428,145	1,513,120
1986	786	22,884	64,302	87,972	0	585,080	585,080	681,363
1987	3422	36,104	71,752	111,278	0	353,012	353,012	469,608
1988	5614	58,380	70,333	134,327	0	752,933	752,933	896,201
1989	10,885	126,405	74,799	212,089	31,168	265,749	296,917	515,914
1990	10,284	146,569	82,298	239,151	91,386	242,083	333,469	477,345
1991	11,121	173,953	64,960	250,034	129,521	172,704	302,225	483,848
1992	22,707	213,926	56,695	293,328	208,669	151,117	359,786	548,067
1993	39,719	234,298	51,487	325,504	516,002	112,992	628,994	890,520
1994	49,856	264,421	52,618	366,895	536,762	95,668	632,430	944,830
1995	56,864	237,337	58,287	352,488	781,313	120,937	902,250	1,178,181
1996	33,413	236,041	56,545	325,999	652,528	113,691	766,219	979,147
1997	46,249	257,248	74,955	378,452	483,631	64,408	548,039	806,393
1998	44,219	244,506	58,455	347,180	670,469	34,424	704,893	1,040,036
1999	73,105	262,898	54,642	390,645	771,456			

Source: McGregor, 2001

All sustainable use programmes, especially ranching and captive breeding, involve the investment of significant manpower and financial resources. As a result of the dramatic growth of ranching and captive breeding since the 1980s an important new constituency has been created among governments, NGOs and the private sector whose interests are compromised by illegal trade. We believe that the creation of this constituency was pivotal to the headway that the parties to CITES began to make against large-scale illegal trade during the 1980s (Anon, 1998) and which appears to have been eliminated during the 1990s. The constituency found a home, coordination and a unified voice in the Crocodile Specialist Group of The World Conservation Union (IUCN) Species Survival Commission. From about 1980 this group exerted a strong influence on the evolution of the various CITES mechanisms dealing with crocodilians as well as on the way that the secretariat and parties responded to unregulated and illegal trade.

The following examples illustrate the measures through which illegal trade was addressed by the parties to CITES:

1. In the early 1980s, a number of important importing countries (notably France, Italy and Japan) were widely criticized[8] for importing Appendix I crocodilian skins under a number of reservations. France and Italy were pressured by the European Community to drop their various reservations in 1984 and Japan dropped its reservation on *Crocodylus porosus* in 1989.
2. Although it did not hold any reservations on crocodilian species, Indonesia was implicated in the illegal trade of its indigenous crocodiles (and other wildlife species) during the late-1980s. In 1994, after almost a decade of deliberation, the CITES standing committee recommended that trade with Indonesia be suspended. The recommendation was not followed through because Indonesia, working with the IUCN/SSC Crocodile Specialist Group, successfully addressed the problem over a five-year period of intensive management in which illegal trade was largely eradicated in favour of a well-regulated legal trade.
3. In 1983, there was a great deal of concern that Bolivia was responsible for laundering caiman skins from Brazil. Concerns in this regard continued until 1985 when the CITES standing committee recommended that trade be suspended – as a result of which Bolivia voluntarily withdrew from all international trade in wildlife.
4. In 1983, it was reported that Japan had imported 45 tonnes of caiman skins from Paraguay, and it was considered likely that these were illegal in origin. Five years later, in 1990, Paraguay resurfaced again amid concerns that 35,000 caiman skins from Brazil had been laundered through that country. As a result of this, and similar problems, the CITES secretariat suspended cooperation with Paraguay and shortly afterward a number of reforms were introduced which were considered to have resolved the problems.
5. In 1990, 6000 illegal caiman skins destined for Italy were seized in Belgium. Concerns about the role of Italy in the illegal trade of caiman skins were reinforced when evidence emerged that at least a further 9000 illegal skins reached Italy that year. By 1992 the problem had become so serious that the CITES standing committee recommended that trade be suspended with Italy. Once again, this most drastic of compliance actions on the part of CITES resulted in a resolution of the situation, and the closure of yet another loophole for illegal trade.
6. Italy was not considered the only 'leaky cauldron' as far as the illegal trade in caiman was concerned, both Thailand and Singapore also had their problems. In 1988 it was reported that Thailand imported an estimated 750,000 illegal caiman skins because it had not passed legislation allowing it to enforce its obligations under CITES. In 1990, after further problems, the CITES secretariat distributed an official notification warning parties about the consequences of trade with Thailand. In 1991, when it was clear that no progress had been made, the CITES standing committee recommended that parties should adopt stricter domestic measures to suspend trade with Thailand. Once again this mechanism had the desired effect. Domestic legislation was enacted and the illegal trade was eradicated.

7 In the early 1990s a great deal of concern was expressed by several South American parties to CITES about the import of caiman skins under reservation by Singapore. It was suggested that many of these skins had been taken illegally from Brazil and laundered through a range of intermediary countries, notably Aruba administered by the Netherlands. After a period of negotiation, characterized by a great deal of recrimination, Singapore decided to drop its reservation on caiman in 1992, closing one of the last of the 'traditional' routes for caiman from 'grey' sources to enter international trade.

8 In 1990 concerns were raised that some crocodile ranching operations in Africa were laundering wild skins in order to maintain their economic viability when experiencing declining prices coupled with high investment and production costs (Hutton, 1992). These fears have receded, not as a result of enforcement, but because a number of the countries most affected have worked within CITES to reintroduce sustainable cropping from the wild. At the same time they have moved away from ranching. Together these developments have removed many of the incentives for illegal trade.

9 In 1992, shortly after Singapore dropped its reservation, the first concerns were raised that wild caiman skins were being exported through captive breeding units (farms) in Colombia. For some years the 'preferred' conservation strategy for crocodilians, and many other species, was 'captive breeding'. However, it was feared that captive breeding provided incentives for the laundering of illegally-taken wild skins in some circumstances.[9] A decade later, these concerns continue in some circles (Ashley, D, pers com, 2002), but no concrete evidence of any wrongdoing has ever come to light.

10 In response to concerns about the possibility that an illegal trade in crocodilian skins could resurface, the parties to CITES responded by introducing a universal system for the tagging of crocodilian skins at the points of origin and re-export. First introduced in 1992, this system was refined on two subsequent occasions to take into account the experiences of the various implementing countries. At the time of writing, all crocodilian skins and parts of skins, have to be recorded and tagged in compliance with Resolution Conf 11.12. This system is considered to have been so successful that the CITES 'TIGERS' database on illegal trade, established in 1997, contained only one report of illegal commercial trade between 1995 and 2000, and on inspection this was found to be in error.[10]

CONCLUSIONS

Within 20 years the crocodilian trade has seen the replacement of skins from unregulated exploitation with skins from sustainable resource management. Today, at least 30 countries may use wild harvests, ranching or captive breeding to produce crocodilian products from 12 species to supply international trade –

but only on the understanding that these programmes do not threaten the future of any species in the wild. As a result, the 11 most commercially valuable species are the species *least* threatened with extinction (Ross, 1998).

In conclusion, in the case of crocodilians it seems clear that:

- Conservation incentives can and have been generated by markets.
- The economic importance of the resource has led directly to stronger institutional arrangements specifically for conservation and sustainable management.
- Illegal international trade, which flourished before CITES encouraged legal trade, has been all but eradicated.

We can therefore reject the hypothesis that legal trade inevitably leads to illegal trade and adopt the hypothesis that legal trade can displace illegal trade. Having established this, this rather sterile debate can move on. The main challenge now must be to establish under exactly what conditions legal trade displaces illegal trade so that wildlife trade systems can be better designed and managed in future.

Notes

1 The total number of alligator skins in trade each year during the period 1870–1902 may have exceeded 110,000 (Elsey, R, pers com, 2001).
2 The taxonomy of the caiman is subject to considerable debate. For the purposes of this paper the term 'caiman' includes all variations of *Caiman crocodilus* including what is sometimes known as *Caiman yacare*.
3 14 species and 2 sub-species of the 21 species recognized
4 A country that takes a 'reservation' against the listing of a species in CITES is not bound by that listing decision.
5 In some cases reservations have played a positive role in conservation and the evolution of CITES (Kievit, 2000)
6 It was decided that the removal of eggs or young animals from the wild for subsequent rearing in captivity should be termed 'ranching' and should not benefit from the trade possibilities provided by 'bred in captivity' exemptions.
7 In the market, alligator and crocodile skins are known as 'classics'. Classic skins and caiman skins are usually considered separately.
8 Notably by TRAFFIC-USA which consistently and successfully focused attention on the illegal and unregulated crocodilian trade during the 1980s.
9 With species of low value or which are difficult to breed in captivity.
10 An alleged illegal shipment of Nile crocodile skins into Zimbabwe proved to have legal permits.

References

Anon (1976) *Proceedings of the Third Working Meeting of the IUCN/SSC Crocodile Specialist Group*, IUCN/SSC Crocodile Specialist Group, IUCN, Gland, Switzerland

Anon (1998) *The International Alligator and Crocodile Trade Study,* WCMC, Cambridge

Ashley, D and David, D N (1985) *Crocodile Hide Marketing: Utilisation, management and conservation implications,* presented at the International Technical Conference on Crocodile Conservation and Management, Darwin. Unpublished

Ashley, D (2002) personal communication, coordinator, International Alligator and Crocodile Trade Study (IACTS)

Barbier, E B, Burgess, J C, Swanson, T M and Pearce, D W (1990) *Elephants, Economics and Ivory,* Earthscan, London

Brazaitis, P (1989) The trade in crocodilians in Ross, C A and Garnett, S (eds) *Crocodiles and Alligators,* Merehurst Press, London

Cott, H B (1961) Scientific results of an inquiry into the ecology and economic status of the Nile crocodile (*Crocodylus niloticus*) in Uganda and Northern Rhodesia, *Transactions of the Zoological Society of London*, 29, pp211–356.

Elsey, R (2001) personal communication, Louisiana Department of Wildlife and Fisheries

Favre, D (1993) Debate within the CITES Community: What Direction for the Future?, *Natural Resources Journal,* 33, pp875–918.

Fernandez, C, and Luxmoore, R (1996) The Crocodile Industry in Papua New Guinea in Swanson, T, Fernandez Ugalde, C and Luxmoore, R (eds) *Survey of Wildlife Management Regimes for Sustainable Utilization*, Darwin Initiative Project, Cambridge

Fuchs, K H P, Ross, C A, Pooley, A C and Whitaker, R (1989) Crocodile Skin Products in Ross, C A and Garnett, S (eds) *Crocodiles and Alligators,* Merehurst Press, London

Games I, Ramandimbison and Lippai, C (1997) *Madagascar Crocodile Survey, July, 1997,* Draft Report to CITES Secretariat, Geneva

Greenpeace (1997) *CITES Under Threat,* Greenpeace International, Amsterdam

Hoyt, J (1994) *How Sustainable Use is Wiping out the World's Wildlife,* Humane Society of the United States

Hutton, J M (1992) *The CITES Nile Crocodile Project,* CITES Secretariat, Lausanne

IFAW (2000) *CITES 2000*, International Fund for Animal Welfare, Yarmouth Port.

Joanen, T, McNease, L, Elsey, R and Staton, M (1997) The commercial consumptive use of the American alligator (*Alligator mississippiensis*) in Louisiana, its effects on conservation in Freese, C (ed) *Harvesting Wild Species: Implications for biodiversity,* The Johns Hopkins University Press, Baltimore

Keller, B (1992) Africa Thinks About Making Wildlife Pay For Its Survival, *New York Times,* 27 Dec 1992

Kievit, H (2000) Conservation of the Nile crocodile: Has CITES helped or hindered? in Hutton, J M and Dikson, B (eds) *Endangered Species: Threatened Convention. The Past, Present and Future of CITES,* Earthscan, London

Loveridge, J (1996) *A Review of Crocodile Management in Zimbabwe*, Mimeo Report, Department of Biological Sciences, University of Zimbabwe

Luxmoore, R and Swanson, T M (1992) Wildlife and wildland utilization and conservation, in Swanson, T M and Barbier, E B (eds) *Economics for the Wilds,* Earthscan, London

McGregor, J (2001) *A Review of the Economics of the Crocodilian Trade,* IUCN/SSC Crocodile Specialist Group.

Roeper, N (1983) WWF-USA, *Traffic-USA Newsletter,* 5 (2), p8

Ross, J P (1998) *Crocodiles: Status survey and conservation action plan,* IUCN – The World Conservation Union, Gland

Thorbjarnarson, J and Velasco, A (1998) *Venezuela's Caiman Harvest Program; A historical perspective and analysis of its conservation benefits.* Wildlife Conservation Society Working Paper no 11

Webb, G J W, Whitehead, P J and Manolis, S C (1987) Crocodile Management in the Northern Territory of Australia in Webb, G J W, Manolis, S C and Whitehead, P J (eds) *Wildlife Management: Crocodiles and alligators,* Surrey Beatty and Sons, Australia

Webb, G J W, Manolis, S C and Whitehead, P J (1987) *Wildlife Management: Crocodiles and alligators,* Surrey Beatty and Sons, Australia

WWF (1992) *Help WWF Stop the Rhino Horn Trade,* WWF-International, Gland

Chapter 12

Regulation of the Timber Trade

Sara Oldfield

INTRODUCTION

Timber is the third largest commodity in international trade. The overall value of international trade in wood products is estimated at over US$100 billion per year and timber is one of the main sources of international revenue for many countries. The timber trade still relies to a large extent on the harvesting of wild material and clearly dwarfs the scale of other forms of trade in wild plant or animal products. The international timber trade is characterized by a wide range of products derived from hundreds of different species. Systems for monitoring the international timber trade are weak and the data, where available, are imprecise. There is, however, increasing evidence that illegality in the international timber trade is rife, with estimates suggesting that half of all the international transactions in tropical timber are in contravention of legislation. The problems are by no means confined to tropical countries. Until recently this major global problem of timber illegality has been largely overlooked and ignored but the issue is now high on the political agenda and solutions are being tentatively sought.

Tackling illegality in the timber trade will require major changes in attitudes and approaches. It has long been in the interests of consumer nations to have a plentiful supply of cheap timber and despite concerns about forest loss, timber is still seen generally as an infinite and renewable global resource. Enforcement of national forestry legislation remains weak and players in the international timber trade have not traditionally embraced regulation for their commodity transactions. Developing mechanisms for international regulation will have to take into account the realities of the current situation and the costs for timber-producing countries in making the major improvements required.

National Legislation

The legal basis for the operation of the timber trade is primarily the domestic legislation of exporting countries. National forestry legislation governing timber exploitation includes concession and licensing policies, fees and royalty payments, restrictions on felling timber of particular species below a certain size, general logging bans, or restrictions on exports of unworked timber. The rationale for the legislation may be to manage and protect the forestry resource, lay down institutional arrangements and to control the revenue derived from forest exploitation. In many cases administrative orders provide supplementary details relating to specific aspects of national forestry laws.

Forest legislation may specify the areas of forest where felling is allowed in relation to a designated national forest estate. Areas where felling is prohibited may include protected watersheds or areas set aside for biodiversity conservation. In addition to area-based controls some timber-exporting countries have felling restrictions on certain specified timber species. Generally, under such legislation, felling is subject to permission from the forestry department. In Côte d'Ivoire, 25 commercially important timbers are listed as protected species under Decree No 66–122 of 1966. Legislation in Mozambique regulates the felling of eight 'precious' timber species including African blackwood *Dalbergia melanoxylon* and other internationally traded timbers. In the Philippines, the Department of Environment and Natural Resources (DENR) Administrative Order No 78 Series of 1987 imposes restriction on the felling of 20 prime commercial timbers which are generally recognized as being of conservation concern.

In general, felling restrictions on species are specified by legislation as minimum girth limits or minimum exploitable diameters. The determination of girth limits for forest exploitation is considered to be a first management regulation, preventing trees being cut before they reach maturity. Cutting limits should be enforced until the forest can be treated under more sophisticated management and silvicultural systems (Schmithusen, 1986). However, it has been noted in Africa that cutting limits are rarely adequately enforced and legal minimum exploitable diameters for timber species in African countries are generally considerably higher than commercial minimum diameters. As noted in Oldfield (1991), it is more profitable to remove all timber of commercial size in one felling than to respect the legal cutting limits.

General logging bans have been put in place under domestic legislation in various countries in response to rapid rates of deforestation, thereby outlawing any timber cutting for commercial purposes. In some cases there are log export bans, which may be general or related to certain species only. Generally, the primary motivation for log export bans has been to promote value-added production within the country as a means of increasing national revenue and employment in forest industry. There may also be an element of concern for species conservation. During the 1980s, Ghana banned the export of 18 timber

BOX 12.1 LOGGING IN AND TIMBER EXPORTS FROM LIBERIA

Within Liberia the recent National Forestry Act, 1999, reconfirms the mandate of the Forestry Development Authority (FDA) which has responsibility for regulation and monitoring of the timber trade. Nearly all the country's forests have been granted as concessions including areas previously designated for national parks or forest reserves. Huge increases in logging have been reported over the past few years with for example, over 600,000 cubic metres recorded for the period January–June 2000, which is more than the total for the previous four years. It is believed that log exports are under-reported by 50 per cent. The main importing countries for Liberian timber are China which imports roughly 50 per cent of the logs exported and France which imports around 18 per cent.

The main timber species exported by Liberia are niangon *Tarrietia utilis* and *Tarrietia densiflora*; tetra *Tetraberlinia tubmaniana* a species recorded as vulnerable by IUCN which is endemic to Liberia; and abura *Hallea ledermannii* and *Hallea stipulosa* the latter of which is another vulnerable species. At present there is not thought to be any degree of protection for these vulnerable species.

species in log form. Côte d'Ivoire operates a log export ban, which is selective by species and is also related to a log supply quota. Nigeria initially banned the export of logs of major hardwood species before introducing a general log export ban. A log export ban on ten species was proposed in Liberia over a decade ago but was not instituted and most previous legislation in the country has been overturned in favour of logging.

In addition to national forestry regulations, biodiversity conservation legislation also provides protection for timber species or forest areas within a domestic context. The Convention on Biological Diversity (CBD) increasingly provides a framework for domestic biodiversity conservation legislation but there is not as yet a similar Multilateral Environmental Agreement (MEA) relating to regulation of forestry activities and forest conservation. In general, for biodiversity purposes, the legal emphasis is on conserving designated areas of forest habitat rather than individual high-value timber species. In a few countries there is, however, specific legislation recognizing the threatened status of individual timber species and specifying legal conservation measures accordingly. Sri Lanka, for example, protects a number of timber species as part of its protected species legislation including 14 dipterocarp species and 11 species of ebony *Diospyros*.

THE SCALE AND IMPACT OF ILLEGAL LOGGING

Generally there are major weaknesses in the enforcement of national forestry and biodiversity conservation legislation as they relate to logging and the trade in timber products. Inadequate resources for enforcement are a major problem and corruption has been reported in a wide range of situations. Poverty is also a major driver of illegal logging at a local scale. The extent of illegality in timber sourcing suggests that it may be considered a 'socially acceptable' crime. Strengthening national forest policy and enforcement of legislation are, however, now recognized as important priorities to reduce the illegality of timber in international trade – at least within the international forums where these issues are being debated. Changes from government to community ownership of forest resources with the legally constituted involvement of local communities may ultimately lead to less evasion of legal harvesting controls. In reality, however, local communities still scarcely benefit from the money generated by the international timber trade and have little sense of ownership of the resource.

The sheer scale of illegality in timber harvesting has been highlighted over recent years, initially as a result of NGO investigations. In the Brazilian Amazon, 80 per cent of the timber harvested is estimated to be illegal; in Indonesia estimates place the level of illegal timber harvesting at around 70 per cent; in Cameroon the figure is approximately 50 per cent; in Gabon, 70 per cent; and in Cambodia up to 90 per cent of the timber is believed to be illegally felled. In Russia at least 20 per cent of the timber is harvested illegally and this figure is thought to be considerably higher in the country's far east. As a high proportion of this timber extracted in all these situations is for export, this leads to a picture of global chaos within the timber trade.

The growing concern about the scale and extent of illegality within the international timber trade centres on environmental, fiscal and basic governance aspects. From an environmental perspective, logging is recognized as a major cause of forest disturbance and biodiversity loss. Logging is claimed to be responsible for about one-third of global deforestation. In addition over 1000 commercial timber species are recorded as threatened with extinction at least in part as a result of logging. This figure on timber species includes, for example, around 250 species of the family *Dipterocarpaceae* which provide commercial timbers such as meranti, keruing and seraya. Collectively dipterocarp trees represent the mainstay of the South-East Asian timber industry. It is not possible to quantify the scale of threat to tree species and forest areas as a whole from illegal as opposed to legal logging, given current levels of information. It is, however, clear that illegal logging threatens some of the most important areas of biodiversity where timber harvesting should not be taking place at all and directly threatens some of the globally threatened tree species, which are harvested in contravention of domestic legislation.

The loss of revenue as a result of illegal logging is substantial. It has been reported for example that Indonesia loses US$125 million per year as a result of the activities of 18 illegal logging syndicates and in Cambodia the government lost over US$180 million in timber revenue due to illegal logging in 1997 (Environmental Investigation Agency, 2001). Avoidance of royalty and fee payments is one of the major motivations for illegal timber harvesting.

From a governance perspective, there are major concerns about the inability of countries to manage their natural resources, implement legislation and to effectively police the outflow of capital. The framework for timber harvesting in forested areas goes to the core of land management and revenue generation contributing significantly to local and national economies. Without adequate controls national and local interests are seriously compromised in favour of multinational timber corporations.

International Regulation

As discussed above, illegal timber on the international market is generally timber harvested in contravention of national laws, for example timber felled within national parks or outside forestry concession areas, timber of protected species, or undersized timber or timber exported without payment of appropriate fees or taxes. The range of forms of illegality in the Asia–Pacific timber trade was described by Callister (1992), and no doubt can be matched in scope and complexity in other parts of the world.

The scale of illegality in timber exports is matched by a corresponding picture of illegal imports for major consuming nations. It has been estimated and widely quoted, for example, that 60 per cent of the timber imported into the UK and around 50 per cent of the timber imported into the EU as a whole may be of illegal origin. The estimates are crude and based largely on inferences but serve to show the size of the problem. The extent of illegality in international trade has also led to calls for strengthened regulation at an international level.

At present there is no effective framework for international regulation of the timber trade. Consideration is being given to further developing the use of existing mechanisms and agreements and to developing new bilateral and regional agreements. For example legislation at a European level to ban imports of timber sourced illegally is proposed.

The Role of CITES

International legislation relating to the trade in timber remains very limited. CITES can be considered the most appropriate international agreement for monitoring and controlling the trade in timber species but as yet its role in this area has been restricted. The licensing of trade in Appendix II species can be an important aspect of the management of commercially valuable wild species, requiring that the exporting countries certify that the export is not detrimental to the survival of wild stocks and that the species has been harvested legally. Appendix II listing also places an obligation on the importing country to monitor imports – currently the only obligation in place for many timber-importing countries.

It is perhaps the emphasis on species that devalues the perception of CITES as a tool for use in controlling the international trade in forest products. Forestry

Box 12.2 Legal Protection for Alerce *Fitzroya cupressoides* in Chile

At a national level, in Chile, alerce is protected by national legislation (DS no 490), which declares the species a natural monument. This legislation bans the cutting of live trees but allows the cutting of dead trees with a death date prior to 1976. This formulation has provided a loophole whereby forests have been deliberately burned so that the valuable timber can be cut. During the period 1998–2000, 17 infractions of this legislation, concerning illegal cutting and transport of alerce were recorded by the government agency CONAF (Reyes and Lobos, 2000). Alerce is also protected within four national parks and one natural monument. In total, 17 per cent of the 260,000 hectares of Chilean natural forest, where the species occurs is under protection.

General forest law in Chile (DL no 701) promotes forestry and in particular the development of pine and eucalyptus plantations. This legislation also establishes fines for illegal actions in native forests. During the period 1998–2000, 20 infractions of this legislation concerning illegal felling were recorded by the CONAF (Reyes and Lobos, 2000). Natural forests are still being cleared for pine and eucalyptus plantations and the legislation is considered too weak to prevent this.

management for production and conservation generally take an area-based approach. There are, however, advantages in tackling the timber trade at a species level. Often, the main motivation for opening up a forest area for commercial loggers is the presence of one or more high value timber species, which are required by international markets. The management of exploitation of those species has implications for the forest as a whole. Furthermore, in many cases, timber products on the international market derive an identity and value from the species they are produced from rather than the area from which they are sourced. CITES, of course, provides a mechanism for linking the management of species with international markets.

Nineteen timber species are currently listed on the CITES appendices, several of which are important in international trade. Many more timber-bearing species meet the CITES listing criteria (WCMC, 1998). Several species were included in the appendices from the early days of the convention. One such species is alerce *Fitzroya cupressoides* a slow-growing and endangered conifer species which is native to Argentina and Chile. The species has been included in CITES Appendix I since the convention came into force. In 1983, the Chilean population of the species was down-listed to Appendix II to allow exports from the country. In 1987 this decision was reversed with all populations again listed on Appendix I. Chile entered a reservation against this listing and has continued to trade in the species internationally with exports to other CITES countries recorded as pre-convention stocks, that is from stocks acquired before 1 July 1975. Illegally imported consignments of the timber have been confiscated in the UK. The main importing countries in 2000, the last year for which export figures are available are Taiwan and Tahiti which are not parties to the convention.

Listing *Fitzroya cupressoides* on CITES Appendix I has probably been beneficial to the conservation of the species and the forests it defines, not least by providing a focus for international attention and a basis for dealing with illegal imports. Illegal exploitation of this valuable timber species does, however, continue to be a problem at a domestic level as shown in Box 12.2.

Over the past 15 years there have been varying levels of interest in expanding the use of CITES to control and monitor trade in timber species within both producer and consumer countries. Proposals to list a range of valuable African hardwood species were prepared, for example, for the 1987 Conference of the Parties to CITES in Ottawa. Ghana had agreed to introduce them but the proposals were not put forward before the official deadline. In the early 1990s the Philippines collected information on a number of over-exploited timber species with a view to CITES listing. At around the same time the European Commission (EC) supported the preparation of a review of timber species for listing on annexes of its regulation to implement CITES. This followed the development of an EC strategy on tropical forests, one of the five elements of which related to the timber trade. The Commission requested that CITES, 'should be examined to see if protection given especially to endangered species of tropical forest trees is adequate. Here, preliminary enquiry appears to indicate that the CITES listing of such species needs urgently to be updated' (European Commission, 1989). Listing of a range of timber species on Annexe D of the European regulation on CITES did not, however, proceed as it was considered by the Commission to be incompatible with development interests.

In 1992 and 1994 various proposals were put forward to list commercially valuable timber species in the CITES Appendices. One such species is African teak or afrormosia *Pericopsis elata*, a species currently listed as endangered by The World Conservation Union (IUCN). This species which occurs in West and Central Africa was added to Appendix II of the convention in 1992. Implementation of the CITES provisions for afrormosia has not been straightforward and there have been considerable enforcement problems. Nevertheless the convention has provided a mechanism both for monitoring international trade and for reinforcing national legislation. Recently four multinational companies were prosecuted in Cameroon for exporting sawn timber of afrormosia in contravention of CITES controls.

The listing of big-leafed mahogany, *Swietenia macrophylla* on CITES has been an ongoing issue for nearly a decade. The two other species of this valuable timber genus, *S. humilis* and *S. mahagoni* which have more limited natural distributions and in the case of *S. mahagoni* has been heavily exploited for centuries, are included in Appendix II. Attempts to list big-leafed mahogany in Appendix II based on proposals in 1992, 1994 and 1997 have been unsuccessful. Bolivia, Brazil, Colombia, Costa Rica, Mexico and Peru do, however, list their populations of this valuable commercial species in Appendix III of the convention and regulate exports under a system of permits. Bolivia, Brazil and Peru are the major exporters. A mahogany working group was established by the CITES parties in 1997 and has addressed a range of issues including illegal trade in the species. CITES authorities in exporting countries contacted by TRAFFIC in 2001, generally believed that the Appendix III listing had helped in the detection and reduction of illegal trade (TRAFFIC Network, 2001).

The idea of using CITES for timber species has aroused considerable resistance in certain countries because it has been perceived as an affront to national sovereignty in timber-producing nations rather than a framework for international cooperation. It probably also reflects the general resistance to regulation by the timber trade and resistance to the idea of commercial timbers as endangered species. In order to increase understanding between different interest groups, the CITES Timber Working Group was established in 1994 and reported to the subsequent Conference of the Parties in 1997. The working group considered practical problems which have frequently been cited (and probably over-exaggerated) as making the enforcement of CITES difficult for timber species. These include the difficulty of identification of timber products, in the form in which they are traded, and the issue of trading in split consignments of timber at sea where buyers are located after the timber has left the country of origin. The working group also considered relationships with other international organizations which are more widely recognized as having competence with regard to the timber trade.

The CITES Timber Working Group effectively helped to tackle the various problems outlined in its remit and helped to resolve some misconceptions and misunderstandings of the roles and workings of CITES. The group did not look specifically at the role of CITES in relation to legality of the timber trade and explicitly did not consider the potential to list additional timber species. It did however tentatively note that:

> *there may be timber species which are under threat because of detrimental levels of use and international trade* and recommended *range states to pay particular attention to internationally traded timber species for which knowledge of biological status and silvicultural requirements indicates concern.*

There have been no significant changes in the way countries choose to use CITES as a result of the deliberations of the working group but recently there has been a growing interest in the use of CITES Appendix III for timber species. This provides a means for a country to make a unilateral decision on cooperative international measures to regulate trade in a species about which it has concerns. Peru placed its populations of the commercially valuable *Cedrela odorata* on Appendix III in 2001, together with *Swietenia macrophylla*. Indonesia has chosen this mechanism to reinforce a national moratorium on the felling and export of ramin *Gonystylus* spp, the timber of which has been extensively sourced illegally in protected areas.

For CITES to become an important measure in the monitoring and control of rare and threatened tropical timber species in international trade considerable political will and allocation of resources will be necessary. There have been fears that if CITES is used to deal with timber, the convention will be overwhelmed. It is clear that CITES can only be part of the solution, given the root causes and scale of illegal logging.

OTHER INTERNATIONAL REMEDIES

A common perception remains that CITES is a mechanism primarily for controlling trade in animals and animal products and that different ways and institutions should be used for the timber trade. The International Tropical Timber Agreement (ITTA) has been suggested as an appropriate vehicle.

As a forum to discuss aspects of the timber trade, the International Tropical Timber Organization (ITTO) established under the ITTA, has the advantage of balanced membership of producer and consumer nations, a commitment to sustainable forest management to maintain the tropical timber trade and some capacity to record international timber trade flows. The organization does not, however, have any enforcement powers in relation to particular issues. Problems associated with illegal timber in trade are now being addressed by ITTO. At its meeting in November 2001, the International Tropical Timber Council – ITTO's governing body – passed a decision calling for and initiating action to promote transparency in the tropical timber trade. The intention to launch a range of new activities on forest law enforcement and combating illegal trade was announced. These activities will be at a national level in response to requests from member states. A study is also taking place to identify problems in reporting systems for timber trade statistics with a view to tackling discrepancies caused by illegal trade.

Other components of the international policy framework which may have some relevance in tackling the illegal timber trade include the UN Forum on Forests (UNFF), CBD, and forest certification schemes such as that of the Forest Stewardship Council (FSC). These bodies and agreements present a range of possibilities for debate and action but do not have the backing of legal force. Illegal logging has also been identified as one of five key areas of action within the intergovernmental G8 Action Programme on Forests. The UK government is taking the lead on this issue. As a result of the 2000 G8 summit, major timber importing countries are examining procurement policies. The UK government, for example, announced in July 2000 that all government departments and their agencies would be required to actively seek to buy timber and timber-related products from legal and sustainable sources. The intent is excellent but in practice this will be a difficult requirement to implement.

The role of forest certification with regard to legality of the timber trade is an issue receiving considerable attention as solutions to the legally out-of-control timber trade are sought. One advantage of this approach is that independently certified chain-of-custody mechanisms have been developed which trace the supply of timber from its source to end market. Ultimately product tracking of this nature provides the best guarantee of legality. The monitoring of timber to source goes considerably beyond the requirements of licensing under CITES. Unfortunately, however, independent certification, to the relatively exacting standards of the FSC, is not well developed in the majority of countries where pressures of illegal logging are strongest, and indeed currently less than one per cent of tropical timber imports to the EU are FSC-certified (FOE, 2001).

Conclusions

There is no doubt that controlling the timber trade is an international responsibility, given that international markets are a major driving force in timber exploitation. At present importing countries benefit from cheap timber from overseas but do not have adequate international mechanisms on which to base import controls. Generally, despite inadequacies, there are better systems in place for the monitoring and reporting of timber exports than imports particularly at species level. It is in the best interests of exporting countries to monitor timber exports and the differential values accrued by different species exported. Exporting countries do, however, need to ensure major improvements in checking the legality of timber exports.

Organizations are at last facing up to the problems of trade in illegal timber but overcoming these is going to be a huge undertaking. Short-term steps which will help include ensuring access to information on the relevant legislation concerning timber harvesting and legislation in exporting countries – information which is notoriously difficult to find; commitment by publicly-accountable timber companies to respect national legislation at all times; increased support for forest management and certification schemes in countries where action is most needed; capacity building in aspects of legal enforcement; bilateral agreements between trading countries and a much more urgent consideration of the role of CITES and other MEAs.

References

Callister, D J (1992) *Illegal Tropical Timber Trade: Asia-Pacific*, TRAFFIC International, Cambridge

Environmental Investigation Agency (EIA) and Telepak Indonesia (2001) *Timber Trafficking. Illegal Logging in Indonesia, South East Asia and International Consumption of Illegally Sourced Timber*, EIA, London and Telepak Indonsia, Bogor

European Commission (1989) The conservation of tropical forests: the role of the Community, *The Official Journal of the European Communities,* 16 October 1989

FOE (2001) *European League Table of Imports of Illegal Tropical Timber,* Friends of the Earth briefing

Oldfield, S (ed) (1991) *Pre-project Study on the Conservation Status of Tropical Timbers in Trade. Report to International Tropical Timber Organization*, World Conservation Monitoring Centre, Cambridge

Reyes, R and Lobos, H (2000) Estado de Conservacion del tipo forestal Alerce (*Fitzroya cupressoides* (Mol.) Johnston): Amenazas y Oportunidades, *Bosque Nativo,* 27 Edición Especial: Conservación del Alerce.

Schmithusen, F (1986) *Forest Legislation in Selected African Countries,* FAO Forestry Paper 65, FAO, Rome

TRAFFIC Network (2001) *CITES Appendix III Implementation for Big-leaved Mahogany* Swietenia macrophylla. Unpublished manuscript

WCMC (1998) *Contribution to an Evaluation of Tree Species Using the New CITES Listing Criteria*, unpublished report compiled on behalf of the CITES Management Authority of the Netherlands, World Conservation Monitoring Centre, Cambridge

Chapter 13

Bushmeat: Traditional Regulation or Adaptation to Market Forces

Evan Bowen-Jones

INTRODUCTION

Bushmeat, or more accurately wild meat, can be defined as wild animal protein that is hunted for human consumption. The current unsustainable levels of trade in this resource in tropical regions are now considered one of the most pressing and insidious conservation problems. This chapter will evaluate the current situation concerning the bushmeat trade and the problems associated with it. It will then consider whether currently proposed solutions are likely to work, addressing whether the agendas of international animal welfare and protectionist groups are justified, and will consider where regulation is most likely to be effective at controlling the trade.

BUSHMEAT AS A CONSERVATION ISSUE

Bushmeat has always been harvested by human beings in the tropics, where attention is currently focused, as well as in other terrestrial ecosystems from the Arctic to the deserts of Australia. The scale of the trade associated with the gathering of non-domesticated meat for human consumption has continued to escalate beyond sustainable levels. Current conservation concern is concentrated on hunting in the tropics since this has some particularly worrying characteristics.

What is the scale of the current trade?

The true level of hunting in most of the tropics is unknown. However, it has been quantified in an approximate way, in both economic and biological terms, for tropical Africa and in a more limited way for the trade in the Americas. In economic terms the Central and West African country-level estimates vary from US$24–205 million per annum. In biological terms, overall estimates of bushmeat harvested in the Congo Basin are between three and five million tonnes per annum (Wilkie and Carpenter, 1999; Fa and Peres, 2001). At least 3.5 million animals per year are known to be taken from the Amazon (Bennett and Robinson, 2000). For tropical Asia, the scale of the trade appears to be less well known.

Implications for biodiversity

Tropical ecosystems are some of the most biologically diverse and complex in the world. They are priority areas for conserving global biological diversity – a goal that most nations have formally accepted through the Convention on Biological Diversity (CBD). Unlike most temperate areas tropical ecosystems typically support a high number of large vertebrate species at low densities. Indeed, tropical forests have intrinsically low rates of animal production because the majority of available food for herbivores is in the canopy and much of this vegetation contains chemical defences to protect it against browsers.

Because of the high variety and low density of animal species, bushmeat hunting in the tropics tends to be for many species and to be highly opportunistic. People catch what they can when they can. The range of species taken is, therefore, vast and includes anything from snails to reptiles and amphibians, birds and mammals.

Bushmeat species include common agricultural pests like grasscutter rats, which breed fast and need to be controlled. Other game species such as smaller forest antelopes thrive in secondary forest, and may be able to sustain quite high levels of hunting.

Rare, globally threatened, and protected species make up a small percentage of the total trade, because they are encountered less often, but this level of off-take is enough to be a real problem. For example, great apes generally make up less than one per cent of the trade in West and Central Africa but this is still unsustainable for these species (Bowen-Jones and Pendry, 1999) and could ultimately lead to global extinctions.

Although, it may be difficult to drive a naturally rare and elusive forest species to total extinction, it may well be possible to reduce its population to the stage where it is no longer viable. Combined with habitat fragmentation or conversion and ever-increasing pressure from fast-growing, demanding human populations the potential for the extinction of large numbers of vertebrate species in the tropics through bushmeat consumption is very real. The resultant loss of biodiversity through secondary extinctions in other plant and animal groups could have wider implications.

The recent confirmed loss of Miss Waldron's colobus (Oates et al, 2000) sparked some debate on whether the cause was purely hunting or hunting in combination with other resource pressures such as deforestation. Overkill, and habitat destruction and fragmentation are two of Jared Diamond's *Evil Quartet* (Diamond, 1989) leading to modern extinctions. In most of the tropics there is also the impact of introduced species, and there are likely to be chains of extinction. When one or more of these factors act together the likelihood of extinction is much greater. Therefore, regulation must be aimed at controlling bushmeat hunting within the broader context of other environmental problems if it is to succeed in preventing species losses.

SOCIO-ECONOMIC CHARACTERISTICS OF THE TRADE

The following characterization of the bushmeat trade is based on work in West and Central Africa (Bowen-Jones et al, 2001) but is used here to describe the trade throughout the tropics. Due to the variability in terms of biological, social and economic drivers, occurring between geographical regions, it is difficult to avoid some over-simplification. However, it is apparent that the trade generally is a large, but often invisible, contributor to the economies of the regions in which it occurs.

The level of trade appears to be increasing universally even though it is already considered to be biologically unsustainable at various local levels. Even relatively low rates of off-take through hunting for subsistence use, using traditional low impact technologies such as nets, bows and arrows and log-fall traps, may be locally unsustainable. Hunting has typically become more efficient with the increasing use of modern technology such as wire snares and guns.

The bushmeat trade has significant impacts on the rural poor, providing both an affordable source of animal protein and income-generating opportunities. Income is provided both for men who are usually hunters, often hunting opportunistically as time permits between other activities, and women who are often bushmeat traders. The supply of bushmeat is part of a complex commodity chain, linking rural hunters to urban and rural consumers.

As a source of protein, bushmeat is particularly important in rural areas since smoked meat is often the only method of maintaining a protein store, and hence there are real food security implications to the trade. At the consumer end, bushmeat is often a favoured food item preferable to domestic animal meat. With this demand driving increased hunting, the line between subsistence hunting and hunting for profit is becoming increasingly blurred.

Commercial hunting is certainly becoming more prevalent. This ranges from farmers selling extra meat that is surplus to immediate requirements in order to buy and trade other foodstuffs, tobacco or alcohol; to professional full-time hunting as a business that supplies dedicated bushmeat markets in growing urban centres.

Finally, there is an important connection with the logging industry, and other extractive industries, that either facilitate or encourage the trade through allowing access to, or attracting people into, more remote forest areas. This is part of a social pattern that sees tropical forest areas as centres of immigration for colonists, as populations in the developing world increase rapidly.

Thus, through access, population growth, technology and demand overall hunting pressure is increasing. So, what of the institutions, laws and policies, that are being used to regulate the trade?

Policies and institutions

Historically, the laws and institutions that govern hunting in Africa, South America and certain areas of South-East Asia were established by the respective colonial authorities, whether French, English, German or Hispanic. These laws were, by and large, put in place to prevent native inhabitants exploiting wildlife resources while conserving the stocks for aesthetic or sporting reasons for the colonists. Consequently, the legislation had little popular support, with most indigenous groups either ignoring the laws or being unaware of their existence. The same type of situation occurred in Britain where the Norman edict, which allowed only noblemen to hunt deer in the royal forests, was subject to wide-scale poaching.

Generally current policies, laws, and supporting institutions in equatorial countries exhibit characteristics that do not encourage sustainability for the bushmeat trade. The policy and legal framework covers several major issues that need to be addressed in order to promote solutions to over-hunting: land ownership, land use policy including forest concession allocation, and protected areas are some of the most critical and relevant in terms of regulation. Species-specific regulation is clearly important for species which are over-exploited but this is not considered in detail here.

Land ownership

The existing structure of land ownership in the tropics does not generally favour the sustainable management of the bushmeat trade. In the tropics:

- There are few areas where tenurial rights have been given to forest-dwelling and dependent human populations.
- There is therefore little incentive for these people to favour long-term resource management over short-term economic gain.
- There is also little incentive to dissuade outsiders from using their local resources.

Forest concession policy

Given the link between bushmeat supply and the logging industry the mechanisms for regulating hunting within concessions are of importance. Licences for timber extraction are often given out on a short-term basis. In

Southern Belize, for example, a firm may be given the rights to an area for three to five years and further licences are then granted to different companies within the same concession straight afterwards (Bowen-Jones and Pop, 2001). Alternatively, licences may be given out for small parcels within larger concessions, such as in Cameroon where permit areas may cover 2500 hectares or less (Auzel and Hardin, 2001). In these cases the economic drivers favour a company to take as much timber out of an area as possible, in as short a time as possible, while spending as little money as possible. Bringing large numbers of cheap labourers into an area, without access to food supplies, and allowing them to hunt using the logging roads and vehicles makes perfect economic sense.

The implementation of policies and regulations for sustainable forest management in many parts of the tropics is notoriously weak. The reasons for this are complex and are essentially economic and political rather than technical. Economic factors include a lack of investment in forestry, debt servicing and the global demand for cheap timber. There is little policing of timber harvesting in many countries let alone policing of secondary bushmeat extraction, and generally few national resources are available for enforcement of hunting regulations.

Protected areas

With less and less habitat available, protected areas such as national parks and reserves are important as landscape units where larger animals can survive. Consequently they have also become important areas of supply for the growing bushmeat trade. Many protected area managers regard illegal poaching for food as one of their most serious problems. For surrounding communities there is often little understanding of the rationale for such reserves. Regulations usually prevent people hunting within these areas and are seen as unfair. Since the capacity of the management authorities involved is usually insufficient to enforce these regulations they are routinely flouted. With other breaches of regulation the term 'paper parks' has been coined because these protected areas are not achieving on-the-ground species or habitat conservation.

Most of the time in-country authorities have overlooked non-traditional protected area management schemes that allow local stakeholders to access game stocks in a controlled manner. This has happened even when those authorities have questioned the rationale behind existing, high maintenance and failing reserves. The potential of protected areas as sources of food, with attendant revenue generation, has not been considered as an alternative rationale for maintaining those protected areas. Often the only perceived values to set-aside areas of habitat are through direct resource exploitation, particularly timber and mining. Therefore, legal frameworks favouring rational use of non-timber forest products such as bushmeat have not been developed.

In summary existing policies and institutions are inadequate, underused and inappropriate to promote a controlled off-take to supply the trade in bushmeat.

SEARCHING FOR SOLUTIONS

Ethics or science?

To some minds, the current bushmeat debate has been hijacked by those who focus on the ethical issues of whether or not it is right to eat our closest relatives – the great apes. Indeed, in some quarters the bushmeat issue could be argued to hinge upon such ethical quandaries. However, the situation is not as clear cut as it is made out to be by campaigning organizations. Given the relatively small proportion of primate meat as a component of the bushmeat trade, the ethical considerations relating to these species can be considered peripheral to the real debate about continued use of a vast range of species to sustain an ever-growing human populace. At worst the narrow focus may risk alienating people with whom constructive dialogue is needed in order to try and mitigate this complex issue with pragmatic conservation solutions.

It is not possible to generalize about the cultural preferences of forest-dwelling communities. Traditionally communities have held a wide range of viewpoints from having taboos against eating chimpanzees, gorillas and orangutans because they 'look too human' to eating apes whenever they could kill them.

It is alarmist to paint a picture of the bushmeat trade based solely upon gory images of dead gorillas and such images do not represent the true nature of the situation. Although these species can be used as 'flagships' for wider conservation, successful conservation depends on the cooperation of local people. One mechanism that can work in more stable areas, is the use of apes as living revenue generators through tourism – as proven by the International Gorilla Conservation Programme. In this instance African armies have been deployed to protect the mountain gorillas because their importance has been recognized nationally through the demonstration of their worth by practical, innovative conservation measures.

Cultural diversity

One of the problems with simplistic campaigning approaches to the bushmeat trade is that they ignore the reasons that people hunt in the first place, whether this is for subsistence, for profit, or for cultural reasons.

This is not to say that priority for hunting should automatically be given when a group claims cultural rights over conservation legislation. However, the recognition that deep cultural conviction often exists, and that this is as much a modern phenomenon in relatively 'advanced' situations as well as for indigenous peoples, is important in determining what strategies are most appropriate. One example of this is in Trinidad where a pop song released in 2001 had a chorus that stated '*wild meat, is the only meat we eat*'.

It is interesting to note that the trend for bushmeat is not confined to the developing world either. A 1997 *Boston Phoenix* article relates how farmed animals including lion, cheetah, musk ox and black bear are on the menu at an up-and-coming restaurant chain with branches in Boston, Johannesburg and Frankfurt. This may be written off as an establishment appealing to the novelty factor, rather than deep-held cultural preference, but perhaps it indicates that caution should be exercised when defining differences between developing and developed-world tastes.

The deep cultural attachment to bushmeat, and the resultant profits to be made from its trade, explain why international laws are broken to import meat from one country into another. Bushmeat is now available in many European capitals, and is regularly brought in inside airline hand-luggage. Any in-country enforcement approaches which do not address these cultural issues are doomed to failure because they will be seen as being imposed by 'outsiders'.

Promotion of indigenous hunting rights?

Those campaigning to halt the 'bushmeat crisis' also say that the livelihood of indigenous peoples is being threatened by the increase in commercialized trade in bushmeat. This is undoubtedly true, but the logic then becomes more questionable from a conservation point of view, as they follow by suggesting that one should permit hunting by indigenous people and not allow hunting by non-indigenous people.

This ignores the fact that there are very few indigenous communities that hunt purely for the pot. The concept of the 'ecologically noble savage' is being widely questioned as it is established that this form of subsistence hunting is often locally unsustainable due to the use of non-traditional technology, such as the transfer from using relatively inefficient nets, or bows and arrows to rifles capable of bringing down larger prey at greater distances.

Once more over-simplification seems to be the order of the day, and there are few instances where 'native' peoples can be simply left to do what they are doing in the hope that they will still be more 'in harmony with nature' than other peoples. Regulation needs to be applied in these cases too, the art is going to be in instituting mechanisms that favour indigenous tenure over colonists while promoting lower impact hunting from both groups.

A conservation problem not a livelihood one

Some argue that bushmeat issues should be viewed purely in terms of conservation, with no livelihood aspect, and that discussing bushmeat in the context of development confuses the policy analysis. In some ways the purist lobby may be correct. After all, the highest trade value estimates for bushmeat in West and Central Africa are from Ghana, a country that has already depleted its larger fauna through a combination of habitat loss and hunting. Here this large trade (which may prove to be on an economic par with agriculture) seems to be based on smaller mammals such as cane rats and porcupines to which both consumers and hunters have switched. Thus, the livelihood dimension is still present and many of the conservation priority species have been lost.

However, we are not learning the lessons of the past century if we don't respond to the current livelihood importance of the trade in other areas where larger animals persist. Conservation has evolved from a protectionist agenda based upon highly restricted use for the minority, to looking at ways to allow use by the local communities who will eventually determine the success of conservation.

In taking this step forwards and thinking in terms of use we have entered a new age of regulation and accept that success requires demonstrable links between conservation and benefit for those most directly dependent on wildlife. Surely we have to recognize the human complexity of this issue and find realistic mechanisms to regulate the trade.

Enforcement of existing legislation

One of the most often cited arguments is that to control the bushmeat trade in the tropics all that is necessary is to enforce existing regulations. Legislation is not, however, the full answer since regulations are not widely respected, or enforced in an equitable manner or, in many cases, understood by the groups that they target. This indicates that there are deeper problems to be addressed. It is not just a question of the availability of money for enforcement, it is also whether existing legislation is appropriate to deal with the scale of the modern bushmeat phenomenon.

The argument tends to be extended to protected areas on the basis that there need to be large areas free from hunting. This is going to have to be part of an overall strategy to regulate bushmeat hunting. However, the way that this is promoted and the mechanisms that are used to allow resource allocation within them do not fit with a protectionist agenda. Many of the countries involved are economically poor at all levels. Non-transparent governmental systems tend to siphon-off available money through bureaucracy at one level, and poverty is a strong force encouraging people to break laws controlling resource exploitation at the local level. Generally governments cannot afford to pay for effective ranger controls. Protectionism in the biodiverse 'South' has generally failed to date. There needs to be more forward thinking about the context in which protected areas and species controls are likely to function.

Regulation of the Bushmeat Trade

The level of the trade, the fact that bans are usually unenforceable and that so many people are reliant on bushmeat for income and protein leaves us with one option. The aim has to be towards engineering a sustainable trade in bushmeat, with exception for globally endangered species, which operates internationally, regionally, and within the countries involved.

What do we mean by sustainable? Most recent definitions of sustainability recognize ecological, social and economic criteria, and ultimately we should be talking about trying to meet all of them.

Discussions about the merging of social, environmental and economic interests which are becoming more common in other sectors, should also be applied to conservation. More astute businesses worldwide are beginning to accept that they have a social responsibility, which extends beyond their shareholders' pockets. On the other hand the conservation sector is beginning to realize that a purely protectionist agenda is often unrealistic, unworkable, and morally suspect as it sometimes denies people access to resources that in the 'West' are taken for granted.

Achieving truly sustainable use at a purely biological level is, as many critics point out, extremely difficult. Furthermore parallels with the fishing industry where there is a greater level of information available on stock levels, but which also deals with multi-species catches are not encouraging. However, modern thinking on fisheries – often not yet applied – advocates an approach with zero-off-take zones, specific conservation measures for declining stocks, temporal restrictions based on breeding and appropriate use of technology. This is the kind of multi-stranded solution that needs to be applied to the bushmeat trade, suggesting a landscape-level planning approach within which appropriate regulation can be couched.

Where could such regulation be applied?

In identifying potential solutions perhaps we should be trying to engineer landscape conservation within which non-traditional protected areas are tied to long-term sustainable funding sources that allow integrated, realistic community conservation initiatives based on natural resource use. Biodiversity conservation by local communities is not a panacea – its success being ultimately reliant on human nature – neither is traditional protected area management. Other management units for conservation of bushmeat stocks outside protected areas will have to provide physical linkages between reserves for the whole system to be viable.

In-country government regulations

Conventional regulation in the country where bushmeat is being harvested is to some extent still the preferred option so long as this is accompanied by an improvement of out-of-date impractical legislation, such as blanket bans on snaring which are generally ignored. However, enforcement of such laws usually requires a large outlay of capital, which simply does not exist or is required for other more pressing and usually humanitarian concerns.

However, if the points at which interventions are attempted are selected with sufficient care and there is enough understanding of the importance of effective enforcement, regulation can be put in place. Recent examples of this include the application of new wildlife laws in Sarawak where one is now only allowed to consume bushmeat caught for personal use. This is designed to eliminate the potential for supply to urban markets while maintaining the right for true subsistence hunting. Although, the long-term sustainability of this scheme cannot yet be assessed, early indications are that there has been a considerable reduction in the bushmeat trade.

More recently, the government of Gabon has instituted a ban on bushmeat consumption following a series of fatalities from ebola outbreaks thought to have originated from eating primate carcasses. In reality this is unlikely to have much impact in the rural areas where people are by and large unaware of health risks, and all too aware of the health benefits of having a reliable source of cheap protein.

Clearly there cannot continue to be an unregulated free-for-all as far as the current hunting situation in most tropical countries goes. There needs to be the right balance of strict reserves, and multiple-use areas enabling species conservation through sustainable use. This will still be expensive to implement and the adoption of such a strategy is dependent on governments realizing the economic significance of the current trade and its long-term financial and food security potential. This is the one way in which the needs of conservation and people can be met and that financially sustainable mechanisms which meet biological sustainability criteria can be instituted in inaccessible areas.

At the demand side, appropriate taxation on market-stall holders in urban centres carried out by a centralized agency that deals with income from bushmeat (and therefore gains national revenue from this lucrative trade) could be combined with non-regulatory awareness-related measures to control the sales of this product without driving it underground. Generation of taxes could also fund enforcement of the revised legislation that was being applied.

Of course, the prerequisite for such systems is that corruption is minimized, and since much of the development work required to institute such complex systems will be funded through international donors, the burden of responsibility of ensuring that such pitfalls are avoided lies with the international community.

Regulation and logging companies

Wherever one stands within the logging debate it is clear that with the amount of land devoted to timber concessions there is a need to get the industry to deliver on conservation outside the protected areas systems. Voluntary certification schemes such as that of the Forest Stewardship Council (FSC) have been developed partially to address this need. Large logging companies that may wish to get involved in controlling the bushmeat trade have the potential to offer a real mechanism for landscape level conservation initiatives. Some of the concessions involved are millions of hectares in size, and bigger than most national parks. They also have the potential, if managed in a sustainable manner, to generate income for the countries involved over the medium and long term. Formal international forestry mechanisms have not yet found a way to harness this potential, but we should not give up.

Constructive dialogue with sympathetic elements of the timber trade is required. A pilot project looking at what can be done is being established by Congolaise Industrielle des Bois (CIB) and the Wildlife Conservation Society (WCS). WCS are providing technical expertise to evaluate the level of off-take and potential regulatory mechanisms within CIB's concessions. This project has unfortunately attracted considerable hostile criticism. Some consider it is wrong for an NGO to be paying (through a grant) for something CIB should be doing themselves while others point out that they would not be happy if WCS accepted the company's money because their neutrality would be called into question. Given the potential for conservation gain, however, there has to be a role for innovative partnerships between the timber industry and conservation NGOs.

Self-regulation by the timber industry with technical assistance has considerable potential. Ideally this should become a matter of course. Many logging companies are legally based in countries where forestry regulations are quite stringent. In such cases these companies could, in theory, be subject to simpler and more effective regulation than other sectors because of their countries of origin. The EU, for example, should consider mandatory guidelines on bushmeat for European companies operating overseas. In reality, however, companies from the Far East are now dominant in the global tropical timber trade – and such companies are not noted for their environmental conscience.

The knock-on effects of sustainable forestry could be that governments in developing countries, in dialogue with bilateral donors, might start to see the potential for sustained income generation and other social benefits from non-wood forest products (NWFPs) such as bushmeat. If this led to longer contracts on concessions this could favour companies operating under good-practice guidelines. Ultimately, it might spark changes to in-country governmental regulation of concession allocation.

Regulation and local communities

A similar model of community self-regulation with external technical assistance is being built through experience of wildlife management for food production in South America (Bodmer and Puertas, 2000). Quotas and non-hunting areas are components of this scheme. In order to make sure that the biological reasoning, for example, in establishing bag-limits is sound, outside biologists assist with monitoring game populations. Therefore, to sustain this type of initiative there has to be long-term funding from external agencies aimed at capacity building and training. An important element of this type of system is internal community regulation based upon existing social hierarchies, or appropriate systems of authority.

Some of these systems can be instituted without tenurial rights being granted to the community in question but as previously explained, in order to promote sustainable wildlife management the question of land ownership has to be addressed. This is where changes of national legislation need to be pursued in combination with technical assistance to assist with community resource management. The danger of instituting land ownership without this support is that the following usage patterns will be biased towards short-term natural resource exploitation.

Regulation of trade within regions and in relation to CITES

The international trade in bushmeat is very minor in comparison with the enormous internal national markets for meat. However, there are areas where international trade is likely to be more significant than others. There is an established cross-border trade in West Africa for example. One case is the trade in Liberian bushmeat exported to the Côte d'Ivoire. Anecdotal evidence suggests that bushmeat supplies have run low in Côte d'Ivoire and that demand is now being met from the larger, richer forests of Liberia. There is also evidence for significant international trade in South-East Asia in endangered species. The forests of Laos, Burma and Cambodia may be providing this meat for consumption and in the past Vietnam was the Mecca for Asian businessmen looking for exotic aphrodisiac meats including sun bear, langur monkeys and clouded leopard. This trade caused a great deal of negative publicity for Vietnam and there has apparently been a tightening of internal laws, which has led to (at least a temporary) closing down of some restaurants. Consequentially, some of this trade seems to have moved to other countries in the region. This illustrates that the best way to deal with cross-border trade within regions is by dealing with underlying causes and looking at the internal markets across the whole of the region.

Recognizing cross-border movements in the bushmeat trade, CITES established a Bushmeat Working Group at the 11th Conference of the Parties. The working group is focusing on West and Central Africa, and is considering what needs to be done within the member countries. One of the successes of CITES in this case has been to gain acceptance from the member states involved of the significance of the bushmeat problem. The baseline information was present to make this clear, as included in the UK government working paper presented to the 11th Conference of the Parties. It is hoped that a similar approach based on sound information is developed for other tropical regions.

The current CITES mandate with regard to the bushmeat issue is to promote awareness and action to achieve better and sustainable management of the bushmeat trade. Therefore, in this instance we are not talking about regulation per se but about the institution of management systems aimed at sustainable exploitation.

Regulation of trade between regions

A more traditional role that CITES can play is in the prevention of shipments of meat of listed species going from one continent to another. Recent incidents, for example, suggest a growing trade in meat from Africa to ethnic minority communities emanating from that region and now living in Western Europe.

In order to address this trade, relevant officials need to be able to identify meat of CITES-listed species from non-listed commoner species. The technology to make this possible is being developed as new DNA sampling kits are being produced for field use. This is the only way that some of the animal carcasses will become identifiable, given that much of the imported meat is smoked, and this in turn is dependent on having a sufficiently comprehensive bank of species-specific genetic reference material. With sufficient political will-power producing sufficient funds these could be made available to enforcement officials. This is clearly something that many in the 'West' would identify as a real priority and a mechanism that should be put in place to enforce existing commitments to CITES throughout the EU.

This is particularly important given that there is considerable risk of repeating the UK epidemic of foot-and-mouth disease by importing infected meat. Indeed, a recent seizure of meat coming into the UK from West Africa included monkey carcasses. Primates in the region have been shown to carry several simian viruses, and can carry communicable diseases including ebola. These diseases are potentially transmissible during food preparation, or directly from consumption (since prions in particular are notoriously resistant to temperature changes including cooking and freezing). Given the suspected origin of HIV, from eating primates, the potential for such diseases to be passed on from consumers to others, and the current focus on emerging viruses, this is something we can ill afford to ignore. Perhaps this is where CITES together with improved customs and environmental health enforcement can really make a difference.

Conclusion

The scale of the trade in bushmeat and its cultural significance suggest that pure protectionism cannot be an effective response. There are, however, emerging alternatives. Governmental regulation and policy have the potential to limit the supply of bushmeat to within sustainable levels through appropriately designed protected areas, linked to well-managed logging concessions and community hunting reserves. Internal markets can be regulated to control demand and in the long term urban consumer attitudes could be changed. Coupled with international controls on the movement of protected species between and within regions there is then the potential to control the bushmeat trade and make it sustainable by adapting to market forces.

Integrated policy approaches are needed to tackle the over-exploitation of bushmeat, building on the traditional species conservation laws and protected area management. Elements of bushmeat policy need to be integrated into overall conservation and development strategies by incorporating the issue into overall local, national and international planning. Discussions within the FAO, CBD and CITES might assist in promoting such initiatives. Successful implementation of both policy and regulation will require the recognition that bushmeat has different but important functions for different sectors of society worldwide.

References

Auzel, P and Hardin, R (2001) Colonial history, concessionary politics and collaborative management of equatorial African rainforests, in Bakarr, M I, da Fonseca, G A B, Mittermeier, R, Rylands, A B and Painemilla, K W (eds) *Hunting and Bushmeat Utilization in the African Rainforest*, Centre for Applied Biodiversity Conservation, Washington DC

Bennett, E L and Robinson, J G (2000) Hunting for the Snark, in Robinson, J G and Bennett, E L (eds) *Hunting for Sustainability in Tropical Forests*, Columbia University Press, New York

Bodmer, R E and Puertas, P E (2000) Community-based comanagement of wildlife in the Peruvian Amazon, in Robinson, J G and Bennett, E L (eds) *Hunting for Sustainability in Tropical Forests*, Columbia University Press, New York

Bowen-Jones, E, Brown, D and Robinson, E (2001) *Bushmeat: A pilot study. Draft Report Including Feasibility and Prioritisation of Current and Further-Required Research Activities and Potential Solutions*, produced for DEFRA Wildlife and Countryside Directorate, UK

Bowen-Jones, E and Pendry, S (1999) The threat to primates and other mammals from the bushmeat trade in Africa, and how this threat could be diminished, *Oryx*, 33(3), pp233–247

Bowen-Jones, E and Pop, J (2001) *Biodiversity Assessment of the Golden Stream Corridor Preserve*, Fauna & Flora International, Cambridge

Diamond, J M (1989) The present, past and future of human caused extinction, *Philos Trans Soc B*, vol 325, pp469–478

Fa, J E and Peres, C A (2001) Game vertebrate extraction in African and Neotropical forests: an Intercontinental comparison, in Reynolds, J D, Mace, G M, Redford, K H and Robinson, J G (eds) *Conservation of Exploited Species*, Cambridge University Press, Cambridge

Oates, J F, Abedi-Lartey, M, McGraw, W S, Struhsaker, T T and Whitesides, G H (2000) Extinction of a west African red colobus monkey, *Conservation Biology*, 14, pp1526—1532

Wilkie, D S and Carpenter, J F (1999) Bushmeat hunting in the Congo Basin: An assessment of impacts and options for mitigation, *Biodiversity and Conservation*, 8(7), pp927–955

Chapter 14

The Impact of the Proposal to List Devil's Claw on Appendix II of CITES

Cyril Lombard and Pierre du Plessis

Introduction

In late 1999 Germany proposed that the Southern African medicinal herb devil's claw be listed on Appendix II of CITES. Range states (Namibia, Botswana and South Africa) opposed the listing, which was consequently withdrawn to allow further research. Despite range-state opposition and NGO protest, the CITES proposal had immediate and measurable short-term impacts (some of which are likely to have medium- or long-term effects). This chapter examines such impacts on trade volumes, rural incomes, research commitments, perceptions of commercial risk and efforts to replace wild-harvesting with commercial cultivation.

Background

Devil's claw is a common name (derived from the hard spiny fruits) for two related species of Pedaliaceae, *Harpagophytum procumbens* and *Harpagophytum zeyherii*, which are endemic to the Kalahari sands and surrounding areas of Southern Africa. Both species are prostrate perennial vines with central taproots and radial secondary tubers. These secondary tubers are dug out, sliced, dried and exported as a phyto-medicinal raw material.

Devil's claw's medicinal properties include anti-inflammatory and analgesic effects. Its use as a natural remedy for arthritis and related ailments is well documented (Wegener, 2000) and in this market segment it has, importantly, few side-effects compared to synthetic alternatives. *Harpagophytum procumbens* is the preferred species, listed in the European *Pharmacopoeia* and internationally traded for more than 40 years. A substantial but unknown quantity of *Harpagophytum zeyherii* – which contains similar biologically active ingredients, but in lower concentrations and different ratios – also enters the trade. The principal markets are currently in the EU, with increasing interest in the US and Asia.

The harvesting, slicing, drying and primary selling of devil's claw provide incomes for rural people from some of Southern Africa's poorest and most marginalized communities. The devil's claw industry was established exclusively on the basis of wild-harvested material supplied by these people (Cole and du Plessis, 2001; Wynberg, 2002).

The Namibian Context

Namibia is presently by far the largest supplier of devil's claw to international markets, followed by Botswana and then South Africa. For illustrative purposes the approximate annual volume in trade is:

- Namibia more than 600 tonnes (see Figure 14.1);
- Botswana less than 75 tonnes;
- South Africa less than 50 tonnes. (South Africa exports more than this, but much is procured from Namibian and Botswana operators with poor market contacts and agreements, and is re-exported.)

Industry views are that the 2002 season will see exports of at least 600 tonnes and possibly over 700 tonnes of devil's claw from Namibia.

Estimates of the number of harvesters in Namibia and Botswana range from 9000 to 15,000. Assuming 10,000 Namibian harvesters and an annual production of 600 tonnes, each harvester supplies an average of 60 kg, which at N$8 (US$0.8)/kg gives an average income per harvester of N$480 (US$48)/annum. To put this sum in context a rural household of eight people in Namibia's Omaheke Region can survive for three months on N$480 (US$48). Under such extreme conditions of poverty, where most households rely for their daily sustenance on government food aid and old-age pensions (N$250 (US$25)/month, typically shared between ten people) it is hard to over-emphasize the role of the devil's claw trade. This sector of Namibian society has very few, if any, other cash-income opportunities.

From an industry perspective, assuming a (reasonable) average free on board (FoB) value of N$22 (US$2.2)/kg for exports, 600 tonnes exported yearly generates some N$13,200,000 (US$1,320,000) in foreign exchange for the Namibian economy. This will probably be more in 2002, due to sharp exchange rate declines in late 2001. Subject to environmental sustainability, Namibian stakeholders in the industry would obviously like to see trade increase

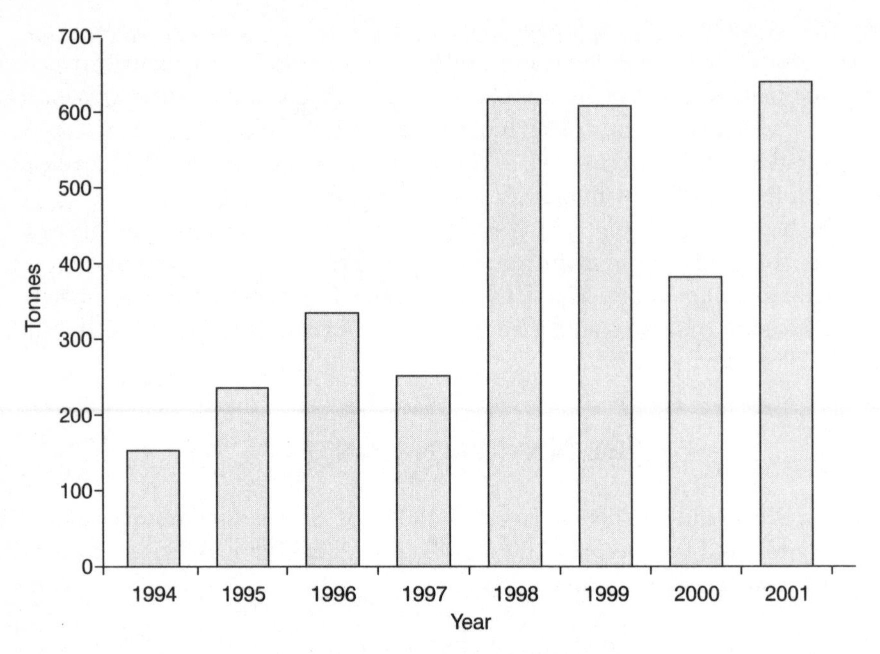

Source: Ministry of Environment and Tourism – export permit records

Figure 14.1 *Exports of Devil's Claw from Namibia*

significantly, partly through new export markets and, if possible, through value-adding operations established in the country. Realizing these hopes and expectations requires investment in markets, product development and new processing capacity, all of which demand that industry and investors are confident about Namibia's ability to supply raw material sustainably and reliably.

Namibian stakeholders acknowledge that it is sometimes necessary to domesticate and cultivate medicinal plants previously secured from wild-harvested systems, but they are nonetheless concerned about the potential implications for rural harvesters who could not take up cultivation opportunities. The vast majority of existing harvesters live and operate under conditions unsuitable for all but the simplest forms of cultivation. The main concern is that large-scale cultivation on commercial farms could replace wild-harvested sources as the preferred supply source of industry, thereby eliminating a crucial cash-income opportunity for marginalized producers. Namibian stakeholders generally agree on the need to research and develop simple cultivation methods suitable for uptake by at least some sectors of the existing wild-harvesting fraternity, but are constrained by a lack of capacity at various levels. There is a sense of a 'race against time' in this respect, not only to develop low-technology cultivation methods, but also to secure niche markets for the wild-harvested product that will assure continued participation in the industry by traditional harvesters, no matter what developments unfold around commercial cultivation.

Namibian stakeholders are generally committed to the sustainable use of devil's claw – including the implications for national resource management responsibilities. *Harpagophytum* species are protected in Namibia under Schedule 9 of the Nature Conservation Ordinance of 1975. Initially this required permits for collection, transport, possession and export of the species. After a review in 1986 had indicated that the implementation of this policy was ineffective, Namibian authorities abandoned all but the requirement to obtain export permits. This allowed continued monitoring of the level of trade. In response to a significant and sustained increase in exports from 1997 to 1999, the permit system has been reviewed and overhauled. Harvesting permits have been reintroduced and are only issued to individuals or registered groups for specific harvesting areas with the written consent of the landowner. Traders are now compelled to keep detailed records of transactions, including permit numbers of the sellers from whom they buy their supplies. Trading records are cross-checked before export permits are issued.

Proposal to List *Harpagophytum* Species on Appendix II of CITES

The increased trade in devil's claw between 1997 and 1998 caused concern in various national and international quarters. In 1999 Cologne University carried out a study, funded by the German government, on the exploitation, trade and population status of devil's claw in Southern Africa.

At the end of 1999 Germany proposed that *Harpagophytum* species be listed on Appendix II of CITES. Namibia and other Southern African range states did not support the listing, citing inadequate range-state consultation, lack of data, ongoing national efforts to regulate resource use, and the unpredictable effects on the livelihoods of extremely poor harvesters. The proposal was later withdrawn, partly as a result of protests by NGOs.

In the terms of a CITES resolution adopted at the 11th Conference of Parties (CoP11) in Nairobi in March 2000, Namibia and other range states that are exporters of devil's claw are required 'to submit to the Secretariat all available information concerning the trade, management, regulatory measures and biological status of *Harpagophytum* species'. This information is to be submitted before the next CoP, towards the end of 2002.

Impacts of the CITES Proposal

Exports and rural incomes

Figure 14.1 clearly suggests that the CITES proposal at the end of 1999 led to a dramatic drop (of some 230 tonnes) in exports in 2000. Using the estimated average prices above, this could be argued to have:

- cost Namibia some N$5,000,000 in foreign exchange;
- led to some 3,500 fewer harvesters earning an average of N$480 (US$48) in 2000; or
- 10,000 harvesters earned on average some N$168 (US$16.8) less in 2000 than in 1998, 1999 and 2001.

Research commitments and perceptions of commercial risk

The following are but a few examples of comments made to the authors during late 1999, 2000 and 2001 by companies and individuals involved in the trade in devil's claw, or researching the possibility of developing products based on *Harpagophytum* species:

- 'We've just heard that devil's claw is actually a threatened species and that supply will be a problem.'
- 'I've just heard that devil's claw is going on to the red list of plants.'
- 'We have looked at the possibility of products from devil's claw but we're worried about the CITES issue.'

In numerous conversations with research and development departments it became clear that the CITES proposal had – in the minds of the decision-makers – presented an additional barrier to product development and investment. It is important to understand that it was not the scientific facts behind the proposal (which were scanty) that scared off investors, but the perception that any CITES proposal – even one based purely on precautionary principles – automatically implies a problem with the conservation status of the resource, and therefore an additional and serious commercial risk.

Industry sources report that even large botanical raw material traders stockpiled devil's claw ahead of CoP11 – 'just in case'. These companies routinely deal with CITES-listed plants and should, presumably, be aware of the subtle distinctions between Appendix I, II and III listings. The same cannot be assumed about the general public in consuming countries, who have their perception of CITES shaped by the mass media that prefer to concentrate on the photogenic wildlife aspects of the convention. For many of these people, to mention any resource in the same breath as CITES equates that resource with elephants and whales, and therefore makes it off-limits to ethical consumers. In the case of devil's claw it is likely that the damage will be compounded by the fact that a significant proportion of its potential consumers – that is, people who prefer natural remedies – are also deeply concerned about wider conservation issues. Seen in the light of this public perception, the industry perception outlined above may seem justified.

Accelerated drive towards cultivation

During 1999, 2000 and 2001 several domestication and cultivation proposals were presented to various funding forums. These usually made reference to the 'endangered' status of devil's claw as part of their justification.

In 1999 a major purchaser of devil's claw is said to have had contracts with three farmers to develop cultivated supplies. In 2001 this company is said to have had seven such contracts. In other expressions of the same nervousness about wild supplies, some formulators of retail preparations have started making (sometimes spurious) claims about the 'sustainably harvested' or 'cultivated' devil's claw in their products.

In an article promoting devil's claw as an alternative crop for commercial farmers, the South African *Farmer's Weekly* (11 August, 2000) misrepresented the CITES proposal thus:

> *A motion* to ban the international trade *in harvested wild Devil's Claw put forward at the … CITES conference in Nairobi in April was withdrawn … temporarily* – on condition that agricultural production supersedes the harvesting of wild Devil's Claw by … 2004 (emphasis added).

While there is probably nothing that Namibia or anyone else can or should do to stop South African researchers, farmers and entrepreneurs from developing a cultivated devil's claw industry, it is unfortunate that repercussions on the livelihoods of rural people in Namibia and Botswana cannot be taken into account. This is particularly the case when international development agencies are involved. There are inherent contradictions in international development and cooperation policy in that this research has been funded by the US Agency for International Development (USAID) and Deutsche Gesellschaft für Technische Zusammenarbeit (GTZ) – large international development agencies also active in Namibia and Botswana. It would be desirable to consider not only the impact of devil's claw cultivation on the livelihoods of marginalized people, but also how the benefits of research work can be shared with the regional owners of indigenous knowledge, and what levels of agrotechnology would be suitable to agroecological conditions in all range states.

Comments and Observations

It can be clearly stated that, under Namibian circumstances, the proposal to list *Harpagophytum* species on Appendix II of CITES has not proved helpful in encouraging sustainable use. At the regional devil's claw conference held in February 2002 in Windhoek, Namibia, delegates included in their common statement the following regarding CITES and devil's claw:

- listing and trade controls are only acceptable where they contribute to sustainable development; and

- CITES should promote awareness that listing does not mean that trade is unsustainable.

Clearly, in the public eye CITES is most commonly associated with endangered fauna, despite the fact that many more plants are listed than animals. In Southern Africa the intentions of CITES are widely distrusted because of its ban on ivory trade, which deprives range states with stable and burgeoning elephant populations from a sustainable source of income – ivory sales from legal culling – that could be used for conservation.

Because negative impressions are easily created and hard to counteract, the prevailing consumer and industry perceptions of CITES can make it a dangerous and risky tool for those working with resources such as devil's claw, especially under such complex socio-economic factors as prevail in Namibia and Botswana.

This 'image problem' appears to be a serious challenge to CITES, at least in certain countries. The convention needs to find creative ways to adapt itself to an era increasingly focused on sustainable use of natural resources under community management, rather than appearing to remain fixated on policing – an emphasis from which it originated.

References

Cole, D and du Plessis, P (2001) *Namibian Devil's Claw (Harpagophytum spp.) – A Case Study on Benefit-Sharing Arrangements,* prepared for the Ministry of Environment and Tourism, Directorate of Environmental Affairs

Nott, K (1986) *A Survey of the Harvesting and Export of* Harpagophytum procumbens *and* Harpagophytum zeyheri *in SWA / Namibia,* Etosha Ecological Institute

Wegener, T (2000) *Devil's Claw: From African Traditional Remedy to Modern Analgesic and Antiinflammatory,* HerbalGram no 50

Wynberg, R (2002) *Devil's Claw Case Study*, Prepared for the Rainforest Alliance – Sustainable Botanicals Project

Chapter 15

The Need for a Better Understanding of Context when Applying CITES Regulations: The Case of an Indonesian Parrot – Tanimbar Corella

Paul Jepson

INTRODUCTION

CITES is one response to the social value which maintains that human use of nature carries with it a moral responsibility to ensure the survival of threatened life forms. The fact that 158 countries have signed CITES is testimony to the international appeal of this value. In line with the growth of scientific rationalism, conservation policy has sought to accommodate the recognition that scientific knowledge concerning the utility value of species and the consequences of species extinction lag far behind the rate of human-induced environmental change. In the case of CITES, this is evident in the adoption of the 'precautionary principle' (Resolution Conf 9.2) and along with it the requirement that range states make a 'non-detriment finding' employing scientific methodologies before setting catch quotas for species entering international trade.

Wildlife trade regulations that set a requirement for biological data on aspects such as population size and demography make sense but, to have effect, such regulations need to take into account the wider conservation context within which they are applied. The present case study illustrates how good intentions can go astray if local context is ignored. Local context enables an assessment of the relevance and meaning of scientific data and method, and thereby provides a guide to how CITES regulations should be interpreted and applied. The importance of understanding the context was illuminated following the

Appendix I listing of an Indonesia parrot, the Tanimbar corella *Cacatua goffini* in 1992. In this short personal account, I describe some of the consequences and impacts of this listing to the conservation programme that I was managing at the time. My hope is that this story will, in some small way, better equip wildlife trade professionals to apply CITES regulations to species or regions that are little known in the West.

THE CASE OF TANIMBAR CORELLA

The Tanimbar corella *Cacatua goffini* is endemic to the Tanimbar Islands of south-east Maluku, Indonesia. These islands exhibit high levels of bird endemism and form part of the Banda Sea Islands Endemic Bird Area (ICBP, 1992; Stattersfield et al, 1998). Tanimbar corella was listed as threatened in 1989 (Collar and Andrew, 1989). This was on the basis of its limited geographical range and the level of international trade in the species recorded by CITES member countries. Based on the above threat categorization and evidence that recorded imports exceeded the quantities reported as exported by Indonesia, the US, a major importer of the parrots, proposed the species for transfer from Appendix II to Appendix I of CITES at the eighth Conference of the Parties in Tokyo, March 1992. The US proposal lacked population data, while the Indonesian delegation presented reports from field staff of the Directorate General of Forest Protection and Nature Conservation (PHPA) that the species was still plentiful and that flocks of Tanimbar corella raided maize crops. Nonetheless the parties resolved to put Tanimbar corella on Appendix I.

Following the CITES Appendix I listing, the newly established PHPA-BirdLife International Indonesia programme conducted field surveys to ascertain key aspects of the management context of the species. The surveys, undertaken in 1993, aimed to determine the status of the wild populations of Tanimbar corella on Yamdena the largest island in the Tanimbar group. The distribution and activity of the human population was also considered together with the interaction between Tanimbar corella and agriculture and the structure of the local commodity-chain for wild-caught parrots.

The survey of the parrot populations was based on a mapping exercise to determine the areas of major habitat types, selection of transects to represent these and a parrot population census using a point count distance sampling technique. The results showed that the parrot species was widely distributed and present at relatively high densities across Yamdena. As a result of the preliminary findings (Cahyadin et al, 1994) the species was removed from the revised list of globally threatened bird species (Collar et al, 1994).

The work by PHPA-BirdLife International Indonesia programme also demonstrated that catching of parrots was limited to agricultural areas and to certain times of the year. The catching was of birds raiding crops and probably involved mainly immature and non-reproductive birds. The survey results suggest that the harvesting of Tanimbar corella for the ten-year period from 1982 to 1992 was sustainable at an annual harvest of several thousand. The income derived from the sale of this species, estimated at between US$37,500–65,000, was significant on an island where other sources of cash income are limited to a few jobs in government offices, logging and the sale of copra. The average household income for the Maluku Tenggara regency, of which Yamdena is part, was under US$250 per annum in the late 1980s and is not thought to have risen significantly since (Jepson et al, 2001).

Following the 1993 survey work, PHPA took a down-listing proposal to the ninth Conference of the Parties held in Fort Lauderdale in 1994 but were forced to withdraw this in the face of strong NGO opposition. Influential bodies such as IUCN, WWF and TRAFFIC recommended rejection on the basis that the PHPA-BirdLife population data were suspect. Sceptics variously argued that:

1. prior circulation of three different population estimates showed the data to be unreliable;
2. observers may have double-counted birds;
3. the survey team may have counted a group of captive corellas released as a result of an initiative of a British-based parrot charity (see below); and
4. that down-listing proposals should demonstrate a population trend, which requires surveys at least five years apart.

Points 1 to 3 were a misrepresentation of the facts and point 4 a 'moving of the goal posts'. The three different populations were the result of the fast-moving nature of distance sampling at this time, in particular the release of DISTANCE 2 software and the recommendation (Buckland et al, 1993) that aerial bird contacts should be excluded from analysis. Protocol to minimize this risk of double-counting were employed in the 1993 Tanimbar surveys and the corella release site was about 30 km from the nearest forest sampled.

Those involved directly in the PHPA-BirdLife surveys formed two interpretations concerning the motivations behind the rejection of the down-listing proposal and the undermining of PHPA-BirdLife Indonesia field surveys. Firstly, CITES-related bodies were frustrated at Indonesia's poor progress at meeting its obligations under the treaty and many were canvassing support for a trade ban. Trade bans are highly political and the CITES standing committee needs evidence of persistent infractions to enact such a ban. CITES I listing of Tanimbar corella constituted evidence of an infraction. New data questioning the basis of this listing was unwelcome, especially as it brought into question the reliability of the threat categorizations for other Indonesian parrots. Secondly, several NGOs, particularly those with an animal welfare emphasis, portray the listing of a species on Appendix I as a conservation gain and organizational achievement to their public constituencies. Having to report back to supporters that they got it wrong would be awkward, not least because this would raise questions about their 'expert' status.

The 1992 CITES export ban and rejection of the 1994 down-listing proposal created perceptions with unforeseen, yet important implications, for the conservation and management of parrots at the local and national level in Indonesia. The Fort Lauderdale meeting in April coincided with the March catching season for corellas on Yamdena. At this time thousands of birds were already in the chain of traders comprising local buyers in Yamdena selling to traders in Ambon who, in turn, sold on to exporters in Jakarta. Payment was on the basis of numbers of birds received in good health by the trader at the next step up the trade chain. When the Appendix I listing decision was taken, exporters cancelled their orders leaving local traders with stock which they had paid for but had no market. At the time there were reports of 1000 corellas languishing in Bali and 500 birds on Yamdena.

Public interest surrounding the 1992 CITES conference led 'The Cook Report', a popular UK investigative journalism TV show, to feature the wildlife trade and the cause of the Tanimbar corella. As part of their show, they enlisted a British-based parrot charity to run a public appeal to buy and release 500 captive corellas from a local bird trader (Reynolds, 1992; World Parrot Trust, 1993). This idea came as a godsend to the local corella trader. Eager to recoup his investment he sold on this 'contract to buy' to a powerful Chinese business family in Samulaki, the capital of south Yamdena. At the request of PHPA, an evaluation of the proposal to release these birds was conducted in November 1992. The family concerned was interviewed and their holding facility visited. The family was angry because the payment for the birds had not come through as promised. Moreover they explained the motivations for the releases in terms consistent with the Chinese and Buddhist practice of releasing birds to gain good karma. Release was recommended against, mainly because the birds were housed on a chicken farm which created a risk of introducing diseases into wild populations (Jepson & Soewoko, 1993). In a final effort to prompt payment, the Chinese family secured a permit from the regent of South Yamdena to release the surviving 319 birds in February 1993. The fate of other corellas 'stuck' in the Indonesian trade chain is unclear. Some were sold on to the domestic market in Java where sellers tried to pass them off as young sulphur-crested cockatoos *Cacatua sulphurea* that had not yet grown their crest. Others probably perished or were released when traders could no longer afford to house and feed them.

The trade ban and release incident created a mistrust of conservationists and a misunderstanding of their purpose on Yamdena. The culture and economy of Maluku is based on the centuries-old trade of spices, birds and other natural resources to Europe. Difficulties of communication mean that verbal contracts and established trade chains are afforded high importance. The reason for suspending the trade in the parrots and reneging on verbal contracts was, at the time, largely beyond the comprehension of the people of Yamdena, most of whom view the Tanimbar corella as an abundant and unattractive bird. This mistrust extended to the provincial forestry department in Maluku. As a result of the trade ban and activist campaigns against logging, the department became highly suspicious of NGO activities on Yamdena, which they perceived as politically motivated and concerned with spreading misinformation. This situation compromised BirdLife plans to pursue a larger conservation goal, namely the establishment of a major ecosystem reserve on Yamdena (see Jepson, 1995). Under the Suharto new order regime, government trust concerning the intentions of NGOs was crucial to the process of protected area establishment. Because this was lacking with respect to Yamdena, the focus of BirdLife's activity was reorientated away from South Maluku in favour of North Maluku (the islands of Halmahera and Buru). More generally, the events described above created an image of parrot conservation as a thankless conservation activity that runs the risk of embroiling an agency and individuals in organizational politics. As a result, the original idea that assisting PHPA to meet its obligations under CITES should be a central theme of the PHPA-BirdLife Indonesia Programme was down-played, and instead parrot surveys were included in integrated packages of assessments related to reserve designation.

Ironically, the fact that the BirdLife Indonesia Programme, as much as the PHPA, bore the brunt of vitriolic criticism concerning the survey findings, generated a new level of trust among the small community of Indonesian bureaucrats, scientists and traders who decided wildlife trade issues. This facilitated some important conservation gains. BirdLife was invited to join the government committee that sets annual trade quotas, thus setting a precedent for NGO participation that has since widened. Through this involvement, trade quotas of parrots have been steadily reduced and PHPA has taken up-listing proposals to CITES rather than these being imposed from outside. A relevant example is the red and blue lory *Eos histrio*, which Indonesia successfully proposed for inclusion on Appendix I in 1996.

Conclusions

The findings of the PHPA-BirdLife surveys indicate that the Tanimbar corella did not meet the criteria for inclusion on CITES Appendix 1 and that the export ban for the species was unnecessary. This case study describes how the regulatory action had unplanned impacts, namely:

1 reorientation of a conservation programme away from the range of the species whose conservation status the regulation was intend to assist;
2 creation of local distrust of conservationists and confusion over aims and purpose;
3 undermining the 'expert' status and credibility of certain individuals, organizations, and conservation threat classifications;
4 embroiling a British-based parrot charity in an issue and location where it lacked expertise;

5 causing suffering to corellas in the trade chain and selling the species on the domestic market where no demand existed previously; and
6 inclusion of NGOs on the quota-setting committee of the Indonesian CITES scientific committee.

A prior assessment of management context would have helped to avoid the negative impacts. Indeed the one positive impact (6) came about because the BirdLife programme, which resulted from an understanding of the way local context shaped our use and interpretations of science, demonstrated professional integrity in the eyes of the Indonesian wildlife-trade community.

In conclusion, one lesson we can draw from the Tanimbar corella issue, is the need for activists and professionals working under the CITES umbrella to give greater emphasis to the implications of management context. The resource management philosophy of Aldo Leopold (1933) proposes that a management initiative should be considered on at least two levels: first as a cell and then as a cell in context. A management cell can be conceived of as a species or action, for example, a regulatory act. Adopting a contextualist approach would encourage deeper understandings of the cultural, social and political aspects of CITES implementation as they relate to place. This would help clarify the role of science in CITES and give voice to other perspectives on how to deliver and internationalize the social values that the convention embodies. While this would increase complexity and require a more flexible and nuanced approach to CITES implementation, I believe it would promote public support for CITES in developing tropical countries and thereby the effectiveness of the convention.

REFERENCES

Buckland, S T, Anderson, D R, Burnham, K P and Laake, J L (1993) *Distance Sampling: Estimatimg abundance of biological populations*, Chapman and Hall, London

Cahyadin, Y, Jepson, P and Manoppo, B I (1994) *The Status of* Cacatua goffini *and* Eos reticulata *on the Tanimbar Islands*, PHPA-BirdLife International Indonesia Programme, Bogor

Collar, N J and Andrew, P (1989) *Birds to Watch: The world list of threatened birds,* International Council for Bird Preservation, Cambridge

Collar, N J, Crosby, M J and Stattersfield, A J (1994) *Birds to Watch II: The world list of threatened birds,* BirdLife International, Cambridge

ICBP (1992) *Putting Biodiversity on the Map: Priority areas for global conservation*, International Council for Bird Preservation, Cambridge

Jepson, P (1995) *Summary Report of an Evaluation of Boundaries for a Protected Area in the Tanimbar Islands, South-east Maluku*, Technical Memorandum no 1, PHPA/BirdLife International – Indonesia Programme, Bogor

Jepson, P, Brickle, N and Chayadin, Y (2001) The conservation status of Tanimbar corella and blue-streaked lory on the Tanimbar Islands, Indonesia: results of a rapid contextual survey, *Oryx,* 35 (3), pp224–233

Jepson, P and Soewoko, S (1993) *An Evaluation of the Conservation Merit of Returning 500 Captive Goffin's Cockatoos* Cacatua goffini *to the Wild on Pulua Yamdena, Tanimbar Maluku,* PHPA/BirdLife International Indonesia Programme, Bogor

Leopold, A (1933) *Game Management*, Chales Scribner's Sons, New York and London

Reynolds, M (1992) Emergency in Indonesia. World Parrot Trust seeks to achieve release of 535 Goffin's cockatoos, *Psittascene*, vol 4, pp1–2

Stattersfield, A J, Crosby, MJ, Long, AJ and Wedge, DC (1998) *Endemic Bird Areas of the World: Priorities for biodiversity conservation*, BirdLife International, Cambridge

World Parrot Trust (1993) A world first in wildlife conservation. Trust secures the release of captive Goffin's cockatoos on Tanimbar, Indonesia, *Psittascene*, vol 5, p1

Part 4

Lessons from Illegal Trade in Other Goods

Chapter 16

Lessons from the Control of the Illegal Trade in Ozone-depleting Substances, Timber and Fisheries

Duncan Brack

Introduction

Over the last three decades the protection of the natural environment has climbed steadily up the ladder of public and governmental concern. Countries have adopted laws and taxes, and established policy, regulatory and enforcement institutions to deal with the problems of pollution, resource depletion and destruction of biodiversity.

At the international level, almost 250 multilateral environmental agreements (MEAs) now exist, and several more are currently under negotiation or have been agreed but are yet to enter into force. All of them place specific or general obligations upon their signatory countries, and many of them establish particular bodies to deal with their implementation and enforcement. A number of international institutions deal with environmental protection, including most notably the United Nations Environment Programme (UNEP).

Needless to say, the more extensive is the framework of national and international legislation, the more opportunities there are to evade it. Deliberate evasion of environmental laws and regulations by individuals and companies in the pursuit of personal financial benefit can be termed 'environmental crime'. Where these activities involve movements across national boundaries, or impacts upon the world as a whole, they can be termed 'international environmental crime' (UNEP, 1999)

TYPES OF ENVIRONMENTAL CRIME

The most commonly known examples of this type of criminal activity fall under four major categories.

Biodiversity

In the area of biodiversity, illegal trade in endangered species of wild flora and fauna and their products – evasion of the controls instituted under CITES – is probably the best known instance of international environmental crime, and is considered extensively throughout this book. Other examples include illegal whaling, in breach of the controls instituted by the International Whaling Commission (IWC), and biopiracy – the illegal use of genetic resources or information, for example for development and commercialization as pharmaceutical products, removed from indigenous habitats without permission or licensing. There is also the future possibility of illegal trade in genetically modified products, in breach of the provisions of the 2000 Cartagena Protocol to the Biodiversity Convention (agreed but not yet in force), which establishes a system for regulating such trade.

Natural-resources-related crime

Natural-resources-related crime covers two main areas: illegal fishing and illegal logging. Illegal fishing – for example, banned driftnet catches, or fishing beyond quota – is a relatively recent phenomenon. As 60 per cent of the ocean fisheries are currently being exploited at or beyond their sustainable yield, it is also a matter of growing concern. Illegal logging and trade in timber and timber products is widespread and represents not only a threat to biodiversity (and in some cases a breach of CITES controls), but also a major loss of revenue to many developing economies. These two examples could fit into the category of 'biodiversity-related' crime, but they are slightly different in that each is an example of broader activities that could be legal if restrained to a particular level but are being carried out at an unsustainable level, in breach of various controls and regulations.

Wastes

In the areas of wastes, the illegal movement of hazardous wastes – in breach of the 1989 Basel Convention – is probably the newest area of international environmental crime. Rising standards of waste disposal in many industrialized countries are leading to rising costs and hence a growing incentive for illegal disposal. The illegal disposal of nuclear waste is a closely related topic, regulation being the responsibility of the International Atomic Energy Authority. The dumping of waste oil at sea, in breach of the International Convention for the Prevention of Pollution from Ships at Sea (Marpol), is a matter of concern to many countries with long coastlines.

Banned substances

Environmental crime related to banned substances currently has one example: the illegal production of and trade in ozone-depleting substances (ODS), in breach of the controls required by the 1987 Montreal Protocol on substances that deplete the ozone layer. There are in addition, however, possible future candidates, including evasion of the controls of the 1998 Rotterdam Convention on chemicals and pesticides, and the 2001 Stockholm Convention on persistent organic pollutants (POPs), which have both been agreed but are not yet in force.

THE DRIVERS BEHIND BLACK MARKETS

There are several reasons, or drivers, behind the emergence of international environmental crime and environmental black markets:

1 Differential costs or values: where illegal activities are driven by regulations creating cost differentials between legal and illegal products; by differential compliance costs, or different consumer prices, in different countries; by demand for scarce products for which substitutes are not available or accepted and by a lack of concern for or valuation of the environment. Examples include wildlife, logging, whaling, ODS and wastes.
2 Regulatory failure: where illegal activities result from a lack of appropriate regulation, including failures to determine and/or protect property rights (open access problems). Examples include wildlife, logging, fishing and wastes.
3 Enforcement failure: where illegal activities exist because of problems with enforcement, including suitability of regulation/enforcement methodology and costs of compliance; regulatory capture; lack of resources and infrastructure; political will and/or expertise; corruption; and political and economic disruption. Examples include wildlife, logging, ODS, and wastes.

The reported incidence of illegal environmental activities has undoubtedly grown in recent years, partly because the implementation of new MEAs has provided new opportunities for evasion, and partly because greater public and governmental awareness has led to more investigation into the issues. Other contributory factors include the general trend towards trade liberalization and deregulation, which makes border controls more difficult and the growth of transnational corporations and activities, among whom regulations are often difficult to enforce. Furthermore, the transformation of the Comecon Bloc, with difficulties of environmental law-making and law enforcement, and the rise of organized crime, in such transition economies is an additional factor contributing to the growth of environmental crime. The growing involvement of developing countries in MEAs is obviously a welcome step, but many lack adequate resources to implement their provisions effectively. For all these reasons, it seems very likely that international environmental crime will continue to expand in the coming decades.

The rest of this chapter looks at three of these areas in more depth: illegal trade in ozone-depleting substances, illegal logging and illegal fishing. The chapter ends with some general conclusions about the growth and control of international environmental crime, and suggests some broad recommendations for action.

Illegal Trade in Ozone-depleting Substances

The emergence of illegal trade in ODS is a good example of a problem springing directly from the negotiation and implementation of an international treaty. With hindsight, it could have been foreseen, and if it had been, the agreement would have been written slightly differently (UNEP DTIE, 2001; UNEP Ozone Secretariat, 2002).

The Montreal Protocol on substances that deplete the ozone layer was agreed in 1987. It was designed to eliminate the production and consumption of a family of industrial chemicals, including chlorofluorocarbons (CFCs), which were widely used, because of their cheapness, lack of toxicity and effectiveness, in refrigeration, air conditioning, foam blowing and aerosols. CFCs, along with other ODS, damage the Earth's stratospheric ozone layer, letting through increased amounts of ultraviolet light, with an accompanying impact on human, animal and plant health, such as an increased incidence of skin cancer and eye damage.

The Montreal Protocol has turned out to be one of the most effective – if not the most effective – MEA in existence, with its phase-out schedules being accelerated on no less than five occasions. With a few exceptions, production and consumption of the main categories of ODS came to an end in the industrialized world at the end of 1995, and will do so in developing countries by the end of 2010.

Criminal Activities: Scale, Sources and Methods

One of the remaining threats to the success of the ozone regime, however, has been the emergence, since the mid-1990s, of illegal trade in ODS, primarily in the US and EU, but now also in developing countries. In 1994–1995, CFCs were the second most valuable contraband smuggled through Miami, after cocaine. Precise figures are of course impossible to come by, but government and industry estimates suggest global totals of 16,000–38,000 tonnes in 1995 – the probable peak year. The higher figure is equivalent to 15 per cent of consumption worldwide, worth more than US$0.5 billion. CFC smuggling appears to have declined since then, particularly in the US and probably in the EU, but many developing countries are now experiencing illicit trade as they steadily move towards phase-out.

The incentive for illegal use arises not from the higher cost of the ODS alternatives – they have often proved to be cheaper and more effective than the substances they replaced – but from the cost of adaptation or replacement of the machinery in question, which can be relatively high. Since most refrigeration and air-conditioning equipment has relatively long lifetimes, this implies a continued incentive for illegal use in the short- and medium-term.

There are two main sources of the material. As noted above, developing countries do not have to phase out CFCs until 2010; the main source of the illegal material now entering the EU appears to be China, and for the US, probably China and Mexico. Second, the Russian Federation continued to produce in breach of its commitments after 1995, though Russian production should have ceased by the end of 2000. It is also possible that some substances illegally entering the EU and US may in fact have been legally produced there, exported and then clandestinely reimported. There is little evidence for the involvement of organized crime; possibly the business is too specialized for this to occur.

There are five major methods of illegal trade:

1. Mislabelling of containers (for example, as HFCs or hydrocarbons, or as recycled ODS) and of accompanying documentation (including the use of false customs codes); ODS are colourless, odourless gases at room temperature, and chemical analysis is needed to determine precisely what substances are present.
2. Concealment of material, for example by constructing cylinders with hidden compartments containing illegal material, or, more simply, by concealing cylinders in the midst of legitimate cargo.
3. Disguise: virgin CFCs can be deliberately contaminated, for example with water vapour, to make them appear as recycled material.
4. Diversion of material destined for legal markets in developing countries into domestic markets in non-developing countries, with false documentation. This was a common problem in the US, with Miami an important source as a major trans-shipment port.
5. Diversion of material from legal uses (feedstock and essential use exemptions, for example) into illegal uses. This is probably the least likely of the five routes examined here, particularly for essential use exemptions, where purity requirements imply strict monitoring.

Methods of Control

Reducing demand

Unlike many other instances of international environmental crime, the problem of illegal trade in ODS will, in due course, solve itself, as all ODS-using equipment is eventually replaced by new machinery using replacements. The replacement process can be accelerated by applying use controls in particular sectors, and instituting ODS sales bans, stockpile bans, or import bans (for recycled or virgin material) in industrialized countries. This implies additional costs to industry as equipment is retired before the end of its working life, but is probably the easiest option to implement and enforce.

Reducing supply

Again unlike most other forms of international environmental crime, this method of control is feasible and, indeed, is possibly the most cost-effective option. A special World Bank initiative raised funding to phase out Russian production by the end of 2000. Six developing countries produce CFCs, of which the largest are China (40 per cent) and India (20 per cent); China also accounts for 90 per cent of developing country halon production. So far, production sector phase-out plans have been agreed with China and India, and could possibly be accelerated if more funding was available through the protocol's financial mechanism.

Controlling the illegal trade

Enforcement action directed against the illegal trade in ODS was initially slow to develop. The US was the first to take action, and national inter-agency cooperation (involving the Environmental Protection Agency (EPA), Internal Revenue Service (IRS), Customs Service and Departments of Commerce and Justice), concentrating on tracking imports and licences, and on border checks, has proved effective. The existence of the US excise tax on ODS, designed to accelerate phase-out, provided an additional incentive for illegal trade (tax evasion) but also, importantly, helped spur enforcement action.

EU authorities were slower to react, with customs agencies in general being disinclined to accept, or to investigate, the scale of the problem. The absence of border controls within the EU also acts to undercut individual agencies' efforts. Coordination, mainly through an ad hoc working group of the European Commission (comprising representatives of member states' environment departments and customs agencies, and of industry) has now improved.

At the international scale, the third major amendment to the protocol, agreed in Montreal in 1997, requires parties to the treaty to establish a system of import and export licences for trade in the various categories of ODS. This was introduced primarily to control illegal trade, and with the benefit of hindsight should have been written into the treaty from the beginning. Somewhat belatedly, the parties to the protocol agreed, in late 2000, to commission a study of the options for controlling illegal trade; the conclusions of that study will be considered at the Meeting of the Parties in Rome in November 2002.

ILLEGAL LOGGING

Criminal activities: scale, sources and methods

Of all the different varieties of international environmental crime, illegal logging and the illegal trade in timber and timber products is almost certainly the most economically significant. Some estimates suggest that the illegal timber trade may comprise over a tenth of a global business worth over US$150 billion a year. It seems likely that at least half of all the logging activities in particularly vulnerable regions – the Amazon Basin, Central Africa, South-East Asia and the Russian Federation – is illegal (Brack and Hayman, 2001; Brack et al, 2002).

Illegal logging takes place when timber is harvested, transported, bought or sold in violation of national laws. The harvesting procedure itself may be illegal, including corrupt means to gain access to forests, extraction without permission or from a protected area, cutting of protected species or extraction of timber in excess of agreed limits. Illegalities may also occur during transport, including illegal processing and export, misdeclaration to customs, and avoidance of taxes and other charges.

Illegal logging is not confined to developing countries, but the problems there are much worse, as resources are limited, international companies which offer investment are proportionately more powerful, and civil society is weaker. Allocation of timber concessions has often been used as a mechanism of mobilizing wealth to reward allies and engender patronage. Protected by powerful patrons, timber companies may evade national regulations with relative impunity. State forestry institutions may be subject to regulatory capture, becoming clients of concession-holding industrial interests of the ruling elite, exercising their powers as a form of private property rather than as a public service.

As in other areas, the clandestine nature of the illegal trade makes its scale and value difficult to estimate, but it is true to say that extensive unlawful operations have been uncovered whenever and wherever authorities have tried to find them. As the World Bank's 1999 review of its global forest policy observed:

> *countries with tropical moist forest have continued to log on a massive scale, often illegally and unsustainably. In many countries, illegal logging is similar in size to legal production. In others, it exceeds legal logging by a substantial margin... poor governance, corruption, and political alliances between parts of the private sector and ruling elites combined with minimal enforcement capacity at local and regional levels, all played a part* (World Bank, 1999b).

To give a few examples, a joint UK-Indonesia study of the timber industry in Indonesia in 1998 suggested that about 40 per cent of throughput was illegal, with a value in excess of US$365 million; more recent estimates suggest over 70 per cent of logging in the country is illegal in some way. Similarly, over 80 per cent of logging in the Amazon may not be compliant with government controls. A World Resources Institute comparison of import and export data for Myanmar in 1997 revealed substantial under-declaration, accounting for forgone revenue of US$86 million, equivalent to almost half of official timber export revenues. Studies in Cambodia in 1997 commissioned by the World Bank suggested illegal extraction may be over 4 million cubic metres, at least ten times the size of the legal harvest, worth between US$0.5–1billion (Development Alternatives, Inc, 1998; World Bank, 1999a). If this level of extraction continued, the country would be logged out in just ten years from when the industry officially began.

The scale of illegal logging represents a major loss of revenue to many developing economies and can lead to widespread associated environmental damage; it is also a threat to biodiversity, and in some cases a breach of CITES controls. A senate committee in the Philippines estimated that the country lost as much as US$1.8 billion per year from illegal logging during the 1980s. The substantial revenues from illegal logging sometimes fund and thereby exacerbate national and regional conflict, the strongest recent example being Cambodia, where Khmer Rouge forces were sustained primarily by logging revenues for several years in the mid-1990s.

The illegal trade may also distort the entire global marketplace for a number of key timber products, making it difficult for sustainable management – which has to endure additional costs from good husbandry and proper tax declaration – to survive. As the World Bank reported: 'widespread illegal extraction makes it pointless to invest in improved logging [practices]. This is a classic case of concurrent government and market failure.'

Methods of control

Unlike the case of ozone-depleting substances, there is no global MEA on forestry. An attempt was made to agree one at the Earth Summit in 1992, but most developing countries regarded it as an infringement of their national sovereignty. A series of generally ineffective international bodies has been created to act as a forum for debate; the latest incarnation, the UN Forum on Forests (UNFF), came into being in 2001. This lack of an overall framework for international enforcement means that even the rather poor levels of international action achieved on ODS have not generally been managed on timber.

In the last few years, however, several countries have displayed a growing interest in tackling the issue, and in September 2001, countries from East Asia and other regions participated in a forest law enforcement and governance ministerial conference in Indonesia, an important initiative designed to establish a framework through which producer-country governments could work together with each other and with governments of consumer countries to tackle illegal activities. Further such conferences are planned for other regions with significant forest resources.

Reducing demand

Reducing the demand for illegal logs essentially requires replacing it with a demand for legally produced material – which in turn requires some means of identification all along the 'chain of custody'. No such system yet exists (though there is growing interest in one), though schemes established to identify sustainability of production – such as the Forest Stewardship Council certification scheme – generally imply legality of production as well. There are several international forums under which such a system could be developed, including the UNFF, CITES, International Tropical Timber Organization (ITTO), and the Organisation for Economic Co-operation and Development (OECD) anti-bribery convention, but it may also be possible to introduce them through bilateral agreements between individual producer and consumer nations – an agreement signed in April 2002 between the governments of the UK and Indonesia contains a commitment to do just that. Government procurement policy, which in some countries (including the UK) is increasingly being targeted on sustainably sourced timber, is a potentially important tool.

Reducing supply

Much illegal logging stems from over-allocation of logging concessions and processing licences frequently associated with corruption. Reform of the systems therefore usually requires thorough-going reform of legislation (which is often outdated and inadequate) and of the administrative systems which implement it. The reform of taxation systems, which are currently often volume based, thereby encouraging maximum exploitation of concessions, is also a valuable route to follow.

Controlling the illegal trade

There are a number of points along the chain of production and supply at which enforcement efforts can be aimed. In producer countries, specialized enforcement units – such as the Malaysian task force set up by the police, anti-corruption agency, forestry department and the army – which bypass local bureaucracies have been used with some success. Private industrial surveillance companies can also be used; the Swiss firm Société Générale de Surveillance (SGS), for example, has been called in to monitor customs departments, and increase revenue collection, in a number of countries including Cameroon, Ghana, Indonesia and Malaysia. Close cooperation with local communities is helpful, both because they are good sources of intelligence and because the provision of alternative employment opportunities is usually necessary to end small-scale illegal activity.

In importer countries, as noted, any action by customs and other enforcement agencies depends on the development of a mechanism for detecting illegal products, and, in many countries, new legislation making it illegal for products produced illegally overseas to be imported or put on sale. Greater cooperation between different agencies, and between agencies for different countries, is a prerequisite for success.

ILLEGAL FISHING

Criminal activities: scale, sources and methods

Illegal fishing is a relatively recent phenomenon. As most of the world's major fishing grounds are now facing over-exploitation, it is also a matter of growing concern, both in terms of the threats posed to species survival (including other species caught alongside the fish, such as sea turtles and albatrosses), but also the economic costs of exhaustion of fish stocks. Studies suggest that over two-thirds of global fish stocks are now being exploited at or above their maximum sustainable yield, and a 30–50 per cent reduction in fishing worldwide is required to return fisheries to a sustainable level.

Key global fishing fleets are heavily subsidized – though much less so than in the 1970s and 1980s – so even entirely legal fishing is posing a substantial threat to the survival of fish stocks. However, the problem is significantly exacerbated by various forms of 'illegal, unreported and unregulated (IUU) fishing. In UN terminology, illegal fishing takes place where the fishery is against the law; unreported fishing takes place where legal instruments are in place to control the fishery, but no requirements for reporting, or penalties for non-reporting, exist; and unregulated fishing occurs where legal instruments are not required, not applied, or not adequate.

There is no global estimate of the extent of IUU fishing, but there is evidence from particular fisheries and regions. One of the best known examples is that of the Patagonian toothfish, a large, long-lived and slow-growing deepwater fish increasingly in demand as a replacement for over-exploited whitefish such as cod. Systematic commercial exploitation started only in the late 1980s, but has already exhausted stocks off Argentina and South Africa. In 1996–1997, authorized catches under the Convention on Conservation of Antarctic Marine Living Resources (CCAMLR) amounted to 10,370 tonnes (with an additional 22,386 tonnes in catches in exclusive economic zones), but estimates from port landings and trade data suggested that an additional 42,800 tonnes was caught illegally. The price of the toothfish fell drastically, and illegal fishing in 1997–1998 was estimated to have reached the lower figure of 33,500 tonnes.

Two main types of poaching operation can be identified. The so-called 'Vikings' are mostly Norwegian and Faroese nationals working from relatively new, high technology boats often equipped with modern blast freezers. The majority of these boats operate out of Mauritius, which is not a member of the convention; 15 such vessels, almost all those known, were recorded landing 10,000 tonnes of toothfish at Port Louis at the end of the illegal season in 1997, earning between US$30–35million. In contrast, the so-called 'Spanish Armada' consists of a large number of somewhat older Chilean, Argentinean and Spanish boats. With less capital at risk and fishing in less deep waters, they seem to accept a higher risk of arrest and tend to fish illegally in exclusive economic zones around sub-Antarctic islands. Almost 100 of these longliners have been involved in IUU fishing over the last two years. As convention member states have gradually closed their ports to unlicensed landings, the pirate ships have switched to trans-shipping their haul directly to freighters at sea; the catch is then processed on land, passing in most cases through the Punta Arenas free trade zone in Chile or Montevideo in Uruguay. China and South Korea are more recent landing points.

The example of the Patagonian toothfish demonstrates many of the problems connected with controlling IUU fishing: non-signatory states to the relevant convention; ships flying flags of convenience to escape domestic controls, and the enormous difficulty of tracking illegal activities across a huge area of ocean. These problems have been demonstrated in many other cases. Even in comparatively well-regulated European waters, illegal fishing is rife, created largely by the shrinking quotas (including those set under the EU's Common Fisheries Policy) for commercially valuable human consumption stocks. Misreporting of catches and retention of undersized fish or fish caught over the allowed quotas is common; recent estimates suggest that up to 40 per cent of the total catch of the Scottish fleet, for example, may be illegal. Financial and contractual pressure from retailers (usually supermarket chains) to supply regular quantities of fresh fish often force the processors to buy from the black market, which in turn undercuts legitimate sales.

No single global agreement governs fisheries management. The UN Convention on the Law of the Sea (UNCLOS), which entered into force in 1992, establishes 200-mile exclusive economic zones (EEZs) as the sovereign territory of the coastal nation. This covers some 40 per cent of the world's oceans, including an estimated 95 per cent of the total marine fish catch. Although enforcement of fishing regulations within EEZs is by no means straightforward, it is at least slightly easier than control of IUU fishing on the high seas and among straddling, or migratory, stocks. The 1995 UNCLOS straddling stocks agreement, when it enters into force, will require states to belong to a regional management organization or agreed management arrangement before they can have access to areas where conservation and management efforts are being applied. The FAO compliance agreement, adopted in 1993, will require flag states to keep registers of vessels authorized to fish on the high seas, and to exchange them with other signatories; it also charges parties to assume enforcement responsibilities. Although the agreement is not yet in force, its provisions have already been incorporated into international agreements and decisions of parties to conventions. The FAO is also currently drawing up an IUU plan of action.

A number of important regional fisheries agreements are now in force. In addition to CCAMLR, which specifies quotas for species such as the toothfish, others include the International Convention for the Conservation of Atlantic Tunas (ICCAT), the Convention for the Conservation of Southern Bluefin Tuna, and the Convention on the Prohibition of Fishing with Long Driftnets in the South Pacific. Both CCAMLR and ICCAT have agreed to prohibit landings and trans-shipments of the relevant fish and products from non-parties and non-complying parties, with some effect. CCAMLR has also recently adopted a catch documentation scheme to better regulate activities. But all these agreements must rely on gunboat enforcement by their member states, which is impracticable on a large scale.

Methods of control

Of all the areas of international environmental crime, IUU fishing is probably the most difficult to prevent. Added to the familiar problems of lack of enforcement capability and the difficulties in detection of illegal material (that is, distinguishing it from legally caught fish) there is the problem of detection of the illegal activity in the first place.

Reducing demand

As with illegal logging, reducing the demand for illegally caught fish requires some means of identification of the products along the 'chain of custody'. Again as with timber, no such system yet exists, though the Marine Stewardship Council (MSC), an independent organization established by WWF and Unilever, operates a labelling scheme identifying sustainability of production, which should imply legality as well. Coverage of world fisheries is tiny, but growing. The FAO is reportedly also considering a certification scheme.

Reducing supply

Again as with illegal logging, some of the pressure behind IUU fishing stems from government subsidies for the fishing industry resulting in over-capacity of fishing vessels and equipment. In 1989 total government support for the fishing industry worldwide came to US$92 billion (compared with a total catch value of only US$70 billion). This fell steadily throughout the 1990s, along with the general deregulatory drive in many Western economies, and the collapse of the Soviet economy, previously one of the biggest source of subsidies – down to US$54 billion in 1992 and possibly as low as US$14 billion in 1997. There are obvious political problems involved in reducing subsidies for an industry which is often the main employer in some coastal communities, but further downwards pressure on subsidies would help reduce excessive capacity.

Controlling the illegal trade

Worldwide, nearly 100 million tonnes of fish catches are reported and regulated to some degree. Enforcing regulations over a significant fraction of these operations demands very substantial resources; for example, the total value of UK fish landings is only £550 million annually, and government expenditure on regulation comes to £45 million. Even with this level of spending (and the UK level is relatively high compared to other EU countries), inspections of individual boats are necessarily limited. EU enforcement authorities carried out a total of 20,357 inspections in 1990; given 50,000 fishing vessels, the average chance of inspection was then once every two years. The EU fleet made nearly 2.5 million recorded trips that year, while the number of offences detected was 2393. Inspection is never entirely random and some boats commit more than one offence but, in general, some ten per cent of vessels inspected were found guilty of an infringement. Across the entire fleet, there may be approximately 250,000 infringements per year, or five infringements per boat per year

AREAS FOR ACTION

Serious though all these problems are, they are at least beginning to be addressed. Some effective enforcement has taken place in several countries, including control of the illegal trade in wildlife and wildlife products (the oldest problem), and of smuggling of ODS. These experiences provide useful lessons to be learned for the control of such activities more widely.

G8 summits have, since 1996, called for more effective and better coordinated action to combat international environmental crime. The first meeting of the G8 Nations' Senior Experts Group on Transnational Organised Crime (the Lyon Group) law enforcement project on environmental crime took place in July 1999, aiming to improve information exchange, data analysis and investigative cooperation among law enforcement agencies, regulators and international organizations. Options for the control of illegal logging are being considered under the G8 forestry initiative, due to report in mid-2002. Interpol, the World Customs Organization and UNEP have all begun to work on the issue, and are establishing cooperative frameworks between themselves and MEA secretariats. And the 1990s also saw the creation of the International Network for Environmental Compliance and Enforcement (INECE) and the European Network for the Implementation and Enforcement of Environmental Law (IMPEL); a number of other similar networks of enforcement agencies are also being established.

There are many policy options available for combating international environmental crime in the areas considered here. Rather than list them all, I concentrate on the broad cross-cutting solutions applicable to all, or most, areas.

Reducing demand

ODS crime is the exception here, as the one area in which demand will eventually disappear of its own accord. In all other areas, two factors are necessary if the demand for the illegal products is to be successfully curtailed.

First, there must be some means of identifying illegal material, probably through licensing or certification systems. The growth of certification systems based on sustainability criteria offer one possibility for an identification method for legality of production, though it may be easier in some cases simply to identify legality. This requires effective means both of issuing and verifying the licences or certificates, implying separate systems for administration and monitoring, and also a legal framework which allows material lacking a valid licence to be seized at the border, or when put on sale. This is a particular problem for areas of criminal activity where a global MEA is not in existence (such as fishing or logging), and there may be a case for the negotiation of global agreements on illegal activity (possibly starting at a smaller, regional, scale). There are also possible complications with World Trade Organization (WTO) regulations which could usefully be discussed.

Second, consumers, retailers and importers of the products need to be educated to look for and demand the licence or certificate, and to refuse products which lack it. Often ignored in many discussions of enforcing environmental crime, public awareness campaigns have proved of value in some cases (for example, in enforcement of CITES) and could usefully be extended. Central and local government procurement programmes can also play an important role.

Reducing supply

Strategies aimed to reduce the supply of illegal materials need to concentrate on the underlying economic, social and political drivers behind the illegal activity – and are accordingly difficult and complex to implement. Once again, ODS crime is the 'easy' area, where supply will be phased out in any case under the Montreal Protocol. In other areas, including fishing and logging, policy options include reform of the systems for granting exploitation rights, taxes, subsidies and regulation, and the involvement of local communities and the availability of alternative forms of employment and economic activity.

Controlling the illegal trade

Most discussions of controlling international environmental crime tend to concentrate, not unnaturally, on improving enforcement, and there is indeed a wide range of policy options available. They include:

- Greater cooperation between environment and enforcement agencies at the international, regional and national levels. Intelligence gathering, information exchange, guidance (such as codes of best practice) and training can all be coordinated and delivered effectively at international or regional level. In some cases there may be a need for new legal instruments such as MEAs. At national level there is a strong case for establishing environmental crime units or working parties, as recommended by Interpol, involving all relevant agencies, NGOs, and industry. Some harmonization of relevant legislation (for example, in terms of penalties) would be helpful.
- Enhanced means of tracking and identification of the illegal trade, including more research and effort in collecting data; the development of independent verification of data reported under MEAs; possible extension of the WCO's harmonized system of customs codes; greater investment in tracking mechanisms, identification of country/factory/area of origin, requirements for export and import licences, preshipment inspections and certification systems, for example; the establishment of registers of licensed traders; and the greater use of new technology in tracking movements.
- The allocation of greater resources, in terms of finance and personnel, to tackling the problem. This includes a higher priority for environmental issues within police and customs agencies (which is often about awareness-raising as much as anything else); greater resources devoted to implementing and monitoring MEAs; and financial, technical and capacity-building assistance for developing countries and transition economies. As many cases of environmental crime may involve unpaid taxes or charges, however, investment here can reap financial as well as environmental dividends.

CONCLUSIONS

The growth of environmental crime is a serious side-effect of the development of policies aimed at protecting the environment. Unlike most other kinds of crime, it harms not just individual victims, but society as a whole. International environmental crime potentially damages the global environment.

The total value of the illegal activities involved in international environmental crime may be in the order of US$20–40 billion a year, about five to ten per cent of the size of the global drugs trade. Compared to the 'war on drugs', however, the resources and political will devoted to tackling international environmental crime are derisory – yet the problem threatens every citizen of the world, and undermines several key environmental treaties.

There is no shortage of policy options available for improving the enforcement of environmental regulations and controlling illegal activity. What are still lacking are political will and resources.

References

Brack, D and Hayman, G (2001) *Intergovernmental Actions on Illegal Logging*, Royal Institute of International Affairs; available from www.riia.org

Brack, D, Hayman, G and Gray, K (2002) *Controlling the International Trade in Illegally Logged Timber and Wood Products*, Royal Institute of International Affairs; available from www.riia.org

Development Alternatives, Inc (1998) *Findings and Recommendations of the Log Monitoring and Logging Control Project*, Main Report, submitted to the Royal Government of Cambodia, Ministry of Economy and Finance, Ministry of Agriculture, Forestry and Fisheries, financed by IDA Credit 2664-KH, September, DAI, Bethesda, Maryland

UNEP (1999) *Enforcement of and Compliance with MEAs: The Experiences of CITES, Montreal Protocol and Basel Convention,* vol I, p24, Nairobi

UNEP DTIE (2001) *Illegal Trade in Ozone-Depleting Substances: Is There a Hole in the Montreal Protocol?* OzonAction Newsletter Special Supplement no 6, Paris

UNEP Ozone Secretariat (2002) *Monitoring of International Trade and Prevention of Illegal Trade in Ozone-Depleting Substances,* report to the 2002 meeting of the parties of the Montreal Protocol

World Bank (1999a) *Cambodia: A Vision for Forestry Sector Development*, Background Note for the Cambodia Consultative Group Meeting, 1 February, World Bank, Washington, DC

World Bank (1999b) *Forest Sector Review*, p xii , New York

Chapter 17

The Controlled Trade in Drugs

Dave Lowe

Introduction

This chapter provides a discussion on the implications of a restricted trade against a total ban in drugs from which some parallels may be drawn with the debate on banning and or controlling wildlife trade. The starting point for this chapter seems simple and straightforward; there is an absolute ban on trading drugs throughout the world, supported by commitments to UN charters, international and domestic criminal law. Quite simply, there should be no such thing as the drugs trade. Even where there is toleration of the supply, sale and consumption of illicit drugs, there remains legislation banning it. We know, however, that there are ample supplies of banned and controlled drugs wherever there is a demand.

But what is meant by the term drugs? And what does illicit mean? There is a global business in drugs that is perfectly legitimate – those substances developed to assist and help with the various ailments and conditions suffered by people and animals. Owing to the powerful, sometimes dangerous effects, there is a range of controls on their manufacture and supply. Equally, this legitimate trade is controlled for commercial purposes, supported by copyright and patent laws.

Collectively these restrictions mean that there are various layers of control on the manufacture and supply of drugs throughout the world. Manufacturing quality and content are established and maintained by systems of licensing, supply is restricted through systems of authorized prescription and consumption can be monitored and supervised. Some of these drugs include those that are proscribed by society: morphine and cocaine, are but two obvious examples. So there is indeed a substantial legitimate trade in drugs and we need to examine the relationship between it and the illicit trade.

Problems Associated with the Legitimate Drugs Trade

Like any other commodity, if there is an opportunity to make money then all sorts of people will be attracted to it, including criminals. But with such a scale of business in drugs there are other fundamental influences of politics, ethics and commerce that complicate the dynamics. The overt criminal attacks upon the legitimate trade fall into three broad categories

The counterfeiting of trade drugs

There is a massive trade in counterfeit prescription drugs, because criminals have the ability to make profits. On the socio-economic side, the case is often made that counterfeits are the only way to get drugs to those that need them because of the political and commercial interests controlling the legitimate supply. The counterfeiting of intellectual property rights mirrors this.

The use of supposed consignments to support a fraud

Whenever there is a trading situation, there is the potential for a fraudster to abuse the normal systems of commerce and business. What looks like a contract to trade a commodity is in fact nothing more than a paper trail. A prime example is cigarette and tobacco fraud, particularly popular in eastern Europe but with one case of note in the UK. In 1992 David George Wilson was shot dead at his home in Lancashire. Subsequently an American, Michael David Austin, also known as Colonel Portillo, was convicted of murder. He had set up a huge fraud using the supposed shipment of cigarettes. Wilson was the accountant and was killed because Austin thought that he was going to compromise the operation.

The illegal supply of prescribed drugs

In the main this is associated with alternative uses of prescribed drugs, the best example being steroids, but also with corrupt or misguided licensed pharmacists and dispensers.

So within the legitimate market there are numerous options for criminals to infiltrate and profit. Governments, industry, law enforcement and regulating bodies have responded by establishing a wide range of measures to combat this and they fall into four categories.

1. Targeting offenders. There have been many international investigations directed at clandestine laboratories and dealers in counterfeit drugs.
2. Linking up series of crimes. There are a number of international cooperation forums where information is shared and a better picture of the illegal business formed.

3 Dealing with hotspots. These may be geographical – for example, Eastern Europe, India – or commodity – for example, steroids, temazepan, viagra.
4 Preventive Measures. In addition to the traditional forms of crime prevention, such as target hardening, control and licensing systems, preventive measures include market manipulation, education, legal and financial incentives and sanctions.

The result is that there is a balance between the legitimate business in drugs and the criminality that is inevitably associated with it. While there may be peaks and troughs the weight is heavily biased towards the legitimate, but is only maintained by the pressure of the activities described. The outcome is that a balance between the legitimate business in drugs and the criminal business is reached. For the legal trade to survive the balance is weighted towards it and, through a mixture of the activities described above, a check kept on the illegal trade.

CHARACTERISTICS OF THE ILLICIT DRUGS TRADE

The illicit drugs (or narcotics) trade is separate from the illegal trade in prescription drugs, even though there are some drugs that feature in both. The motivators for the illicit trade are:

- demand;
- ability to produce;
- ability to supply;
- ability to avoid detection and disruption.

Where the drugs are the same, the legal market sources are entirely separate from the illegal because of the requirement for quality control and accountability. No such restraints apply to the criminal market. The whole business is clandestine and subject to its own influences.

The global supply of illicit drugs is centred around the producing countries in South America, Africa, the Middle East and the Far East, with Europe and the US featuring highly on synthetic drugs. The illicit trade is so vast that it heavily influences the macro-politics of countries and regions and has such a corrupting influence that the normal institutions of the state are not able to control or manage the situation. The producing cartels are the dominant factors in the availability of illicit drugs and there is little evidence to show that any action against drugs has anything other than a local impact (despite having had many operational successes). The transportation and supply routes are all intact and so integrated into the normal commercial world that it is virtually impossible to separate them.

The local dealerships that ultimately supply the demand for illicit drugs are still capable of supplying their wares, wherever required and under whatever regime, however restrictive, is in power. That is not to say that nothing can or is being done about illicit drugs. On the contrary, illicit drugs are a minority activity globally and locally and it is in relatively few places that organized drug criminals have effectively infiltrated national and international institutions.

Tackling the Crime

There is a different balance between the criminals and their opponents in the illicit trade than that in the legal trade because fundamentally different factors influence them. It is only by looking at the margins of the two areas that it is possible to identify issues that can assist with the examination of other commodities such as the illegal trafficking of wildlife.

For example, there is a stupefying herbal drug called khat, which is popular in the Somali community. It is not proscribed in the UK, but is in many other parts of the world, especially Canada, where possession is a criminal offence and trafficking attracts a maximum ten-year prison sentence. Consequently, the UK is a major shipment centre for the herb. The point is that any difference in approach to a drug, leading to a difference in legality creates a market opportunity, rather like tariff differences create opportunities for smugglers. There can be no better example of this that the growth of alcohol and tobacco smuggling from France to the UK since the opening of the Channel Tunnel.

The rise in use of steroids has presented a dilemma for society. It is illicit, but with only weak sanction and low priority enforcement. Yet the use is closely connected to nightclubs and the bodybuilding scene, which in turn are intimately linked to the supply of other illicit drugs, especially amphetamine-based substances such as Ecstasy, a Class A proscribed drug and currently a UK government priority. At one point consideration was given to proscribing steroids because of the potential sensitivity around hosting the Commonwealth Games. This would have taken steroids into a completely different law enforcement environment and it would have been interesting to see if that made a difference to the balance between criminal and legal supply.

The point is that whether or not the supply of a commodity is legal, if there is a demand then it will be met and in meeting it a unique set of influencing factors will emerge. In turn these will affect the demand and so a cycle will be established.

Conclusion

Only by careful study and an accurate understanding of the dynamics of the legitimate and illicit business can rational decisions be made to affect it in any particular direction. While it may be perfectly understandable to take an ethical stance, say to ban the trade in certain animal products, if the desired outcome is to sustain a population, the effect that ban may have on the other factors supporting its survival must be considered.

Similarly with drugs, while banning has been shown not to work in terms of stopping the supply, that does not mean that there is no use in banning. It means that to achieve the desired outcome – for example a reduced demand, many more factors have to be understood and taken into account.

Chapter 18

Lessons from the Trade in Illicit Antiquities

Neil Brodie

INTRODUCTION

The trade in illicit antiquities has exploded over the past 40 years. They are torn from standing monuments, secretly dug out from the ground, or stolen from museums. Sites that have a historical, cultural or religious significance are vandalized or destroyed to supply antiquities that are traded around the world before eventually coming to rest in the public and private collections of Europe and North America, and increasingly the Far East. Links have been demonstrated with other illegal activities including drugs trafficking and timber extraction.

The trade is largely underground so that its size, or the damage it causes, cannot easily be quantified. Estimates of its monetary value vary wildly from as little as US$400 million up to US$4 billion per year. More is known about damage caused on the ground. One study in 1982 showed that 58 per cent of all Mayan sites in Belize had been visited by looters (Gutchen, 1983). A regional survey in Mali in 1991 discovered 830 archaeological sites but 45 per cent had already been damaged, 17 per cent badly. In 1996 a sample of 80 were revisited and the incidence of looting had increased by 20 per cent (Bedaux and Rowlands, 2001). In Pakistan's northern Charsadda district nearly half of Buddhist shrines, stupas and monasteries have been badly damaged or destroyed by illegal excavations for saleable antiquities (Ali and Coningham, 1998).

Today, most countries have placed their archaeological heritage under some kind of state control, so that the unlicensed excavation or export of antiquities is illegal. This control may be strong, when the heritage is taken into state ownership, or weak, when private ownership of material is allowed within a country but its export is regulated. These protectionist laws usually grow out of a desire to hold on to what is seen to be a national patrimony.

Archaeologists are more concerned with questions of access and preservation than of ownership, though when working as guests in a foreign country they are bound to respect the (sometimes onerous) rules that govern their activities. Occasionally they conspire to ignore them, or circumvent them, although this happens much less often today than it did in the past. That it doesn't is due in no small part to a reorientation of archaeological aims, away from the recovery of 'works of art' or the identification of historical events, towards what might be called the 'total reconstruction' of past societies and environments. This new research focus places less emphasis on the recovery of individual objects, and requires instead that more attention be paid to context: in effect, where an object is found and what is found with it.

The importance of context was recognized as archaeology came of age in the late 19th and early 20th centuries when the principles of stratigraphic excavation were first worked out, and wide-ranging chronological frameworks were constructed using objects of known age to date other material (of unknown age) which was found in close association. Both of these techniques were dependent upon the existence of discrete and undisturbed strata, or contexts. Since then, the introduction of scientific methods of dating, artefact analysis and environmental (including climatic) reconstruction have elevated the importance of context still further. So today, sites are excavated carefully and a full record is kept of all relationships, both among objects and between objects and their matrices. Indeed, in the expectation that methods of analysis will continue to improve, and given the fact that the archaeological record is a limited resource, there is growing recognition that where possible archaeological sites should be conserved intact for future generations.

Thus the interests of archaeologists and governments are concurrent, but not actually coincident. In theory, any laws which regulate the free flow of archaeological material should constrain the market and help to protect the integrity of archaeological sites. However, this is not a logic to which everybody subscribes. There is a countervailing view that overly strong regulation can deter people from declaring material which is discovered by chance, so that its find-spot and possible context are lost, and any subsequent trade is driven underground, with the criminalization and corruption that this entails. Rather than strong regulation, dealers and collectors, and some archaeologists too, favour the development of what they see to be more lenient and equitable laws, which would protect the most important archaeological finds, while allowing free circulation of the remainder. This would, they suggest, have the added cultural and educational benefits of allowing a large number of people to come into contact with pieces of the past, either as owners or museum visitors.

There is a sense in which these two viewpoints, of archaeologists on the one hand and dealers and collectors on the other, are not so much opposed as incompatible. Members of the trade (understandably) are concerned with individual objects, and will make judgements about their significance which are based on aesthetic or monetary criteria. This is how it is possible for them to talk about important and unimportant pieces. For many archaeologists though the informational value of a piece is dependent upon context and cannot be judged from intrinsic qualities alone. What might appear to be an unimportant or mundane object might actually be highly significant if found in situ: the single coin that dates a site or the small pot that proves a trade contact. It is the integrity of the site that needs to be protected, not the individual objects it contains.

There is also a fundamental disagreement over causality. Proponents of more relaxed regulation adopt the premise that most archaeological objects coming on to the market are chance finds. In other words, they would be found anyway, but in the absence of a market thrown away or destroyed. In effect, the market rescues them. Most archaeologists are not convinced about the predominance of chance finds, although there are obviously some, and believe that the major part of new material has been deliberately looted, and without the market it would still be safely in the ground.

Comparative Perspectives

The dual object of any strategy aimed at combating the trade in illicit antiquities is to take it out of the hands of criminals while at the same time protecting the archaeological resource. To this end, the effects of regulatory solutions on other illegal trades are often used for purposes of comparison. Many archaeologists, for instance, who are generally in favour of regulation, look to what is the perceived success of CITES, while opponents of regulation point to the failure of prohibition to stem the trade in drugs or alcohol. However, it is not at all clear that all comparisons are equally valid, because while all illicit trades might share some broad resemblances, there are also likely to be significant points of difference. For example, there are several similarities between the trade in illicit antiquities and the drugs trade: they are both demand-driven, they are international in scope, and they are both socially harmful. However, these are generic characteristics and are probably also typical of the various trades in endangered species. For a more focused response to an illicit trade it is necessary to go beyond generalities, and identify what might be the unique or defining features of the trade in question. Otherwise there is a danger of adopting inappropriate countermeasures that are expensive and ineffective, and which might even be counterproductive.

One characteristic of the antiquities trade that has attracted attention is that it is neither completely licit, nor completely illicit. Nor are there parallel licit and illicit trades. The trade is, in effect, sequential. Material that at source is illegally excavated or exported is eventually sold openly and legally in the salesrooms and auction houses of Europe and North America. At some point in the trading-chain it is 'laundered' by passage through what Polk (2000) terms a 'portal', which facilitates entry on to the legitimate market. A portal is a jurisdiction that allows free trade of material and supplies documentation that will legitimize exports for import into a third country. Hong Kong and to a lesser extent Taiwan play this role for China; Brussels and Paris for West Africa, and Switzerland for Italy. Provenances can easily be lost or invented when an object passes through a portal, and information about illicit origins is suppressed. It is this peculiarity of the antiquities trade which led to the adoption of the rather loose term 'illicit antiquity' to describe an antiquity whose first means of acquisition was illicit, whatever its subsequent status in law. Thus the trade in illicit antiquities is different from, and much larger than, the illicit trade in antiquities. It is a nice distinction, but unfortunately one that has no legal basis.

This division of the trade into two discrete spheres, legal on the demand side but with a largely illegal supply, is matched by its geographical and economic polarity. Ultimate demand is located in the rich G7 countries, while supply is concentrated in poorer countries, the so-called source countries. There are some exceptions: archaeological sites in the US and UK are open to plunder, and Italy takes an ambiguous place in the ranks of the source countries, but the generalization remains broadly true. It has some unfortunate consequences. The social costs associated with the trade, which can briefly be summarized as loss or destruction of cultural heritage (which might also in the long term be an economic resource) and the socially harmful behaviour associated with criminal activity or the disbursement and laundering of criminal proceeds, are also concentrated on the supply side. The benefits accrue on the demand side. Museums fill up with material for public edification and there is a legal economic gain derived from sales and from increased employment in museums and the market. This marked imbalance between costs and benefits finds its reflection in regulation. The source countries that bear most of the costs have strong protectionist legislation, while the laws of beneficiary countries facilitate free trade.

A second but related point is that demand is socially circumscribed, or it was until very recently. Antiquities collecting has traditionally been a rich person's pastime. Part of the allure is that an antiquities collection allows easy entry into the gala world of museum receptions and gallery tours. The investment opportunities that antiquities present have not been overlooked either. However, the advent on the Internet of virtual auctions has reinforced a drive down-market that was already apparent with the development of mail-order sales and the move out of specialist salesrooms into department stores. Nevertheless, it remains the case the market receives its impetus from the big collectors and museums.

The move down-market has a bearing on the evolving debate over regulation. Internet and mail-order sales are obvious marketing strategies aimed at enlarging the demand base, and particularly at creating a demand for poorer quality antiquities that in the past would have been discarded. Antiquities are now as likely to be sold as ornaments as works of art. This suggests that although the trade is demand led, demand can be manufactured to fit supply. In other words, if supply increases, the trade becomes more commercialized, and new markets are created. Thus while it can be claimed that the logical counterpart of strong regulation is criminalization, it seems equally true that the corollary of weak regulation is commercialization.

A third distinguishing feature of the antiquities trade is that its commodity is non-renewable. Archaeological sites are a finite resource so that, in the long term, there can be no strategy of legal but sustainable exploitation.

Finally, for the wealthy collector, all antiquities are not alike. There will always be a demand for the exceptional or unique that will not be assuaged by lesser pieces. The collector George Ortiz has called his illustrated catalogue *In Pursuit of the Absolute: Art of the Ancient World* (Ortiz, 1996). Presumably, the absolute is unattainable and the pursuit will never end. If regulation was relaxed around the world, allowing a freer flow of what dealers call less important material, it seems probable that there would still be an illegal market for objects of high monetary value.

Thus, to recap, there are at least four characteristics of the antiquities trade which serve to distinguish it from other illicit trades, and which must be borne in mind when discussing regulation:

1 The importance of portals for laundering illicit material.
2 Demand is geographically and socially circumscribed.
3 The archaeological resource is limited and not renewable.
4 There will always be a demand for the unique piece.

Points 3 and 4 imply that any effort to eradicate illicit trade by the legitimate exploitation of archaeological sites for saleable antiquities will fail both in the short and long term. Point 2 has most relevance for the present discussion. It suggests that any efforts made to combat the trade in illicit antiquities should be aimed at reducing demand, which is relatively accessible and limited in size. The implications of this run through the discussion of regulation that follows.

Export Controls

It is possible to distinguish between two types of export control: total embargo (complete prohibition of export) and screening (whereby the most important pieces are retained but anything else is allowed out). From an archaeological perspective, for reasons already described, it is difficult to subscribe to the object-centred rationale of a screening system, and in any case it can be argued that it doesn't work (Brodie, 2002). However, most source countries have passed laws which embargo export, and so the question that generates most controversy is: Does an export embargo on a broadly-defined category of archaeological material actually prevent its export and thus protect archaeological sites? Unfortunately there is little hard information which can offer a definitive answer to this question.

One revealing set of statistics has been released by the Czech Republic (although the statistics are not strictly archaeological as they pertain to works of art and other objects stolen from religious and cultural institutions). During the 1980s the incidence of theft was at a relatively low level, but then rose dramatically in 1990, followed by a decline which levelled off in the later part of the decade and has perhaps gone into reverse (Figure 18.1). However, pre-1990-levels have not been regained, despite the passage of new, protectionist, laws in 1987 and 1994. The 1990 rise was directly attributable to the opening of borders which followed the fall of the communist regime, although exacerbated by the fact that guardianship of religious and historic buildings had been run down since 1948, and it was only in 1994 that the Czech government was able to establish and fund a new project of protection (Jirásek, 2000).

The Czech statistics show that export regulation is effective, provided it is properly enforced. However, the Czech example is an extreme case, and would probably find few advocates, illustrating as it does the social costs that such enforcement entails. The control was maintained by an authoritarian regime imposing unacceptable restrictions upon personal freedom. Reports from other authoritarian regimes – China and Iraq – that individuals have been executed for illegally excavating archaeological sites sound like 'news from the asylum'.

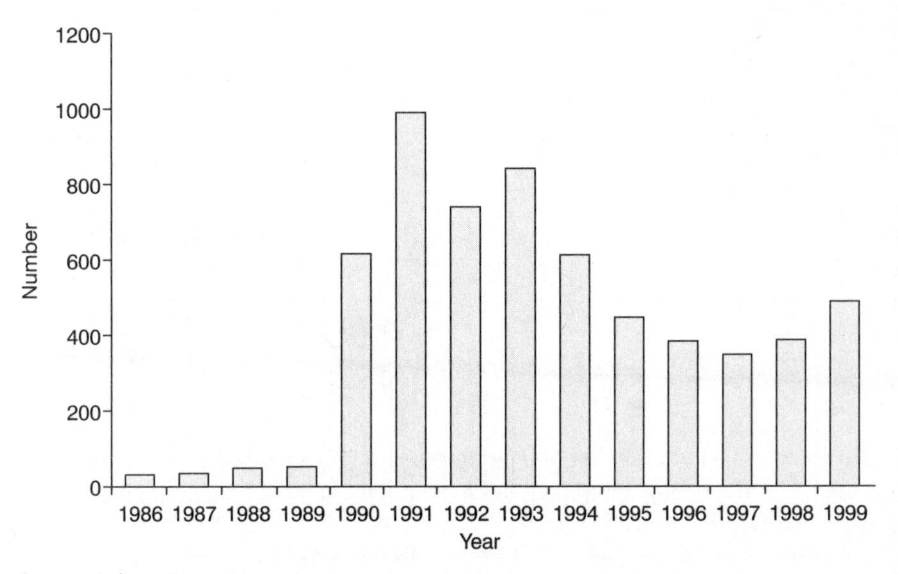

Source: Jirásek, 2000

Figure 18.1 *Registered Thefts from Cultural Institutions and Churches in the Czech Republic (1986–1999)*

An appreciation of the effectiveness of export control in a more liberal country can be pieced together from what is known about Apulian vases. These vases were of Greek inspiration and made during the 4th century BC in what is today the south Italian district of Puglia. They are to be found in all major collections of ancient Greek art and at auction regularly command prices in the region of US$10,000–30,000 each. They comprise an unusual corpus of material in that they have been extensively catalogued (so that any previously unknown piece which arrives on the market must be of questionable origin) and their looting and trade have been investigated by academic research and journalistic exposé.

During the 1980s and early-1990s, large numbers of Apulian vases were offered for sale at Sotheby's auction house in London (Elia, 2001; Figure 18.2). A major part was consigned for sale by a Geneva-based dealer (B), who was shown to be acting as a front for an Italian dealer (M), who bought the vases directly from tomb-robbers in Puglia (Watson, 1997). The tombs (often dug out

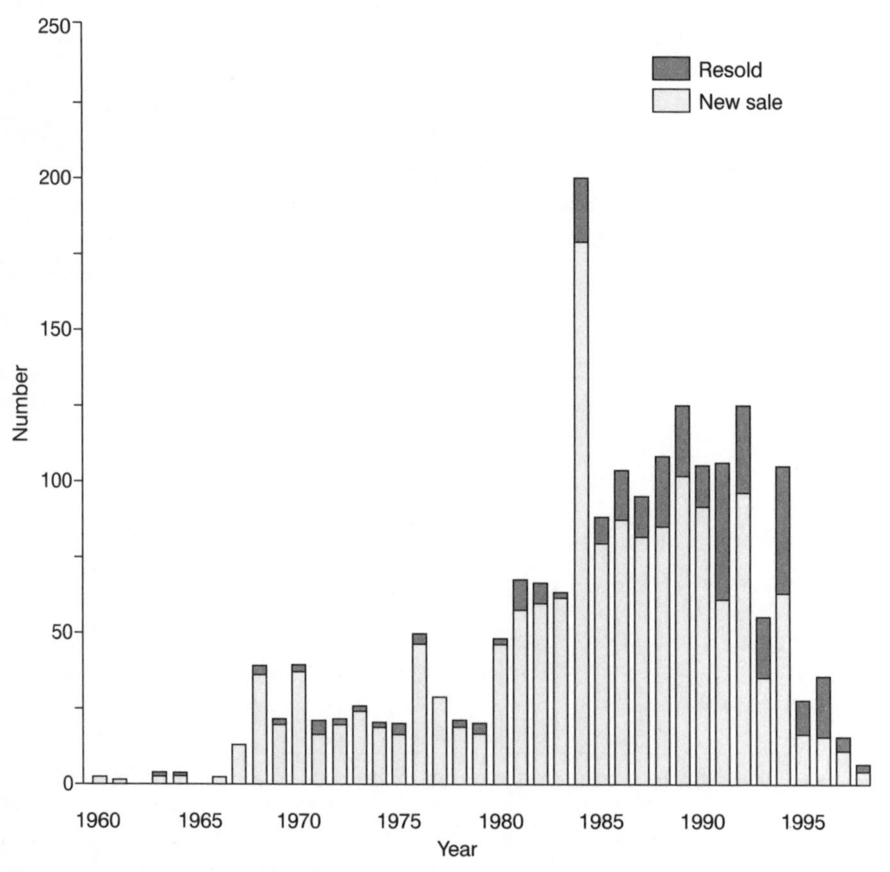

Source: Elia, 2001

Figure 18.2 *Apulian Red-figure Vases Sold at Sotheby's (1960–1998)*

with the aid of mechanical diggers) contained many objects of interest, but only the more valuable pieces were passed on to the international market, and many assemblages were irrevocably broken up (Graepler and Mazzei, 1993). The vases were probably smuggled out of Italy in refrigerated trucks (customs officers are reluctant to search these trucks thoroughly for fear that their legitimate cargoes might perish), in consignments of modern reproduction ceramics, or in personal luggage (after first having been broken) (Pastore, 2001).

Italy has had laws which protect the archaeological heritage since 1939 and which can be traced back as far as the 15th century in some areas. At the present time all archaeological remains are the property of the state, and therefore their illegal excavation and exportation is a criminal offence. Clearly, though, during the 1980s, in the case of the Apulian vases this law was no deterrent.

Between 1994 and 1999, 99,970 archaeological objects were seized in Italy by the art police (Comando Carabinieri Tutela Patrimonio Artistico) and some major smuggling rings were broken up (Pastore, 2001). In 1997, dealer (M) was arrested in Italy and Swiss police seized the contents of his four warehouses in Geneva Freeport. They were found to contain 3000 antiquities from all parts of Italy, worth in total something like 20 million Swiss francs. Also in 1997 the role played by Sotheby's in marketing the vases was exposed in a book and on television (Watson, 1997), and its London branch stopped antiquities auctions soon after. Since 1994 there had already been a decline in the numbers of Apulian vases sold at Sotheby's, perhaps because Italian law enforcement had already begun to bite.

The Italian example is more encouraging than that described for the Czech Republic. Diligent police work within Italy by the Carabinieri coupled with effective international cooperation seems to be having a positive effect. Nevertheless, there is still a cost, in this case to the Italian taxpayer. The Comando Carabinieri Tutela Patrimonio Artistico employs 150 staff which are deployed between its Rome headquarters and seven field units (Pastore, 2001). For comparison, in Britain, Scotland Yard's art and antiques squad has an investigative staff of about three.

Export controls or bans are clearly expensive to enforce and it is futile to expect a poor country, such as Mali, with an area of 744,000 square miles, to police its own borders. Understandably, the protection of archaeological heritage is not a priority in developing countries – health, education and employment rank higher. Even the UK, one of the wealthiest countries in the world, makes very little attempt to control the illegal export of archaeological material. This is one reason why it is sometimes suggested that export controls should be abandoned, as they are expensive to enforce, do not protect the archaeology and, in reality, do little more than encourage criminalization of the trade. Against this it has been pointed out that while export controls do not offer complete protection, it has yet to be demonstrated that they offer no protection whatsoever.

Import Controls

It is now an established precedent in both US and UK courts that the illegal removal or handling of archaeological material from a country which claims ownership can constitute an offence under their respective stolen property laws. There have been a few successful prosecutions, but not as many as might be expected. This is for three reasons. First, there is a severe standard of proof. It must be established beyond doubt when and from where an object was first obtained, a difficult task when it has been excavated secretly and has not previously been seen or published. Second, state ownership must be more than a legal fiction, it must be actively pursued. But again, there are costs attached to domestic enforcement, and many states turn a blind eye to private collections within their own borders. In these circumstances it is doubtful whether a US or UK court will recognize a claim of ownership as valid, and may regard it instead as an export control, which falls outside the purview of US or UK criminal law. Finally, the problems attached to the interpretation and effects of limitation periods are formidable.

What is needed is a cheaper, easier and more reliable method of intercepting material that has been moved illegally out of its country of origin. In theory, the developed countries of Europe and North America have the resources necessary to establish systems of import control but, by and large, until recently, this has not happened. It seems that this is largely because states are reluctant to commit resources to the enforcement of foreign export laws, particularly when, as in the case of antiquities, their contravention causes no obvious harm to the importing society.

However, in recent years, the US has been experimenting with import restrictions placed on certain categories of archaeological material under the auspices of the 1970 United Nations Organization for Education, Science and Culture (UNESCO) Convention on the means of prohibiting and preventing the illicit import, export and transfer of ownership of cultural property. This convention was drafted in the late-1960s to combat the illicit trade in cultural material, and to date it has been ratified by 91 countries. It is a diplomatic instrument and offers the means to effect the return of stolen cultural objects and also to control their trade. The US implemented the convention in 1983 as the Convention on Cultural Property Implementation Act (CPIA). This act enables the US to enter into bilateral agreements with other state parties of the UNESCO Convention, when asked to do so, and place import restrictions on specific categories of threatened archaeological or ethnographic material. The agreements are not retroactive. Restricted objects may only enter the US if accompanied by a valid export licence of the country of origin, or if it can be shown to have left the country of origin before the date of the relevant agreement. This marks an important shift in the burden of proof. Outside CPIA it has to be demonstrated that material is stolen, while within CPIA it is assumed that material is illicit unless proven otherwise. However, the CPIA is not simply an instrument of regulation. It also makes provision for the professional and technical help to promote the long-term protection of heritage in situ by means of educational and economic initiatives.

The US currently has agreements with nine countries, but in the general absence of any reliable data, for reasons outlined above, it is difficult to quantify their effects. One treaty is with Mali, which was signed in 1997. Illegal excavation around the town of Djenné was rampant in the late-1980s, but, in the wake of the agreement, has now virtually stopped. However, this was not due to US import control alone. In Mali there has been a great effort on the ground to win over public support by means of local information campaigns and the enhancement of museums (McIntosh, 2002). Perhaps the potential impact of a bilateral agreement can best be judged from the vociferous opposition on the part of dealers and auction houses in the US to the signing of a wide-ranging agreement with Italy in January 2001. As the agreement is not retroactive, it can only be presumed that it was seen as a credible threat to the ongoing and profitable trade in material that is being smuggled out of Italy.

In general terms, countries whose archaeological heritage is under threat from looting are those with strong laws regarding its ownership or export. Those are also the countries that suffer the adverse cultural, economic and criminal consequences of the trade, and those which can least afford to enforce their own legislation. This injustice could be remedied by shifting the cost of enforcement off the already overloaded shoulders of poor governments and on to Western taxpayers (who benefit culturally and economically from the enlarged museums sector that the trade permits). This is the clear message of the CPIA – the US taxpayer foots the bill.

Conclusion: Beyond Regulation

The fundamental cause of archaeological looting in many countries – and one that is shared by other illegal trades – is rural poverty. The problem is further exacerbated when public order breaks down, most obviously in cases of civil war. The archaeological sites and museums of Cambodia, Afghanistan and Somalia, for example, have suffered particularly badly at the hands of warring factions; and despite the high-profile destruction of the 'idolatrous' Bamiyan Buddhas by the Taliban in 2001, most material is usually stolen for profit, not destroyed for religious or political purposes. Even in less destructive conflicts, when government rule is weak its laws can easily be ignored. In the northern Guatemalan province of Petén in 1997 the Mayan site of Naranjo was occupied by a drugs gang and systematically stripped.

Poverty and public order are problems which fall outside the professional remit of archaeologists, and this can be used as a pretext for inaction. But it should not be. In countries whose archaeology is badly threatened, archaeologists can engage in international partnerships aimed at public and professional education. They can also take care to ensure that the tourist, and thus economic potential of projects is maximized. In this way local communities are included in the archaeological process and are more likely to take sites under their protection.

What else can be said about regulation and enforcement? As noted previously, one of the defining features of the antiquities trade is that demand is restricted to what, in global terms, is a relatively small number of collectors. Antiquities in the developed world are cultural capital: they are objects of scholarship and indicators of taste and style. In this context, even what is at source an unenforceable control places a moral restraint upon their collection, as decent and law-abiding citizens will think twice before they stake their reputations on the product of a seedy and illegal enterprise. This is a compelling reason for the retention of export controls – if they are relaxed or abandoned, the moral restraint is removed.

In the US the CPIA is important as it establishes a new principle of demand-side enforcement of supply-side regulation. Two of the other major market countries, the UK and Switzerland, have long dragged their feet over the 1970 UNESCO Convention, although this has now changed. The UK signed up in July 2002, at which time Switzerland was in the process of drafting implementing legislation. This raises the possibility of opening up US bilateral agreements to multilateral participation and further extending enforcement, an eventuality hoped for when the CPIA was first adopted.

One of the antiquities trade's more distressing inequities is that the actual looters (usually poor farmers) may be punished quite severely if caught, and yet stand to gain only a very small proportion of the true value of anything they find. The real profits are made higher up the trading chain by individuals who often remain out of reach of the law – they might be government officials or foreign diplomats in source countries, or dealers in Europe or North America. Penalties are disproportionate too. Jail sentences and even death penalties are handed out at source, presumably in the hope of 'setting an example', but it is not clear that they have any real effect. On the demand side, archaeology-related crimes are not considered serious, and punishments are correspondingly light. However, this too now looks set to change. In November 2001 the US sentencing commission proposed that harsher penalties, more severe than for general property crimes, be introduced for crimes against archaeological heritage, including contraventions of import restrictions put in place under CPIA.

Increasing enforcement of foreign legislation in Europe and North America may serve to drive the trade there underground too, but this would probably be a good thing. Collecting antiquities is not addictive, at least not in the way that drugs are, and collectors will not want to be associated with a criminal enterprise. They will collect only antiquities which can be shown to have a legal provenance or else find other outlets for their cultural urge – and archaeology will be the safer for it.

References

Ali, I and Coningham, R (1998) Recording and preserving Gandhara's cultural heritage, *Culture Without Context,* 3, pp10–16

Bedaux, R M A and Rowlands, M (2001) The future of Mali's past, *Antiquity*, 75, pp872–876

Brodie, N J (2002) Britannia waives the rules? The licensing of archaeological material for export from the UK in Brodie, N and Tubb, K W (eds) *Illicit Antiquities: The theft of culture and the extinction of archaeology*, Routledge, London

Elia, R J (2001) Analysis of the looting, selling, and collecting of Apulian red-figure vases: a quantitative approach in Brodie, N, Doole, J and Renfrew, C (eds) *Trade in Illicit Antiquities: the Destruction of the World's Archaeological Heritage*, McDonald Institute for Archaeological Research, Cambridge

Graepler, D and Mazzei, M (1993) *Fundort: Unbekannt. Raubgrabungen zerstören das archäologische Erbe,* Walter Biering, Munich

Gutchen, M (1983) The destruction of archaeological resources in Belize, Central America, *Journal of Field Archaeology,* 10, pp217–227

Jirásek, P (2000) *One Hundred Missing Objects: Looting in Europe*, International Council of Museums, Paris

McIntosh, S K (2002) Reducing incentives for illicit trade in antiquities: the US implementation of the 1970 UNESCO Convention, in Brodie, N and Tubb, K W (eds) *Illicit Antiquities: the Theft of Culture and the Extinction of Archaeology*, Routledge, London

Ortiz, G (1996) *In Pursuit of the Absolute: Art of the Ancient World*, Benteli, Berne, Switzerland

Pastore, G (2001) The looting of archaeological sites in Italy in Brodie, N, Doole, J and Renfrew, R (eds) *Trade in Illicit Antiquities: the Destruction of the World's Archaeological Heritage*, McDonald Institute for Archaeological Research, Cambridge

Polk, K (2000) The antiquities market viewed as a criminal market, *Hong Kong Lawyer,* September, pp82–91

Watson, P (1997) *Sotheby's: Inside Story*, Bloomsbury, London

Conclusions: Looking Ahead – International Wildlife Trade Regulation and Enforcement

Rosie Cooney

This examination of regulation and enforcement in the international wildlife trade was prompted by a number of concerns:

- that current regulatory strategies frequently fail;
- that conceptual and empirical foundations of regulatory strategies are frequently faulty or untested;
- that effective enforcement is a persistent problem;
- that the changing nature of conservation challenges requires reassessment of regulatory strategies;
- and that regulatory practice may neglect or even violate values of equity, livelihoods and development.

What have we learned, and where do we go from here? In this concluding chapter we highlight key questions addressed by this work, present some tentative conclusions emerging from the material presented, and raise further issues for future work.

Three questions run through the chapters in this book:

- First, when is regulation the right response to a conservation challenge?
- Second, in a regulatory regime, when is banning the right response, and when is allowing or facilitating a regulated trade the right response?
- Third, when does regulation work?

Work presented here has shed considerable light on all three of these questions in relation to the international wildlife trade, and allows formation of some partial answers. The conclusions presented now are necessarily provisional and contingent – they are prompted by information and analysis and may certainly be modified by more of the same. They represent, however, only the beginnings of understanding of these issues, and themselves prompt more questions, which it is hoped will provide some stimulus to further examination.

When is Regulation the Right Response to a Conservation Challenge?

Regulation is only one of at least three basic responses to a conservation challenge: regulate; create positive incentives for non-detrimental behaviour; or do nothing. Action at the international level to counter conservation threats generally favours regulatory approaches, although the alternative paradigm is demonstrated by the emphasis on positive economic incentives within the Convention on Biological Diversity. But when is regulation the right response?

Regulation will not always, and not alone, effectively address conservation problems

Regulation is sometimes relied on as a response to conservation threats, regardless of utility, implementation, or enforcement. The goal of regulating wildlife trade, however, is to stop detrimental trade, not merely make it illegal. Before regulatory strategies are adopted adequate consideration needs to be given as to whether regulation is an effective response to the conservation threat, and regulation itself should not be considered a conservation gain without consideration of conservation impacts. In the analysis by Nigel Leader-Williams (see Chapter 9) of impacts of trade regulation on the conservation of rhinos, for instance, it is clear that a global ban on all rhino products trade from 1977 onward failed to prevent either trade or precipitous trade-related declines in rhino numbers across Africa and Asia, and has probably contributed little to more recent increases. Likewise, it is argued that adequate regulation for control of bushmeat hunting and trade in Africa is already in place: there is little indication, however, that this should provide any reassurance.

Emphasis on regulatory responses to conservation problems is encouraged by the fact that particularly at the international policy level, regulation may be one of the few actions external organizations can take in response to conservation threats within national borders. It may reflect an underlying conviction that trade in wild species is inherently detrimental or unethical, and that limiting trade must always be desirable. It may be prompted by the fact that regulation presents an achievement 'on the books' without the frustrations and complexity of engaging in on-the-ground management, or regulation as a response may simply minimize costs for bodies responsible for conservation.

One example discussed here is regulation for protection of the red-tailed black cockatoo in Australia: once regulation was achieved, this procedural success effectively obviated any need for the costly, time-intensive substantive conservation procedures of monitoring, research and enforcement.

Regulation, particularly trade bans, can produce negative impacts for both people and conservation

While the benefits of a well-functioning regulatory regime are obvious, regulatory interventions also clearly pose risks to both human needs and attainment of conservation objectives. In terms of negative conservation impacts, limitation or banning of trade can simply drive trade into the black market, with the lack of control, lack of information and monitoring, and substandard practices that this implies. Banning of alcohol in the US during the Prohibition era provides perhaps the clearest example of this effect. Shrinking supply of the resource or species through regulation can lead to inflation of prices, creating powerful incentives for circumventing controls. Brendan Moyle in Chapter 4 pointed to the consequences of Australia's ban on trade in wild parrots, suggesting this reduction of supply inflated the overseas price of parrots, perpetuating and sustaining the black market. Trade bans in particular can decrease or remove the economic incentives for conservation such as the financial benefits derived through sustainable utilization for trade. These incentives have been powerful tools in increasing, for example, conservation of white rhinos on private land in South Africa.

Regulation, as a strategy that seeks to control people's behaviour, can also lead to serious impacts on people's livelihoods. This in turn may have conservation consequences. The listing in Appendix I of the Tanimbar corella as described in Chapter 15, which after investigation turned out to be a locally common agricultural pest, caused significant losses of income to local villagers in Indonesia who had previously trapped and traded them. As described in Chapter 14, the mere submission of a proposal to list devil's claw in Appendix II, on precautionary grounds, precipitated at least a short-term drop in demand for the wild-harvested plant, reported reluctance within the pharmaceutical industry to pursue research and development avenues, and probably a shift to more technology-intensive cultivation which delivers no benefits to the traditional harvesters. Incomes of some of the poorest rural people in Namibia were directly affected. Both these cases have led to a distrust and suspicion of CITES and NGOs among sectors of local society. In the case of the Tanimbar corella, resentment and distrust provoked by the CITES listing led directly to loss of local political support for an important protected area, and the consequent breakdown of this initiative.

The costs and consequences of regulatory approaches should be assessed before decisions and after application

Regulation is likely to be better designed and more effective if any regulatory decision is based on a well-informed effort to assess its impact. Further, the potential for detrimental impacts of regulatory decisions mandates that consequences and costs should be assessed in advance. Such an assessment may lead to the conclusion that non-regulatory approaches are indicated, or that international regulation will only further conservation goals if linked to management interventions at a lower level. Within CITES there is no formal requirement for such assessment and neither parties nor NGOs place adequate emphasis on such assessments.

The precautionary principle is frequently invoked in cases of uncertainty to justify erring on the side of greater regulation. However, the potential for regulation to cause negative impacts implies that the precautionary principle gives insufficient guidance when making such a decision. In deciding regulatory strategy one is always choosing between risk and risk, rather than risk and no risk.

Assessment of regulatory impact may be particularly important if, as in CITES, decisions are difficult to reverse. Here asymmetric requirements exist for increasing and decreasing the level of regulation. To use again the case study of the Tanimbar corella, while comparatively little information was required to support Appendix I listing, a great deal of information and management effort would be required to support down-listing. Such an investment is likely to present a low priority for the limited conservation resources of the agencies involved, meaning the option of reversing this situation is effectively barred.

This prompts the question: who should be obliged to assess and demonstrate the potential consequences of decisions to regulate? Should, for instance, those seeking to limit or ban trade be required to demonstrate that the trade is detrimental, or should those seeking to continue or establish trade need to show it causes no detriment? This must be answered within a context in which the poorest people, in the poorest countries in the world, are frequently those most economically reliant on the trade.

Once regulation is adopted, assessment of whether regulation is achieving the desired aims should be built into an effective regulatory strategy. This is highly desirable both to inform future regulatory interventions and to establish a modicum of accountability for regulatory decisions within forums such as CITES. The complex biological, economic and social systems involved in wildlife trade are dynamic and volatile, and such assessment is also required to ensure often simplistic regulatory responses remain relevant to the conservation challenge. Such assessments of the impact of regulatory strategies are both difficult to do and rarely undertaken. An example presented in Chapter 7 is the EU's attempt to assess the impacts of its 'stricter domestic measures'. While such a review cannot be comprehensive or precise, it gives valuable information about both the limitations and strengths of regulatory strategies. The 'significant trade review' process adopted by the CITES parties provides a good example of a system of review of the impacts of regulatory decisions.

Scientific information should not provide the sole basis for decisions to regulate

The appropriateness and effectiveness of regulation is demonstrated throughout this book to depend on a wide array of social, economic, and political factors, including, for instance, the engagement, understanding and capacity of different interest groups, such as land managers, harvesters and traders, the financial incentives for compliance, and political will within producer states. While scientists can provide vital technical advice on biological aspects, and often have the skills and training to ensure other factors are assessed, the expertise and understanding which will inform effective regulatory decisions extends well beyond the purview of science.

Banning or Regulated Trade as the Right Response

If regulation is adopted as a response to a trade-related conservation challenge, major options include banning trade, or allowing a conditional, regulated trade. Various problems associated with bans are pointed out above: they may have negative consequences for both people and conservation, in terms of affecting livelihoods, promoting black markets, and reducing positive incentives for conservation through reducing options for utilisation. When are these responses indicated?

Bans are sometimes necessary

A primary indicator for the application of a ban on any trade may be the inability of the resource or species to withstand any level of off-take for trade. The extreme case may be demonstrated by antiquities – where there is a finite and limited quantity in the world, there can be no 'sustainable production'. A more problematic situation is where sustainable use might be possible, but where bans on trade or exploitation are necessary to prevent illegal or unregulated trade. This situation is addressed further below. Where well understood and enforced, bans can reduce trade: the domestic experience of strict trade bans within India assessed in Chapter 8 appears to have resulted in comparatively little availability of ivory, skins and fur. In some circumstances bans, even when poorly implemented and enforced may, by their simple existence, reduce demand. Lessons are drawn here from the global trade in antiquities, within which export controls are poorly implemented and virtually unenforceable. However, because antiquities carry cultural cachet as symbols of taste and style, even entirely unenforceable legal restrictions appear to place a moral restraint on the actions of collectors. It is, however, important to point out that in the absence of such specific factors bans do not automatically decrease demand. For example, the banning of trade in wild parrots from Australia does not appear to have decreased overseas demand, but rather led to it being supplied from illegal sources.

Due to generally high costs of enforcement, bans may be best backed up by attempts to decrease demand. This suggestion is made here with reference to the antiquities trade, and such an approach has been adopted in relation to rhino horn through engagement with the traditional Chinese medicine community. In some other areas, such as narcotics, and the historical example of Prohibition, lack of any success in decreasing demand may be an important factor in the relative failure of these bans. It would be worth further examining the proposition, in the context of the international wildlife trade, that if one is working with limited enforcement resources, bans are only likely to present a viable strategy where there exists the potential to substantially decrease or eliminate demand.

Allowing a regulated trade in resource or species will not always stimulate illegal trade

Within CITES and domestic regulatory contexts, the question of whether legal trade stimulates illegal trade has persistently emerged. It appears clear that the existence of an unregulated trade has in some circumstances provided the distribution network and the market to enable a flourishing illegal trade. Some have moved from this observation to the proposition that allowing a regulated trade will promote illegal trade. As divergent answers to this question provide central planks of various opposing arguments within CITES, and substantial conservation and livelihood impacts ride on the answer, answering this question is a high priority.

Work presented here demonstrates at least that a regulated trade does not inevitably stimulate an illegal trade. In the case study of international trade in crocodilian skins (see Chapter 11), the legal, regulated trade can be seen to have effectively displaced the illegal trade over a period of several decades. Moreover, one of the few, perhaps the only, rigorous empirical assessment of the impact of allowing some regulated trade on illegal killing, a study of an elephant population in Zambia found no discernible impact.

However, this lack of impact is unlikely to represent a general rule. The question then becomes: under what circumstances does a regulated trade not stimulate illegal trade? While comprehensive answers to this question remain elusive, some interesting suggestions emerge from studies presented here.

First, legal trade may be likely to suppress illegal trade when the legitimate trade generates sufficient financial resources and political support. This certainly appears to have been an important factor in the case of crocodilian skins. As the skin trade both became an important source of revenue in range countries, and represented an increasingly large investment of management, research and development resources and effort, this was reflected in the level of political will and resources made available to counter the illegal trade.

Second, structural characteristics of trade in some commodities may lend themselves to relatively low cost enforcement. In the case of crocodilians, for instance, the very small number of tanneries through which any high value products are required to pass make for relatively easy control of the vast bulk of the trade.

Third, the crocodilian example emphasises that the availability of effective enforcement measures such as trade suspensions is likely to be a vital component in decreasing the illegal trade.

When does regulation work?

In general, regulation only works if there is widespread and general compliance, which may need to be strengthened through enforcement. What factors lead to regulation working effectively?

Regulation which involves some positive incentives for compliance, rather than relying heavily on intensive enforcement, is more likely to succeed

Enforcement tends, in general, to be difficult, expensive, and under-resourced. It follows that regulation which relies heavily on enforcement for its success is likely to be unstable and unlikely to gain compliance. It has been pointed out here that the organized crime responsible for much illegal wildlife trade is competitive, adaptable, and globally mobile, with ruthless methods and excellent business knowledge, but is combated by enforcement agencies which are bound by jurisdictional borders, are rigid, rule-bound, slow to change, and may be susceptible to corruption. In addition, wildlife trade enforcement tends to be allocated a low priority for resourcing compared to the illegal narcotics or arms trades. While enforcement remains a vital component in effective regulation, regulation that depends on intensive enforcement efforts – negative incentives for compliance – is less likely to be effective than that which provides for some positive incentives. At the international level, regulatory regimes such as CITES rely primarily on negative or punitive incentives. Similar considerations operate at a national scale. Some of the factors which encourage compliance, and decrease reliance on expensive enforcement efforts, may be involvement of local communities in regulatory design, the perceived legitimacy of the management regime, the involvement of all users, and equity of access to the resource under management.

Effective regulation relies on understanding, capacity, training and education

At the most basic level, adequate compliance is only likely where all the interested parties are aware of and understand the regulatory structure, and have the capacity to achieve compliance. In terms of CITES, however, these frequently present major challenges to effective regulation. Lack of compliance with CITES requirements is often based on lack of awareness and understanding of the obligations and procedures involved. The objectives of CITES are unclear to many parties, including wildlife traders themselves, and coupled with this are major gaps in capacity to implement and enforce CITES obligations.

High level regulatory initiatives are more likely to succeed when coupled with national or local action

Most problems involving the use of natural resources and species are determined by the policies and practices of agencies and people at national or lower levels. International policy-making which constructively links to action at these levels will generally be more effective than that which produces a prescriptive formulation to be applied. Within CITES, an increasing role for the convention has emerged in fostering national management strategies to ensure international trade does not lead to over-exploitation, and this is perceived as highly successful. Evidence from the EC (see Chapter 7) suggests that the stricter domestic measures it has instituted have been most successful when they are accompanied by initiatives concentrating on management at a national or lower scale. For instance, import restrictions on wildlife from Indonesia were accompanied by a workshop in Jakarta and a series of discussions which led to changes in the way Indonesian wildlife controls were applied. In the absence of such engagement, the impact of import restrictions was often ambiguous, and sometimes appeared to simply produce shifts in trade routes without decreasing volume. Likewise, in efforts to implement import bans on antiquities, most success has been gained where these have been linked with work with local communities to address the causes of illegal looting. Both these trades are frequently driven at the producer end by rural poverty, and without addressing the causes of illegal take and trade at a national or lower level, high-level policy prescriptions risk irrelevance or futility.

Some Final Thoughts

Over the long term, effective regulation relies on the credibility of regulatory institutions, and acceptance of regulatory norms and practices by the people who are affected by regulation. The stability of international institutions as forums enabling the negotiation and resolution of conflicts around divergent priorities, paradigms and values is crucial. In the arena of international wildlife trade regulation, CITES, in contrast to some other regulatory bodies, enjoys a high degree of legitimacy and acceptance as a negotiating forum. This is evidenced by the relatively few, and declining numbers of reservations entered with respect to important traded species, the acceptance by parties of trade suspensions, and the emphasis on substantive debate rather than obstruction based on technical grounds. However, these efforts can be undermined by mistrust and resentment caused by problematic approaches and flawed thinking, as highlighted in the analyses and case studies presented throughout this book. These include lack of recognition of the livelihood and development needs of local people, lack of assessment of the practical impacts and consequences of regulatory decisions, the lack of accountability of decision-makers on the international stage, and failure to link high-level policy initiatives to management regimes with a closer connection to resource or species use. As we face growing challenges of increasing, shifting and unpredictable patterns of international wildlife trade, effective and equitable regulation to realize conservation objectives demands that these considerations inform our thinking and guide our practice.

Index

Page numbers in *italics* refer to Figures, Tables and Boxes